A DANCE
WITH THE
DEVIL

A DANCE WITH THE DEVIL

A TRUE STORY OF MARRIAGE TO A PSYCHOPATH

Barbara Bentley

BERKLEY BOOKS, NEW YORK

THE BERKLEY PUBLISHING GROUP
Published by the Penguin Group
Penguin Group (USA) Inc.
375 Hudson Street, New York, New York 10014, USA
Penguin Group (Canada), 90 Eglinton Avenue East, Suite 700, Toronto, Ontario M4P 2Y3, Canada
(a division of Pearson Penguin Canada Inc.)
Penguin Books Ltd., 80 Strand, London WC2R 0RL, England
Penguin Group Ireland, 25 St. Stephen's Green, Dublin 2, Ireland (a division of Penguin Books Ltd.)
Penguin Group (Australia), 250 Camberwell Road, Camberwell, Victoria 3124, Australia
(a division of Pearson Australia Group Pty. Ltd.)
Penguin Books India Pvt. Ltd., 11 Community Centre, Panchsheel Park, New Delhi—110 017, India
Penguin Group (NZ), 67 Apollo Drive, Rosedale, North Shore 0632, New Zealand
(a division of Pearson New Zealand Ltd.)
Penguin Books (South Africa) (Pty.) Ltd., 24 Sturdee Avenue, Rosebank, Johannesburg 2196,
South Africa

Penguin Books Ltd., Registered Offices: 80 Strand, London WC2R 0RL, England

This book is an original publication of The Berkley Publishing Group.

The publisher does not have any control over and does not assume any responsibility for author or third-party websites or their content.

This book describes the real experiences of real people. The author has disguised some identities to protect privacy, and in some instances created composite scenes of certain events, but none of these changes has affected the truthfulness and accuracy of her story.

Copyright © 2008 by Barbara Bentley.
Cover photograph courtesy of Barbara Bentley.
Interior text design by Kristin del Rosario.

PRINTING HISTORY
Berkley trade paperback edition / November 2008

Library of Congress Cataloging-in-Publication Data

Bentley, Barbara, 1945–
    A dance with the devil : a true story of marriage to a psychopath / Barbara Bentley.
        p.   cm.
    ISBN 978-0-425-22118-1
  1. Bentley, Barbara, 1945–   2. Attempted murder—United States—Case studies.   3. Divorce—
Law and legislation—California.   I. Title.

    HV6529.B46 2008
    364.152'3092—dc22
    [B]

                                                                                2008024620

PRINTED IN THE UNITED STATES OF AMERICA

10   9   8   7   6   5   4   3   2

I dedicate this book to my husband, Rex;
to the memory of my friend Helen; and
to the memory of Homicide Detective Greg Smith,
who saved my life.

CONTENTS

INTRODUCTION

This is my story, where fairy-tale dreams, trust, and hope collide with the crazymaking world of psychopaths and domestic violence. I could never have imagined my recovery would be so hard won, or that a psychopath would be so hard to lose.

My Prince Charming swept me off my feet, but the euphoria was short lived. Once the honeymoon period was over, he quickly learned how to manipulate my insecurities with his skillful lies. He could be so charming that I didn't recognize how he was using me and our relationship to reach his own goals to achieve the high standard of living and the admiration he craved. At other times, he could terrify me. When he threatened to leave me, my bones froze. In a panic, I did whatever I thought necessary to keep the relationship on track and stop my fear of abandonment and rejection from becoming reality. I was dealing with a psychopath, but I didn't recognize it.

Beneath the façade of a retired rear admiral, my Prince Charming was actually a monster in disguise, a psychopath adept at spotting a woman he could enchant and influence. He fanned the flame of love. He knew just what to say, how to say it, and when to say it to trap me. I was his prey, and it led to at least one attempt on my life. Dr. Robert D. Hare, in his book *Without Conscience,* defines psychopaths as "social predators who charm, manipulate, and ruthlessly plow their way through life, leaving a broad trail of broken hearts, shattered expectations, and empty wallets." Psychopaths are also known as sociopaths, and Dr. Martha Stout, in her book *The Sociopath Next Door,* states that "one in twenty-five everyday Americans...is secretly a sociopath."

Dr. Hare further sets forth: "Psychopaths are often witty and articulate. They can be amusing and entertaining conversationalists, ready with a quick and clever comeback, and can tell unlikely but convincing stories that cast themselves in a good light. They can be very effective in presenting themselves well and are often very likeable and charming."

Psychopaths are experts at manipulating facts and twisting the truth. If I became suspicious and challenged a story, my Prince Charming usually responded without hesitation, offering a plausible explanation that often contained a kernel of truth. At other times he would smoothly glide away from the question. No matter which way he gave his answer, I would be left feeling foolish or crazy, yet I continued to trust him.

Dr. Hare also writes: "Given their personality, it comes as no surprise that psychopaths make good imposters. They have no hesitation in forging and brazenly using impressive credentials to adopt, chameleonlike, professional roles that give them prestige and power." You will see them as lawyers, psychologists, military officers, war heroes, professors, company officers, and two of their favorites, CIA or FBI agents. These professions are usually given unchallenged trust, and the psychopath wants his victims to trust him implicitly.

Psychopaths look for the pot of gold and will use ruthless means to get it. They have no financial responsibility and feel no obligation to develop or maintain a good credit rating. Greed drives them to abuse the victim's credit cards, borrow money, confiscate valuables, encourage second mortgages, and finagle large insurance policies or wills with themselves as beneficiaries. They may even use murder to get what they want. However, if the resource dries up, they casually move along, without conscience, to find the next victim.

The criminal justice system constantly deals with psychopaths who have developed a lifelong pattern of being in trouble with the law. Many use fake IDs. Their rap sheets can be remarkably inventive, but frightening in the potential to do harm. Most practice their deception until the day they die. There is no real cure for a psychopath.

Practicing psychopaths fit the profile of domestic abusers. They are proficient at emotional and financial abuse. They may also revert to physical and sexual abuse to get their way. Domestic violence is about power and control. And a psychopath, who thrives on power and control, knows just how to get and sustain them.

Psychopaths are adept at using the cycle of violence. After an abusive event, they are apologetic and loving, manipulating with their words. "I promise, it will never happen again." The victim is led to believe that the abuse was her fault. This honeymoon stage may be short lived as tensions begin to build, escalate, and eventually lead to the next abuse.

Some verbal abuse is obvious. Harsh words are said in anger. There is yelling, swearing, and name-calling. The victim responds by developing low self-esteem and by becoming emotionally paralyzed.

Verbal abuse may also be subtle, disguised in smooth, manipulating words. Patricia Evans, in her book *The Verbally Abusive Relationship: How to Recognize It and How to Respond,* says, "Covert verbal abuse is subversive because of its indirect quality. It is a covert attack or coercion. This kind of abuse has been described as 'crazymaking.'" The psychopath is a master of its use. He knows just what to say to keep the victim off balance, to make her feel crazy and unable to understand why she feels lost, disconnected, and out of control.

A financial abuser may use obvious tactics such as having the victim account for every penny, not allowing the victim to have any money of her own, and not allowing her to have a career outside the home. Her self-esteem is bruised when she's told she's not responsible enough to handle money or smart enough to hold down a job.

Covert financial abuse is harder to spot. The psychopath, motivated by greed, is a master at this type of abuse. He uses smooth or threatening words to manipulate finances to his advantage. The victim may find herself giving him her credit cards and allowing their misuse, even though she suffers extreme stress and fear when she can't pay them off. The psychopath may con his way onto the deed of the victim's home or clandestinely obtain a second mortgage on her property. When the psychopath moves on, the victim is left financially drained and responsible for the debt.

To the outside world, domestic violence leaves the most easily recognized signs...blackened eyes, broken bones, or dead bodies. For many reasons, including fear, guilt, low self-esteem, financial dependency, and children's welfare, a victim will often continue to put up with physical abuse, even if it leads to her death. Many victims have nowhere to go, no one to help them. Tragically, a misinformed society perpetuates the problem.

Physical abuse can also be covert, especially when the psychopath needs to cover his deceptive actions. A staged car accident or an unexpected fall down the stairs is physical abuse, though the victim may not recognize it as such. The psychopath explains it away with glib words, apologies, and promises.

Another form of abuse is spousal rape. The abuser demands sex as a husband's right or forces the victim to perform acts that are offensive to her. The opposite of rape may also apply. There is no sex. The victim may rationalize this away, too.

During my journey I have been given the right people at the right time to support me emotionally, legally, spiritually, and financially.

For that I am grateful. I thank those who guided me, directly or indirectly, on my path of recovery: Carolyn Pedrotti, LCSW; Melody Beattie; and Lucia Capacchione, Ph.D. I thank those associated with the criminal aftermath of the murder attempt: Lisa, Michelle, Greg Smith, and Theo Stamos. I thank Harriet and Mike Salarno for teaching me about victim advocacy. I thank Dick Rainey, Kim and Peter for supporting my legislative quest. I thank Gregg Jones and Melvin Belli, who believed in my ability to defend myself in court.

I thank those who fostered, encouraged, and mentored my writing, especially Gary and Gail Provost and Hannelore Hahn. They were there at the beginning of my writing journey and continue to be an inspiration to me. I thank Lois Winsen for her advice and editing skills, and Patricia Evans for her encouragement. I thank my literary agent Rachel Vater for her enthusiasm, support, and skill in getting my manuscript sold. I thank my literary agent Nancy Yost for monitoring my progress. I thank my three editors at Berkley: Samantha Mandor for acquiring my manuscript, Katie Day for improving my manuscript with minor changes, and Shannon Jamieson Vazquez for bringing further clarity to a fact-filled story and gracefully handling a first-time author. I also thank my copyeditor, Amy Schneider, for her meticulous work.

I am grateful for the support of my family and friends. I thank my husband, Rex, for his patience as I have pursued my publishing dream. And I wish to thank my departed golden retrievers, Gobi and Gaby, for giving me wet kisses at the times I needed them most.

Some scenes in this book are a compilation of events because everyday life strings out experiences. Facts are represented as accurately as possible, but some names and locations have been changed for privacy. As a survivor of this story, I realize now that I am the product of my upbringing and my life choices, good and bad. Throughout my journey I have encountered many life-altering decisions. What if I had turned away when I met John, instead of running into his arms? Where would I be now? Would I be the whole person I have become, or still a victim of my own ignorance of self? Because of my experiences, I have learned how to survive being a victim and find a truly fulfilling life without shame, and I have had the opportunity to recognize and overcome some of my deepest fears. It is my hope that by sharing my experiences, I can reach others who may see themselves in my story, and that they will find courage, strength, and hope for finding their own freedom before it is too late.

PROLOGUE

To Trust or Not to Trust

I was sitting at my office desk staring at my November day planner when I made what seemed like an innocuous decision—I would invite my recently reconnected friend Rex to the Justice for Murder Victims dinner dance in San Francisco. It was less than two weeks away. I reached for the telephone and paused as a pang of guilt reminded me that I didn't like it when people changed plans on me at the last minute, and inviting Rex meant putting my mother off after she had been my date for the charity affair the last several years. *She won't mind,* I rationalized. *She'll be happy that I will have someone to whisk me around the dance floor.*

My hand grasped the receiver and I shuddered. A sense of impending doom enveloped me. Before the receiver reached my ear, I dropped it back into its cradle as a paralyzing déjà vu washed over me like a ghost from the past, taunting me with memories best left undisturbed. *Was I reacting as I once did? Without abandon? Could I make the same mistake twice?* At least I had learned one lesson—I didn't trust my decision to extend the invitation without bouncing the idea off a neutral party. I grabbed the receiver and quickly punched my friend Pam's number.

"My plan feels too close to how I got started with John," I fretted.

My stomach knotted at the memory.

"This is different," Pam counseled. "Didn't you have a good time at the lunch I arranged a couple of weeks ago?"

"Yes," I conceded, "it was fun reconnecting with him at the Potato Barge."

"You've known Rex since nineteen sixty-nine, even if you hadn't seen him for eight years before the lunch. You know his history and he's already a good friend. You can trust him."

We discussed my feelings of impending doom, and in the end I had to agree with her that I could trust Rex. I knew his background. As former co-workers, we had learned a lot about each other during the six years we tested production samples in the analytical lab at the Excelsior Chemical plant in Martinez, California. Rex, a chemist, transferred from the Midwest in 1969. He specialized in the emerging technology of gas chromatography, and Pam and I occasionally worked directly with him when we rotated into his area as lab assistants. We lost contact when he transferred to another company.

"You're right," I said. "Rex is a kind man without hidden agendas."

I thanked Pam for her friendship and closed by saying that she had helped bolster my resolve to ask Rex to the dinner dance. I had barely returned the receiver to its cradle when the phone jangled with a double ring indicating an outside call, startling me into a nervous jump. I laughed. *Another one of my mother's endearing traits that she passed along to me,* I thought.

My reverie was short lived. The call was from my divorce attorney, who let me know that my now ex-husband had just thrown another monkey wrench into what I thought was a final property settlement. My shoulders tightened. I slammed the receiver down and took a brisk walk to regain my composure.

Later that afternoon I called Rex. He gladly accepted my invitation and, because of logistics, we decided that I would drive. *This is just a date with a friend*, I thought to myself as I hung up the phone. Then I called my mom.

On a brisk, clear Sunday evening Rex escorted me to the flowing staircase in Gabbiano's, an upscale restaurant tucked between the San Francisco Ferry Building and the Bay Bridge. Rex looked dapper in his dark suit that complemented my one-piece black velvet and crepe jumpsuit. I grabbed my point-and-shoot camera from my purse and solicited a passing waiter to snap a picture of us before we climbed the stairs to the dining room overlooking the warmly lit Bay Bridge and twinkling city skyline. We mingled with the guests—all advocates for victim justice—and I proudly introduced Rex as an old friend. Later he shared that it felt strange to be in a group where murder had touched everyone's lives.

Outside on the deck near the shimmering water, over dinner with flickering candlelight, waltzing around the shiny dance floor, sipping mellow Napa Valley cabernet, we rediscovered our common interests. We laughed at lab episodes from the past, like passing Rex around to the ladies in the darkroom at the annual Christmas party or him watching me as I cleaned the inside of the fume hoods wearing a short skirt. He was there when I took my two younger sisters skiing, gladly escorting us to the company ski cabin because his wife and my first husband didn't want to have anything to do with swooshing down slippery slopes. It was all in good fun. At that time we were both married to others and had no designs on crossing the other person's boundaries.

The Ferry Building's ornate clock tower chimed eleven p.m.—not quite the midnight from Cinderella fame but time to head for home nonetheless. I selfishly didn't want the evening to end. I had rediscovered an admirable friend, someone I could talk with freely, and someone with whom I shared a past—a respectable past without any secrets. As I pulled onto the lower deck of the Bay Bridge I remembered another night—my university graduation night—when the fog was held at bay outside the Golden Gate Bridge and bright stars illuminated the dark sky.

"There's a great view of the city from Treasure Island," I said. "The night's so clear. Would you like to stop for a few minutes?"

"Just a few," he laughed. "I have to get up at three thirty in the morning to get ready for work."

I parked the car in the visitors' lot outside the main gate. We got out, climbed onto two rocks, and sat next to each other, savoring the sparkling lights of the city spread before us from the Bay Bridge to the Golden Gate Bridge, like a scrumptious dessert.

"It's a great shot," Rex said, breaking the silence. "Too bad we don't have our thirty-five-millimeter SLR cameras with us."

I loved that he shared my interest in photography beyond the popular point-and-shoot cameras. "We'll have to plan better next time." I laughed. "And bring warmer coats."

I hugged my arms and rubbed them to generate some warmth. I couldn't help but feel like we were two awkward teenagers on a first date at the movies. We shifted a little closer together. Our shoulders touched. Then slowly, and gently, Rex wrapped his arm around my shoulders and I snuggled into his embrace. We sat tranquil for a few moments. It felt good to be able to trust a man again.

"I almost didn't ask you to come tonight," I whispered. "The scenario reminded me too much of how I started dating John."

Rex didn't answer, but I could feel his sympathy as he squeezed me a little tighter. In the warmth of his embrace, I was drawn back to another time and another place, the most dangerous in my life, when misplaced trust had escalated into a nightmare and almost took my life. Of course, I didn't imagine any such thing at the time. Back then, it had started just like this, on what should have been nothing more than a carefree date arranged by a friend. . . .

PART ONE

Passion

ONE

Prince Charming

"Thanks for coming," Debbie said, giving my arm an extra little squeeze of appreciation.

"Hey," I said, "A promise is a promise." She had called me earlier that day while I was at work, preoccupied with testing samples in my analytical lab at the Excelsior Chemical Company. When she'd asked me to round out the double date for a dinner party at her house that evening, she wouldn't take no for an answer, so here I was.

I knew what Debbie was up to. Five months earlier, in February 1981, after I split up with a man who was a close friend of Debbie and her husband, Ted, Debbie somehow saw me as her "perfect single woman" friend. Somehow she'd managed to extract a promise from me: that I would help her keep her dinner table evenly set.

The eternal optimist, I wasn't opposed to meeting new men myself. When I asked about who my date for the night would be, she answered, "Older than you, but you don't have to think of him as a date. The point is, I know you'll find him interesting. His great-grandfather was Admiral Peary. Remember? Peary... North Pole? John works over at Vestico with Ted. You'll like him."

I wasn't holding my breath that we'd be a love match, and I was exhausted from working long shifts, but Debbie had a way of talking me into social events, and so I found myself agreeing. Besides, what harm could it cause? It was only dinner.

By the time I'd arrived and she'd greeted me warmly at the door, I found myself relaxing.

"I knew I could count on you," she said happily, leading me into her living room. "Well, I owe you, big time." Debbie glanced toward the kitchen, then quickly leaned over and whispered in my ear. "Don't be put off when you see John. He showed up in a foam neck brace and said he'll tell us all what happened." She pulled away, then quickly returned to my ear. "I forgot to mention that he wears a toupee, so don't stare." She smiled and, in her sweet normal voice, said, "I'll be back in a minute." *This should be interesting*, I thought. *I've never met anyone who wears a toupee.*

She hurried off to the kitchen, where the men had already begun preparing drinks. I sat down on the sofa and looked around. The brass, ceramics, paintings, and furniture that Debbie had collected during her time in Taiwan never ceased to impress me, and as usual reminded me of how long it had been since I'd gone off to somewhere exciting. I did a fair amount of traveling for Excelsior, but the places I was sent to could hardly be considered exotic.

"Well, hello there," I heard a deep voice call. I turned to see John Perry emerging from the kitchen, carrying two drinks. Ted and Debbie followed. Debbie winked at me.

Despite the medical brace around his neck, John was a dashing figure... tall, light brown hair, good looking with a ruddy complexion and mischievous blue eyes. He was well dressed, too, in his tweed jacket and designer silk tie. He strode confidently across the living room. "Rum and Coke for the lady," he said, offering me the drink with an impish grin. Debbie was right, I thought. This man was already interesting to me... neck brace, toupee, and all.

"Thanks," I said, taking the drink. I felt my cheeks flush as he looked me over. I was glad I'd decided to wear my red knit dress tonight. Everyone said red was my best color, and suddenly that seemed important.

Meanwhile, Debbie had set a tray of appetizers on the glass coffee table. John, I noticed, had already fixed a plate and was holding it out for me to take. I thanked him again.

"Debbie," he said, "you didn't tell me your friend was such a looker."

My cheeks burned once more. John settled into a nearby chair, never taking his eyes off me. This was not going the way I had expected. Trying to exert some control, I blurted out, "Why don't you tell me something about yourself?" And he did. He started out with an apology for the blue-foam neck brace and explained that a baggage cart loaded with heavy equipment had recently plowed into his neck and back while he stood waiting for a taxi at the Mexico City airport. "But it can't stop an old Navy man," he said. He launched into his military career and told me that after his last Vietnam tour in 1969, he'd been denied field duty. Because he hadn't relished the notion of a desk job, retirement was the better choice. He'd been a captain in the Navy, but at retirement received a tombstone promotion to rear admiral.

"Tombstone?" I asked.

"That's when an officer, at retirement, is honored by a raise of one rank. It depends, of course, on the officer's service record. Obviously, it provides higher retirement pay." He raised his glass.

"Guess you got that promotion because of the Congressional Medal of Honor, huh, John?" Ted asked.

I leaned forward. "You received the Medal of Honor?"

We were off and running. John talked about how the VC had swarmed over his unit's position. They'd been completely outnumbered, casualties incredibly high. He was nearly killed trying to save several of his men. John's hand slid to the side of his chest and rested there as he continued. "A fifty-millimeter machine gun opened me up good." He patted the spot on his side. "Real good. Right here." He sighed. "Lost a lung, you know. Still carry the scar."

We were all silent for a moment while John leaned across the table to fix himself a plate of appetizers.

"No disrespect intended," I heard myself say, "but war is always horrible. I believe we had no business being in Vietnam."

John smiled and began to lay out the usual arguments about the importance of fighting communism, but eventually admitted the war had taken its toll on him. "I still have nightmares about the kids I wasn't able to save," he said solemnly. He told us he had to shoot one of his own men who had fallen into a camouflaged, bamboo-stake-filled pit. Debbie gasped and I shuddered. "He begged me to shoot him," John explained. "When you're in the service, you go where duty calls and you do what you have to do."

I looked away, not caring to hear any more war stories. That didn't faze John, who seemed to relish talking about it. If I had only known then what I know now...that most servicemen don't like to talk about their war experiences. But I didn't. So, despite my disinterest in the topic, I found myself listening.

He said he'd been in three wars. He'd lied about his age in order to enlist during World War II, and, at sixteen, joined one of the first Navy SEAL units for underwater demolition. "I was a naval aviator in the Korean War. Got shot down once but landed in the water." He smiled, remembering. "After two tours in the Blue Angels, I went to Vietnam and was given command of the Black Boats, small and swift. They went up the river into North Vietnam. It was dangerous duty. Very dangerous."

It was clear he loved to talk about the military, about his experiences. "It's in the blood," he commented. "I'm tenth-generation Navy. Did you know that, Ted?"

Before Ted could answer, John was already into the topic of a film from the 1940s, starring John Wayne. It was the story of John's father and how he had started the Seabees.

"Because Dad was story consultant on the set," John said, "I got to meet John Wayne. Matter of fact, the Duke and I got to be real good friends."

After offering some inside gossip about the Duke, he joined Ted back in the kitchen to rustle up another round of drinks. Debbie immediately pumped me for my reaction to her guest. I conceded the man was certainly interesting. "But," I cautioned her, "if you're thinking what I think you're thinking, forget it. He's almost as old as my mother."

"Maybe he *is* too old for you." Debbie stood, announced that she was going into the kitchen to put on the finishing touches, and started out of the room. Over her shoulder she added, "Or maybe he's not."

"Not?"

"Too old for you. Maybe he's not."

With everyone settled back in the living room, the conversation turned to family. I shared that I didn't have any children from my first marriage but I did have three sisters and a brother, all younger than me. The two youngest sisters were still at home; the one closest to me (ten years younger) was married and lived in Washington, and my brother had recently been discharged from the Marines. I joked that my parents had two families. I was the first, and when I was old enough to be the live-in babysitter, the rest started popping out. We all laughed.

Ted and Debbie had grown children from their first marriages, and they brought us up-to-date with the latest news of who was where and doing what. Then it was John's turn. I had to try to not let my mouth fall open as he wove a fascinating story.

When John was a young officer he married Sara Brimstone against her father's wishes, because she was from old money and John was not. Together they had had a girl, Sandy, and a boy, Sonny. When John returned early from a long deployment, he found Sara in bed with another man. They divorced. He fought for custody of the children and won. Whenever duty called John to the sea or sky, his Grandmother Dannigan watched the children in Coconut Grove, Florida.

Then John met Cindy Shirrow, an airline stewardess. They married and had one daughter, Estelle Desiree. In less than a year Cindy was killed in an automobile accident. John was in Vietnam when it happened, and his grandmother took one more child under her wing.

John's fourth child came into his family through his father, who had adopted Francesca, the daughter of a faithful servant. When John's father died, John assumed the responsibility. It was the right thing to do, he said.

John saw to it that his children were well taken care of as they grew into adults. When he was home he lived with them in his house in Coconut Grove. When he was away, Grandmother Dannigan and her servants continued to care for them. John made sure they went to the best schools, and all appeared to be successful. Sandy was married and going to MIT, Sonny was at NASA's astronaut school, Desiree was at Juilliard, and Francesca was at Florida International University and living with John's Grandma Dannigan.

Just when we thought he was finished, John hung his head. "We're not very close now. I guess I was away too much when they were growing up. I feel like the black sheep of the family."

Something stirred inside me. I wanted to rush over and put my arms around him and tell him it was all right, he had done his best. But I had just met this charming man, and that would have been too presumptuous. Instead I meekly said, "I'm so sorry."

Later, at the dinner table, Debbie sat John opposite me. He immediately reached up, ripped at the Velcro, and removed the blue-foam neck brace, saying the doctor recommended he wear it only when his pain was excruciating. *Hmmm…looks even better,* I thought. Ted poured the wine, and John lifted his glass.

"A toast," John said. "Here's to the breezes that blow women's chemises past their kneeses." Even I laughed at that.

I looked around at the beautifully, evenly set table and realized I was fully lulled into the spirit of Debbie's dinner party. The meal, as always, was exceptional. Wine was plentiful. John, throughout the meal, was completely captivating. He complimented Debbie's culinary talents, offered lighthearted jokes, and filled the hours that passed with more of his fascinating stories. *A real charmer, this one,* I thought, *who knows all the right moves.*

As the evening wore on, I learned even more about him. Before coming to Vestico as a consultant he was with the Federal Government Contract Administration. The FDA and the CIA, he explained, used the service. He was sent on missions into sensitive areas where it was, as he put it, "best for U.S. government presence to remain unknown."

Before the night was over, he told us he'd been born in Turrialba and that he spoke Spanish fluently, having first learned it as a child living with his mother's family in Costa Rica. That was why, he explained, most of his missions took him to Central America.

I interjected that I was a genuine California girl and that I had lived my whole life in one county—from being born and raised in Pittsburg to settling in Concord during my first marriage to migrating to Antioch for affordable housing after my divorce, all within a twenty-mile radius. "For a world traveler like you it must sound dead boring," I said.

"I envy you." John sighed. "As a child I moved around a lot because my dad was in the Navy; then I enlisted and the rest is history."

"My parents still live in Concord," I added, as if that tacked on some allure to my story. "They moved to California in World War II when Dad's unit was stationed at Camp Stoneman. The weather appealed to them, so they stayed after Dad was discharged."

John added that was exactly why he had settled in the Bay Area, and then he was off on another story. To me, this dinner guest of Debbie's was a regular James Bond. As difficult as it was becoming for me to keep my eyelids from drooping, I wanted to hear every word of the story he was telling about a mission in Panama City.

He and another operative, he said, had rented adjoining offices. They were close to completing their mission of forcing a drug cartel out of Colombia. One day, after lunch, John was at his desk in his office when he heard his partner's office door open. John expected to hear his partner's footsteps, but instead, he heard the loud rattle of machine-gun fire. Instinctively, he hit the deck, scrambled under his desk, held his breath, and waited. The office door opened, and a strange voice said something about "getting the other one next time."

Minutes later John learned his partner had been killed instantly. That might just as easily have happened to John, I thought, realizing that in real life, this James Bond stuff was horrifyingly brutal. As though reading my thoughts, John looked directly at me when he said, "That's when I realized I was getting too old for that line of work. It was time to call it quits."

I sighed deeply. "And it's definitely time for *me* to call it quits now," I announced. "It's nearly midnight."

While Debbie and Ted waved to me from the porch, John escorted me to my car, surprising me with his rapt attention. After I was behind the wheel, he asked me to wait while he walked over to his own car. He returned with a paper bag.

"I wish I had something more to give you," he said, "but this croissant is from a special bakery in San Francisco. I know you'll like it." He grinned. "A special pastry for a special gal."

It was an odd, but interesting, gesture. I thanked him for the croissant and drove away. On the way home I reflected on the entertaining evening and my introduction to an articulate, witty, and amusing man who had impressive credentials and exciting stories, a man who went out of his way to focus his charm and attention on me. But also *an older man,* I reminded myself. Parked in my garage, I grabbed my purse and the paper bag. What was it about me, I wondered, that made this man decide I was "special"? Although I had certainly learned a great deal about him, what exactly had he learned about me?

TWO

The Infatuation

The following week, I kept busy with my normal routine. During the day I analyzed samples at Excelsior. In the evening I either drove to San Francisco to attend classes to earn my bachelor's degree or spread out my textbooks at home on the dining room table to study. Despite my hectic lifestyle I often found myself absorbed with thoughts of Debbie's dinner party and John Perry. With friends I found myself joking about the blind date I'd had with an older man who turned out to be a most singular individual. Spicing up the normal chitchat my friends and I typically exchanged, I went ahead and relayed some of the stories John told about himself, about the famous people he knew, the escapades he'd participated in, and the historical events he'd witnessed. As far as I could tell, my friends appeared as captivated as I had been.

Naturally, I assumed my family would be captivated too. After finishing an early dinner, I had a few minutes to spare before leaving for my evening class. Comfortably seated on my kitchen bar stool, I took time out to call my parents.

My mother hadn't yet gotten over my move away from Concord, where my family and friends lived, nor had she gotten over the divorce that forced my move. Bryan, my first husband, had been unfaithful throughout our thirteen-year marriage, and when I mustered the courage to assuage my Catholic guilt, I divorced him. Bryan remained in the Concord house, and we put it on the market. I stayed with my friend Pam for almost a year until I could afford a home of my own in Antioch. The move to Antioch triggered something in my mother. She had always expected me to be "there" for her, so as I dialed her number I prepared myself for a few negative remarks and guilt trips about "abandoning the family," but I didn't expect the rest.

Mom answered the phone, and as soon as I greeted her, she said, "Hold on," and put the phone down. I could hear her walk off, and then a door closed. It seemed to take forever.

When she was back on the line, I asked, "Why do you always do that?"

"Do what?"

"You know, make me wait while you go turn down the TV, or put on a robe, or whatever else you do. Couldn't you at least say hello first?"

"I don't want flies in the house, Barbara."

"Flies?"

"I was in the garage, doing laundry, when you called. I had to close the door."

"Well, it's irritating to be put on hold, that's all. Oh, never mind. I called to tell you I was at Debbie's the other night for dinner, and you'll never guess who she set me up with—someone from a famous family."

"This is silly. Just tell me. You know I don't like guessing games."

"I met John, the son of Admiral Perry! The Admiral Perry who started the Seabees in World War II."

Without skipping a beat, she said, "Your dad, you know, was a sergeant in the Army Air Corps in World War II." It never failed. At the very mention of World War II, Mom would bring up Dad.

"Yes, I know, Mom. I know. But I wasn't talking about Dad. I was talking about John. Captain John Perry. He's Admiral John Richard Perry's son, and great-grandson, by the way, of the Admiral Peary who went to the North Pole. Now that I think of it, John is an admiral, too. He was promoted when he retired."

"Well, your father served proudly even if he didn't get stationed overseas," she said. Why she felt the need to be defensive or competitive about that, I'll never know.

"Dad certainly did his part, Mom," I said, hoping to appease her. "John did, too. He was a Navy SEAL in that war."

"World War II? What are you saying? How old a man is he?"

I told her.

"What in heaven's name could Debbie have been thinking? A man only two years younger than your mother!"

"What Debbie was thinking, Mom, was that she needed a fourth for dinner. That's all. She wasn't making a match. Look, I'm only mentioning this to you because he was such an interesting man, really special and nice. He's not only straightforward, he's also kind and generous. I was lucky to meet him, that's all.".

"I don't think you should see him again. He's much too old for you."

Here we go, I thought. "Well, you don't have to worry about it, Mom. He didn't ask for my phone number." I knew that even if he had, and even if he'd been the "right" age for me, it wouldn't have mattered. Mom and Dad both would have automatically spoken negatively about him. The fact that I was thirty-five and quite capable of deciding for myself what was or was not in my best interest would never occur to them. They were still stuck back in time, still worried about me getting in with the wrong crowd, and if they could get away with it, even now, they would restrict me from dating anyone at all, as they had done for two endless years when I was in high school. It wasn't my fault that a jealous schoolmate called them and told them I got pregnant at a party, when all I had done was some passionate kissing. Going overboard with discipline was their style, so there was no point in arguing with her. Still, it was impossible to hold back entirely.

"Mother," I said, "don't you think it would be more reasonable for you to hold off making judgments about people until after you've met them?" I wished I'd bitten my tongue.

"If you're referring to this John Perry," she said coolly, "a man twenty years older than you…I don't need to know any more than that."

Our conversation ended quickly. As I hung up the phone after defending John to my mother, I was suddenly aware I was far more interested in him than I had pretended. I envisioned him, placed myself in his aura again…the way he acted, spoke, looked at me. I loved the way he made me feel, as though his own honor had some-how rubbed off on me, making me important, too. Hearing about his heroic exploits had expanded my understanding of military life, and being exposed to the larger-than-life figures of his father and his great-grandfather had strongly heightened my sense of history. In addition, when John mentioned being ostracized by his family despite his unwavering generosity, my caregiving instincts were deeply stirred. After this last ego-battering conversation with my mother, I appreciated John's attentiveness and kind words to me all the more. He made me feel valuable and important.

I glanced over at the kitchen wall clock and realized I should have left for school ten minutes ago. I hated to be late. I hopped off the stool, grabbed my briefcase and jacket, and ran to the car. As I zoomed down the freeway, I couldn't help wondering, might John Perry, despite our age difference, be the salve to heal the abrasions of my soul?

I was still thinking about John the next morning when I noticed that a Johnny Mathis concert was coming up soon on my calendar. Why not offer my extra ticket to John? No big deal. Going together to the Concord Pavilion for the concert would be a fun evening, that's all. There was nothing unusual about a woman inviting a man for a date these days. It was perfectly acceptable.

I called Debbie. She gave me John Perry's work telephone number, the only number she could provide.

John sounded pleased to hear my voice when I called him. He told me how much he had enjoyed meeting me, and revealed that he'd wanted to call me but hadn't wanted to seem forward. He gladly accepted my invitation and, to my delight, invited me to join him for dinner before the concert. I hung up the phone, giddy as a schoolgirl. This famous man wanted to go out with me. Me! I twirled into the lab and circled the center bench, like *West Side Story*'s Maria, singing "I Feel Pretty." Fortunately no one was around to hear me make a fool of myself.

During the two weeks before the concert, John and I kept in touch by telephone. I relished each call and looked forward to our conversations. The night before our Pavilion date, I was surprised when he said he was calling from the Oakland airport. He'd just gotten back from L.A., he told me. He and Ted had gone together on business, and Ted was there with him. They agreed it would be great fun for Debbie and me to meet them for dinner at La Cigale in Walnut Creek. "How about it?" he asked.

"Sure. When?"

"Tonight."

My heart sank. I wanted to go, of course I did, but I already had plans to barbecue with Jenna, my boarder. Jenna was an Excelsior intern, just for the summer, and I loved her company. She had needed a temporary place to stay, and I had just moved into a brand-new, three-bedroom home in Antioch only five months before. My finances were stable, but the extra income she provided was the perfect remedy for my FNS (financial nervousness syndrome), and we'd become friends in the meantime. Much as she and I enjoyed each other's company, we were both so busy we rarely spent an evening at home at the same time. Tonight was to be one of those nights. The charcoal in the Weber was already heating up. "I'm sorry," I said. "I can't."

"Oh, come on. Drive over to Ted's and meet us. We'll probably pull in about the same time. We'll have a drink first, then go together to La Cigale. You'll love its Country French atmosphere, and I know the owners. They'd love to meet you."

"Sorry, I can't, I have other plans. Jenna and I are going to enjoy a quiet, relaxing evening at home."

"You want to relax? Relax over dinner with me. Have your barbecue another night."

"No, I made these plans, and I don't break plans I've made with friends."

"Just a minute."

I heard muffled conversation but could not make out the words. After a few moments John came back on the line. "Okay. This is perfect. Do you know Dan?"

"Debbie's son, Dan?"

"Right. Ted tells me he's home from college this weekend. So it's perfect! Bring Jenna along with you. Dan will come, too."

Stretching the phone cord, I squeezed past the dining room table to look out the sliding glass door to the back deck. Jenna was stretched out, relaxing. Exactly what she sorely needed, and what I needed. No pressure. No expectations. No demands.

"I don't know," I said. "I hate to put her on the spot."

"Why don't you ask her?" he said simply. "What could it hurt?"

I thought about it. Even before I met John at Debbie's dinner party, I learned that as much as I prefer to make plans carefully, spur-of-the-moment decisions often worked out even better. Holding on to that thought, and the delightful feeling that John desperately wanted me with him tonight, I went out to Jenna. She'd already heard all about John from me, of course. Now I told her that he was on the phone, urging us to join him and the others for dinner. "Are you up to it?" I asked. "Please be honest."

"Hmm," Jenna mused. "Tell me, what do you know about Dan?"

"He's a darling, a senior, majoring in physics at UC Berkeley. Very friendly and good-looking, too...blue-eyed, blond, and very athletic." I smiled. This could be a good match.

She grinned, apparently entertaining the same thought. "But, what about the fire and…that?" She pointed to the Pyrex dish filled with our marinated New York steaks.

"Jenna, if you really want to go on this adventure, we'll simply douse the charcoal, refrigerate the meat, and go. You can grill the steak tomorrow night." I walked over to the TV tray beside the grill, saying over my shoulder, "Invite a friend over." I turned and winked at her. "Maybe a 'new' friend."

"I like the way you think," she said. Her eyes widened. "Wait! I haven't got a thing to wear. I didn't bring anything with me decent enough to wear to a place like that."

I picked up the dish of steak and said, "Come." She followed me into the kitchen. I put the dish down and picked up the phone. "You win," I told John. "We'll see you at Debbie's."

Jenna wrapped the not-to-be-eaten-tonight food with plastic wrap. "Barbara, what will I wear?"

"Pick whatever you want from my closet," I offered with a smile. "Except for the red jersey dress." She chose the white summer chiffon with spaghetti straps and a matching sleeveless bolero.

An hour and a half later John held the beveled-glass door to La Cigale open for us, and we stepped into the small reception area. The hostess recognized John and smiled at us warmly. "Welcome," she said in a soft French accent. "Captain Perry, so good to see you again." As she led us to our table I looked around at the charming decor…lace curtains and tablecloths, colorful fresh flowers, the room lit only by candles. The ambience was created for romance.

Dinner was exceptional, each course a culinary delight. John carefully selected a different wine to accompany each of the many courses and, as we indulged ourselves, he regaled us with more of his exciting stories, which fascinated everyone. Even better, I could see that Dan and Jenna appeared fascinated with each other. Yes! Deciding to do this had been the right choice.

We were having dessert when John excused himself and strode off to the kitchen, emerging a few moments later with Marcel, the owner and chef. At our table, John made the introductions. Marcel nervously wiped his hands on his apron and, in a charming soft accent, apologized for his attire. John said something in French to Marcel, who answered in French, and before I knew it they were involved in a lively conversation. It was slightly awkward for the rest of us as we sat there quietly with our eyebrows raised in surprise while we wondered what he might be saying. Finally, Marcel bowed and returned to the kitchen. John resumed his seat.

"I didn't know you spoke French," Ted said.

"Actually, I speak seven languages. English, of course." John grinned, picked up his wine glass and sipped from it. "And Spanish, Dutch, German, Italian. Let's see, what did I leave out?"

"French," Debbie said.

"French, *naturellement*!" He snickered, staring at the six fingers he had extended as he recalled each language. "One more." His eyes stared upward. "Oh, yes, Swahili."

"Why so many?" Jenna asked.

"I've been stationed around the world. Some I learned when I was at the Monterey Naval Language School."

"Swahili!" I said, laughing. "I have a hard enough time with English." I looked into his twinkling blue eyes. "So tell us. What were you and Marcel discussing in French?"

"Nothing, really," John replied sheepishly.

"Come on, John," Ted said. "Out with it."

One by one we cajoled him, until finally John said, "Oh, all right, I'll tell you." He shifted in his chair and lowered his eyes. Slowly, a little smile appeared. Then he looked at me. "I told him I was attracted to you."

My heart began to pound, and I could feel my face burn.

John didn't skip a beat. "Marcel said you were a beautiful woman, a striking combination with brunette hair and fawnlike eyes, so very French. I told him I was interested in pursuing you, but felt I was too old. Marcel replied that age didn't matter in affairs of the heart."

Had I just imagined what John said? After all, my heart had been thumping wildly. I glanced at the others. Each was looking at me, smiling. I knew I should say something, but simply could not speak. Out of the corner of my eye, I saw John watching me as well. The famous Admiral Perry was watching *me*, wanting to pursue *me*. It was a dream. It had to be. Finally, I simply lifted my wineglass, sipped, looked at John, and smiled.

On the following evening, our first planned date started off badly. John was very late, and I began to worry. When he finally arrived, I suppose he sensed my distress and apologized profusely, explaining that he had misjudged the distance out to Antioch. We left immediately and were only a bit tardy for our reservation at the Italian restaurant near the Pavilion. As dinner progressed and John once again charmed me with his manners, attentiveness, and spellbinding tales, the annoyance I had felt earlier vanished completely.

At the Pavilion I spotted Pam and George Rammell. Pam and I worked together, and she was one of my best friends. They were talking to their neighbors, Gretta and Barry, who in turn invited us all to their house after the performance. Later, as we sat around the living room, we discussed Johnny Mathis, and how incredible his voice still sounded after all these years. Barry brought in a round of drinks.

"I'm waiting for them to get Frank Sinatra," Gretta said.

Pam piped up, "Gretta knows everything there is to know about Sinatra. She's a huge fan."

John, seated beside me on the sofa, his long legs stretched out, casually remarked, "I know Sinatra."

"You do?" Gretta leaned toward John. "How so?"

"When he married Ava Gardner in nineteen fifty-two, I stood up for him at their wedding."

"That's odd," Gretta said. "I don't remember you being mentioned in the news stories."

"Reporters never care about who stands up for celebrities," John said.

"Why did he have you as his best man?" I asked.

John beamed. I couldn't wait to hear this story. "Sinatra knew my commanding officer. He ordered me to fly them down to Cuba on a military plane. The guy who was to be the best man couldn't make it, so Sinatra asked me to stand in as a proxy."

"Hmm," Gretta said. "I don't remember a Cuban wedding."

"I was there," John assured her. "They may have staged a public wedding later, but I was at their private ceremony."

Gretta rolled her eyes and opened her mouth, apparently ready to argue. Then, shaking her head, she said she'd get us some more munchies. I figured she knew less about Sinatra than she had thought.

As the evening continued, John dominated the conversation with lively accounts of his experiences. When John told one of his war stories, George spoke up, pointing out that John was mistaken about some of his so-called facts. George tried several times to correct John, but each time John was adamant about his facts being correct. Finally, George dropped the subject, as Gretta had done earlier. John, I thought, was most convincing.

I was so pleased that my friends seemed to look up to him. I wanted them to know more about him. Because they were all bridge buffs, I mentioned that John was a master bridge player.

"Great," Pam said. "Then we'll have to have a bridge dinner sometime soon."

As John and I were the first to leave that night, I had no way of knowing until years later that after we'd gone, my friends discussed John and agreed that he was opinionated and had dominated the conversation. They were convinced John had a serious problem with exaggeration, that he was delusional. They could not understand my attraction to him and argued about whether one of them should talk to me about him. In the end, they agreed I'd probably dismiss their concerns and might even get angry. Because they valued my friendship, they agreed to accept John, exaggerated stories and all.

While they were deciding that, I was deciding something too. Back in Antioch, we pulled up to my house and I invited John in for a brandy. The house was mine and I loved driving up to it and living in it…all two stories, three bedrooms, two-and-a-half baths, and double garage of it. It was a great satisfaction and a point of pride that I could reward myself with such a beautiful place after having worked hard for many years. I could control my life in a way that was visible to everyone.

Despite the late hour, John didn't hesitate to accept my offer for a drink, and soon it was apparent he wanted more. So did I. I took him by the hand and led him upstairs, sure it would be in our mutual best interest if I were to show how very much I cared for him. What better way to do that than to give him all of me? I asked him to stay the night.

Looking back, I now realize that my invitation propelled me into the waiting arms of a cunning psychopath. How could that happen? I thought I was a strong adult, in control of my life, an intelligent woman attending Golden Gate University at night while maintaining a fulfilling career during the day. I owned a brand-new home and a slightly used sports car. At that time, what I didn't recognize was that the exterior trappings I used to gauge success masked an inner void that made me vulnerable.

I now see that my move "over the hill" five months earlier had been more traumatic than I had realized. It started on moving day, when my boyfriend of a year didn't show up as promised and had called with a lame excuse that sounded the death knell to our relationship. I felt abandoned, and I silently grieved. That evening, as I climbed the stairs to bed, a surge of loneliness had swept over me, a loneliness brought on not only by my boyfriend's desertion, but also because all of my family and friends remained fifteen miles on the "other side of the hill." I felt as stranded and alone as if I had been on a deserted island. Several months later I'd had a jealous reaction to my friend Pam's marriage even though I was definitely happy for her and George. In a convoluted sort of way, I once more felt abandoned, as if her marriage would end our friendship. It didn't. When my busy schedule of a full-time job, college studies, and new-home decorating left no time for dating and perhaps finding a new love, I was ripe for the picking.

That night, when I asked John into my house, I realize now that aligned circumstances made me emotionally needy. John recognized it the first night we met. Like a panther on the prowl, he picked up my scent, sized up his prey, and moved in for the kill. I was emotionally defenseless against his attack and fell for his dedicated attention.

THREE

The Courtship

By the following week my emotions were so completely out of control that I was unable to concentrate on running my analytical lab. Me, the woman who practically invented the art of staying focused. John Perry was to blame. Ever since the night I invited him into my heart and my bed, I was blindsided. Now, for me, there was nothing else...only John.

Snap out of it, I scolded myself time and time again. *Pay attention to what you're being paid to do.* Mostly, I'd succeed. But fragments of our blossoming relationship kept interrupting my work with visions and memories...not all perfect, but at least hopeful. I could almost feel it...our bodies coming together, disappointment that our lovemaking had not been better, John's attentiveness with his toupee askew, my belief that practice would make perfect. After all, his neck and back did cause him pain.

John had stayed at my house for the next three days. During that time I believed I had learned all I needed to know. The man sharing my bed was a hero. During that first night, my fingers traced John's scar, a hero's scar. From the middle of his back his badge of honor stretched to the right down toward his waist, then traveled around to the middle of his chest. The first sight of it made me wince.

At the touch he remarked quite simply, "Vietnam. When I lost my lung."

I cuddled him all the tighter, deciding I would somehow erase his terrible memories of war, but each night, as he cried out from his nightmares, I realized that the experience of war ravages not only men's bodies, but their souls, leaving even heroes like John raw with pain. As John thrashed about, I woke to hear him scream, "Zero Charlie! Zero Charlie! Plane going down!"

In my caretaking mode and without any experience of dealing with a psychopath, I was sucked up into John's stories, all of them. Why would I suspect them as lies? Didn't he have the horrific scar that proved his courage under fire and a neck brace for the pain from the recent encounter with a baggage cart? Didn't I see the myriad of pills he swallowed daily to alleviate the pain? Since then, I have learned that extracting pity is a major ploy of a person without conscience because it's so easy to trap a victim who has compassion. John deftly played the pity game with me. His compelling stories kindled my empathy and love. I would learn much later that most of his tales were concoctions of his devious imagination wrapped around microscopic kernels of truth.

Now in the lab, I ordered myself to concentrate on my work. I was supposed to be titrating samples, not dreaming about easing John's pain. It was a losing battle. I wiped a tear from my eye, remembering John's anguish while he explained his recurring, disturbing nightmares, each with its own name, each connected to one of his horrifying war experiences.

"Zero Charlie took place during the Korean conflict," he stammered through his own tears, "when my squadron was attacked. We were outnumbered and retreating." His voice cracked. "I saw the enemy spitfire above Joe's plane. He was my best friend. I kept yelling, 'Zero Charlie, Zero Charlie'…even after he blew up right in front of me." His voice became a whisper. "I couldn't save him. I always ask why...why him and not me? He was the one with a wife, three kids. I wasn't married."

My lab phone rang, jolting me from my reverie. It was John, in Mexico City, calling during a break from his business meeting. How much better could it get?

"Hey, guess what I found in my briefcase?" he said.

"What?" I breathed, knowing full well what he had found. Before he left for the airport, I had slipped my snapshot portrait behind some of his papers.

"I'll never remove it from my briefcase," he gushed. And he never did.

"You honor me, sir." This man of mine made me feel so special. I felt myself melt and glow with each word he spoke.

"Ted won't let up on me, you know," he said. "Keeps chiding me about how worried he was when no one at work heard from me while I was over at your place."

I smiled, remembering those three glorious days. We were a perfect twosome, going to dinner, making awkward love, gushing about each other. It felt wonderful to be the center of someone's attention, but not just *someone*. John was a war hero with a famous family, a celebrity of sorts, and I wanted more than those three days. I wanted to be around him all the time. I had known him for only a month, but he had penetrated my heart and added spice to my ordinary life.

"I've got to come back down here in a couple of weeks," John said.

"Oh," I said, unable to keep the disappointment out of my voice.

"When I do, I want you to come with me."

"Go with you?" I loved to travel, to experience new places. I wanted to say yes with abandon, but I couldn't. "Ship's coming in," I explained. "I have to analyze the incoming products. I'm sorry, John. No can do."

It was so typically me. I had a reputation as someone you could count on, especially here at work. This dependability started when I was ten and my parents began what I called their "second family," three girls and a boy, spread out over the next nine years. I was the live-in babysitter, an immature third parent. But it was because of this dependability that I could afford nice clothes, a nice used car, and a nice home. My finances were stable, but I had to keep a close eye on my pocketbook. With care and prudence, my money situation was under control, and it was important to me to keep it that way.

"Surely you're due a vacation," he argued. "No one's indispensable. Find someone to cover for you."

"I can't."

"C'mon, Barb, I want you with me. Please."

"I don't know. I guess I could miss a few days of work, but I've got a final in my hazardous materials class."

"At the university? That's no big deal."

"It is because I've got an A riding on it."

"Negotiate it. Postpone the final."

"Can I do that?"

"Sure. Hell, I did it lots of times, when I studied for my Ph.D. at Berkeley."

"A doctorate?"

"Didn't I tell you? I've just completed my thesis in psychology and only have some required student teaching to finish." He explained that he had started a school for schizophrenics as research for his thesis. The program offered job training for clients to foster their independence and included typing classes and bird care. Incredibly, my brother had just been diagnosed as schizophrenic, but it didn't seem appropriate to share this fact at this particular moment, on a long-distance call from Mexico.

"John, you never cease to amaze me!" There was always something new, something exciting going on in his life. He was a true Renaissance man. "I don't know, John. I don't think I'd better."

"Honey," he said, "I've already told my business associates down here about you. About how I met the woman I'm going to marry."

I gasped. Had he just mentioned the M-word? I wanted to embrace the words he'd spoken, but my conservative upbringing warned me to beware. No matter how much I wanted to be with him always, this was moving far too fast. All I could utter was, "We'll see."

After ringing off, I called Western Union and sent John a telegram: "You light up my life. You give me hope to carry on." Not exactly original, but it said exactly what I was feeling. From that moment on, I began counting the days until I would pick him up at the San Francisco International Airport, as he had requested, even though I'd have to use a vacation day to do it.

Three days later, I easily spotted John in the baggage claim area. He was a vision to behold, the epitome of a man of the world, the best-looking man in the best-looking suit carrying the most handsome briefcase and garment bag. A shopping bag rested at his feet. As soon as he saw me, his face brightened in a loving smile. I felt so proud.

By the time we crossed the Bay Bridge, John had already showered me with gifts, and such *expensive* gifts: an exquisitely embroidered blouse, a gold Mexican coin, and a handcrafted copper plate. I couldn't believe my good fortune. He was spoiling me, and I had to admit to myself, I loved it.

"Listen, John," I said, "we're making a stop first. I'm bringing you over to meet my parents."

"What? Now? Why?"

"I think it's time." I explained this would be the best way, maybe the only way, for my parents to accept my decision to fly off to Mexico City with a near stranger.

"Fair enough," he said. "Bring 'em on. I can't wait to meet them."

"But, John?"

"Yes?"

"Please, no mention of . . ." I sighed. "Well, please don't mention anything about marriage. Okay?"

He shrugged. "Sure."

Forty minutes later we pulled into my parents' driveway in Concord. I led John through the back gate, through the garage, and into the family room.

"Barbara!" Mom exclaimed testily when she and my father saw us. "What's the matter with you? You know the back door is only for family."

Rather than say John would soon *be* family if things went as I expected, I introduced John as my new friend. Once we were all seated at the kitchen table, I quickly told them about John's recent trip to Mexico City. I even ran out to the car to fetch the gifts he'd given me so that I could show them off.

Yes, I was overanxious, but only because I hoped John and my parents would hit it off. I believed my family could not help but be impressed with the gifts and the man who had chosen them for me. When it appeared my folks had taken the bait, I casually said, "John is going to take me with him on his next trip to Mexico City in two weeks."

I braced myself, waiting for the floodgates of parental negativity to open. When they did, I prayed that John and I would withstand the surge and prevail in the end.

We listened to their warnings about bad water, Montezuma's revenge, and bandits. What about the language barrier? The cost, how could I afford it? I know my parents were concerned for their daughter's safety, but more than that, I knew they wanted to protect my reputation.

To each of their warnings, John countered with soothing words. We'd only drink bottled water; eat in the best restaurants; stay in a first-class hotel in the Zona Rosa, the most exclusive business area in the city. All costs would be covered by his expense account. He even went so far as to offer a religious appeal. We would visit the holy shrine of Our Lady of Guadalupe.

Not even God that day could make it come out right.

"You go ahead and do what you want, Barbara," Mom grumbled, making it perfectly clear that she and my father did not approve.

As usual, when it wasn't worth the battle to change their minds, I changed the subject. I mentioned John's distinguished family and his military career. This was a huge tactical error. Dad leaned forward, and the inquisition began.

"Weren't you a little young for World War II?" he asked.

"I lied about my age," John replied, "and went in against my dad's wishes. When he found out what I'd done, he tried to move me into officer school, but it was too late. I was already a member of the first underwater demolition team."

"The one that became the SEALs?"

"Yep." John's chest seemed to swell, and his eyes sparkled. "Not even my dad's rank could get me out."

"Rank? Oh, right. Barbara told me you said your father was the rear admiral who started the Seabees."

"He was a commodore at the time," John pointed out, "and made rear admiral at the end of the war."

I desperately wanted to find some way for these two men to come together on common ground, so I mentioned to John that my father was a lover of history, an avid reader, and a World War II buff. Mom, unhelpfully, took that moment to roll her eyes and mention that my father had only been stationed stateside. John didn't seem to notice or care.

"Well, sir, if you're a history buff," he said to Dad, "you probably know that my father was at the signing of the armistice with Japan, right there on the USS *Missouri*."

"Really?" Dad said. He stood, quickly crossed the room to the bookshelves, and pulled down a volume of the encyclopedia. He flipped through the pages and returned to us. "Here's a picture of the signing," he said. "It doesn't say anything about Admiral, excuse me, *Commodore* Perry." He handed the book to John.

Mom and I came around to peer over John's shoulder.

"There!" John said. "That's my dad." He tapped one of the

indistinguishable faces in the row behind the signatory table. I strained to see the face of his father but couldn't make out any distinct features, and none of the attendees were identified in the caption beneath the photo.

"Guess we'll just have to take your word for it," my father sneered. I glared at him, but he was not looking my way.

While my mother went into the kitchen to brew some coffee, my father continued to avoid my eyes and pursue his interrogation of John. "Tell me, John, based on your military exploits, why didn't you settle someplace closer to a base, say, a base like Alameda?"

John calmly replied, "Truth is, I never liked Navy social games. Not then. Not now."

John was fine, I thought, just fine. He was handling my father. I could breathe easy, knowing it was safe to leave the two of them to talk, so I excused myself to go into the kitchen to help Mom. John stood, excused himself, and asked for directions to the bathroom.

As I turned toward the kitchen, I noticed my father returning the encyclopedia to the bookshelf. After replacing it, he quickly pulled out another volume. I stopped to observe him as he seemed to study one particular entry until he saw John saunter back into the room. Dad snapped the book closed and shoved it back onto the shelf without a word. What, I wondered, had he been so interested in, and why hadn't he shared whatever it was with John?

As Mom and I served coffee and cake, I tried to steer the conversation away from our previous topics, but my father continued to run the show, and the next wave of questions quickly ensued.

"Barbara tells me your great-grandfather is Admiral Peary of North Pole fame. Why then, do you spell your name P-e-r-r-y instead of P-e-a-r-y?"

Without hesitation John answered. "Simple. He's my great-grandfather on my mother's side of the family." Winking at me, he added, "I'm a real Navy brat."

Dad leaned forward toward John. "Okay, then tell me this. If you're so famous and can run in any social circle you want, what do you see in my daughter?"

My lips parted, but I could not speak. My eyes stung with tears as I tried to make sense out of what had just taken place. Even John was speechless. What in the world was my father implying, that being the daughter of a blue-collar worker had forever cast me in a lower social stratum and that I, his own daughter, wasn't good enough to be with this man...my hero, the country's hero? I was humiliated and embarrassed, not just for myself and for John, but also for my father, for insulting a guest that way.

I stood up, fighting back tears. "He sees a...a....a real person!" I stammered.

John reached out and gently took my hand. He smiled at me and said, "Barbara makes me feel special. She has no airs; she's honest and trusting. I've looked a long, long time for someone like her."

I wiped at the tears that spilled from my eyes. After an uncomfortable silence, I thanked John and sat again. The visit continued with no more of Dad's endless, confrontational questions. That day I never noticed how easily John answered each one. He hadn't skipped a beat.

Later, on our way back to my place, I apologized for my father's unforgivable insensitivity. John laughed it off.

"Please don't apologize. It's typical. Believe me, I know. Even at my age, I catch plenty of grief. I'm considered the black sheep of the family."

"Why, for heaven's sake?"

"I don't live up to their expectations of what I should be doing with my life, or with my inheritance."

I bristled. "Well, John, at least you know it's not your money that attracted me to you. I told you that first night at Debbie's, and I'm telling you now...what I want, what I need more than anything is honesty, plain and simple honesty, especially after my first marriage."

I surprised myself with my own frankness and talked for a while about my first marriage, about enduring thirteen years of sexual infidelities. The pain still hurt.

"I want someone I can trust," I whispered.

"I'll never be anything but honest with you," he said as he reached across to stroke my hair. "You're too precious to hurt." His soothing words made my heart skip a beat. *This man really loves me,* I thought, *and doesn't everyone deserve a chance to be truly loved?*

At that very moment my parents were discussing the man who was promising always to be honest with me. They didn't care whether he was famous. Even though Dad had his suspicions about John, they both could see I was infatuated with him. They had decided they would not interfere in my life. In any event, it would not be proper to discuss their feelings or mine. Silence, not sharing, ruled in our family. Never again did they voice any opposition to John, his family, or his career.

Joyfully, I took their silence as acceptance. When John and I visited them the following week and John began calling them "Mom" and "Dad," they seemed to like it, and they seemed to like John, too. I saw no reason to question why John moved so quickly into my family, much sooner than one would expect in a normal budding relationship, because his presence vanquished my loneliness. In hindsight I should have recognized a red flag but, back then, I was hopelessly color-blind. So although I never had their official approval to go along with John to Mexico City, when I did go, I had the time of my life.

FOUR

Moving In

The Mexico City trip was as exciting as I dreamed it would be. We shared beautiful scenery, exquisite meals, sightseeing excursions, and great shopping. And John wanted to buy, no, *insisted* on buying me expensive gifts throughout the trip. I felt I had stepped into the pages of a fairy tale.

Back home, in real life, things were pretty fantastic as well. John was spending more and more time at my house. When he suggested moving in permanently, he made it seem not just a welcome idea, but an obvious one. Not only would we be together as much as we wished, but "with me around all the time," he said, "your life will be as grand as it deserves to be."

As tempting and right as the idea sounded, something held me back. I didn't say yes.

As though to prove his point, one afternoon John showed up with a twenty-four-by-twenty-eight-inch, $8,000 lithograph from the Collier Art Gallery in Los Angeles. He informed me of the details as he hung the art above my fireplace.

"No, no, no!" I cried out. "I can't have that here. My insurance doesn't cover such expensive art."

He waved away my reaction. "Nothing's going to happen to this, Barbara. Come here and take a close look at this Zapatista, the bold lines, the color, the passion!" I did. I stood beside him and had to admit that what I was examining was stunning and unusual, like John. "It is an exciting piece," I agreed, "but I don't see how...."

"Think about it. When I move in, the painting is protected, you're protected. Now that Jenna's no longer renting I'll help with the expenses. Who can argue with that?"

Bingo! He called my winning number. After I agreed to his plan, he fixed us a drink, remarking offhandedly that he would soon be improving my liquor cabinet, as well. "Grocery store brands," he said, "just don't cut it."

John moved in the next day. He didn't come with much. He brought his clothes, some furniture for the room that would serve as his office for consulting work, the hospital bed he said the doctor had prescribed for his back and neck issues, and most wonderful of all, his golden retriever, Gobi. When I expressed surprise at how little he'd brought with him, he said he had decided to leave most of his furnishings behind for his cousin, Jason Green, to use over in John's Danville house.

"You're so good-hearted, John," I said. He gave a no-big-deal kind of shrug. Then we turned our attention to our newly integrated family: me and my two cats, John and his dog.

The next six weeks provided plenty of ups and downs, as they probably do for any couple that comes together to work through the awkward period when candlelight and stardust meld into the unexciting routines of daily life. It wasn't easy. I knew it would take work and time to achieve a full level of comfort. Yes, I assured myself, we just needed time.

But it wasn't long before time became my adversary. One evening, as I sat at the oak desk in my upstairs study, I looked at the pile of bills before me and shuddered. Before John had come on the scene, I considered bill paying a dull but not unpleasant routine. Bills came in...checks went out promptly in full or at least with minimum amounts due. It was a practical matter, not an emotional one. Now bill paying had become pure torture. Decisions about who would get paid and who would not were getting harder and harder to make. There wasn't enough money to cover them all. Tonight was no exception.

I picked up the phone bill and felt a ripple of anticipation as I ripped open the envelope. The telephone bill held special significance. I'd been waiting, even longing for it, because it would list all the calls John made to his family, calls that hadn't appeared on previous bills.

I had come to think of those as "phantom calls" because John always made them when I was either away at class, at Mass, at work, or at the grocery store. It hurt that John would wait until I was gone before he'd call to speak with his family. Even though I explained many times how I yearned to connect, to talk with them, he continued to make the calls while I was away. When I finally got him to tell me why, the reason hurt even more. His family, he said, believed me to be a gold digger. It was absurd, of course. Each time I expressed how untrue, how unfair that was, John assured me that eventually they would come around.

This night I determined to take matters into my own hands. From the bill I would get the phone numbers and call John's family myself. The plan was sneaky and a little embarrassing, but it had to be done. If I could just meet his family, even by telephone, I'd change their minds. They'd come around and accept me as the woman who made John happy. John would be ecstatic, and love me all the more.

Now I perused the bill closely, pen in hand, ready to put phone numbers into my address book. But there were no calls to Coconut Grove, Boston, Houston, or New York City...cities where he said his family lived. I was disappointed and confused. What about all the times John told me he'd called Sonny, or Grandmother Dannigan? I shook my head to clear my thoughts, and filed this in the things-to-discuss-with-John part of my brain, as I wrote the check for the amount due.

I put that aside and opened my credit card statement. I couldn't believe it was right. The card was at its limit. I scanned through it in disbelief. Most were restaurant charges. I grabbed the bill, ran downstairs, and inserted myself between John and the television set.

"Hey, what gives?" he said, flashing a wide grin.

"This...this!" I sputtered, shoving the bill into his hand. "John, you said you needed to use my credit card for *one* business lunch. *One*. But...but..." I could hardly get the words out. "Look at all the charges!"

"No sweat," he said, tossing the bill on the coffee table.

"No sweat? You haven't paid your share of the expenses yet, and you misused my card. You stomped on my trust!"

"Hey, wait a minute, Barbara. Let's be fair. You never asked for it back, so I assumed it was okay to continue to use it."

He rambled on, rationalizing what he'd done, twisting my actions so they seemed wrong and elevating his into the right. He was a master of words, and his words made me dizzy. Then he said, "You're getting to sound just like the gold digger my family says you are."

I gasped. If there was one thing I knew I was not, it was that. I had an excellent job and an education, owned a sports car, held two house mortgages...held my own. His words struck through me so deeply I felt fighting mad. "I want my card back. Now!"

John stared at me. Scowling, he took out his wallet, yanked out the credit card, and threw it at my feet. "Goddamn Indian giver." He stood and glared at me. "I didn't realize this before, but you're just like your mother."

"No, I am not!" My voice was loud and harsh and filled with fury, completely unlike the calm me, the controlled me, the rational, reasonable, responsible, let's-talk-things-out me. As a child growing up with verbal abuse, I promised myself I would never yell in anger. No. I'd always talk things out calmly with my mate. Yet here I was, raising my voice, and I couldn't stop. "I'm not like my mother," I cried. "I just want to get the bills paid, and damn it, John, you're not helping. You're making it worse."

"I told you from day one, my commission checks are sporadic," John barked as he stood up. "I cannot help that." He shot me a look of disgust before he turned and strode toward the stairs.

"Where are you going?"

"To pack my bags. I can't stand this anymore. I know when I'm not wanted or appreciated."

The bewilderment I felt from anger quickly dissipated into fear as I watched John turn and walk away from me. With each angry stomp of his foot up the stairs, my hidden fears grew, fears I would not fully understand until much later. The fear of loneliness, of financial abandonment, of another failed relationship, each of which in turn triggered a fear of social and parental embarrassment. It was more than I could bear. I decided right then that I would back down and find a way to work it out. I would return to the comfort of John's arms, whatever the cost.

I now know this was not rational thinking for a loving relationship, but back then I had let my idea of a loving relationship slip into an addictive one without noticing the warning signs. This was the beginning of becoming so absorbed in John's needs and trying to fix them that I forgot about my own. I felt compelled—almost forced— to help John solve his financial problems with my unwanted advice and series of suggestions. I just knew I could change him. I would get him to control his spending so our lives would be stable. What I didn't realize then was that, one by one, as I let my boundaries slip, John was gaining more and more control of me—subversive control that made it seem like I was still in control, when I definitely was not. I was being manipulated by a psychopath who knew what he wanted and how to get it out of me. I entered the crazymaking world of the psychopathic verbal abuser. Looking back now, I can see that the pattern became entrenched that night. I continued to unwittingly play my role in the repetitive sordid drama for many years to come.

Just then my kittens, Peaches and Patches, skittered down the stairs. Peaches crossed John's path, and tripped him. "Goddamn cat," he hissed, picking himself up. He grabbed the kitten, raged down the stairs with her, and headed for the back door. Before I could get to him, he hurled Peaches outside. She landed hard, on her head, in the dirt, and began to convulse.

"You son of a bitch!" I screamed, as I tried to push John aside. I rescued Peaches and cradled her to my chest, rocking back and forth. As John came toward me, I shrank away from him.

"I . . . I'm sorry," he whispered. "Cats are supposed to land on all fours."

"Obviously," I managed while weeping, "they don't."

"Here, let me take her," he said. He held out his hands. I stepped back. Things had gotten so horribly out of control I was afraid of what he might do next.

"Please," he said, "let me have the kitten. I've treated convulsions on the battlefield. I have. Honest. I can help Peaches. Let me have her."

We stared at each other for a long time before I relinquished my sweet pet back into his hands. But the hands that had moments ago abused Peaches were now gentle and caring. When we were inside, I watched as John sat in the rocker with Peaches on his chest. "Please, Barb, get me a blanket," he said, "I'll spend the night with her here." I covered the two of them and left them there, listening as John called up to me, apologizing over and over, saying that his temper came from being half Irish and half Latin American. He called it a deadly combination.

I looked again at Peaches. She had calmed down. John had calmed down, as well, and so had I. At the middle landing, I turned around and called down, "John, so help me, if you ever lay a hand on her again, or me, you're out. Out! No second chance."

He didn't reply. I went to bed, but was too uneasy to stay there.

I needed to explore this violent side of John, so I returned downstairs and questioned him. He resisted. I probed some more. He finally acknowledged that he had been violent before, when he was a child and he had tied firecrackers to a cat's tail and lit them. He said he'd laughed. While I silently wondered how he could do such a thing, I acknowledged this was only a boyish childhood prank, no different than a scene from an Our Gang or Three Stooges comedy. Even my father had admitted to me many years earlier that he and his brothers had tormented their pet cat by pushing her through tunnels they had dug in their backyard. But at least they hadn't killed her. When I mentioned that I didn't think it was funny, John quickly added that he had felt bad when his father caught him.

Then he told me that he had also been violent as an adult, but only twice, and both times had occurred with his first wife. She'd asked for sex when he was busy doing the taxes. He shouldn't have, he said, but he did lose his temper with her. The other time was when she woke him from one of his nightmares. "Can you really fault me for that one?" he asked.

I didn't answer, but I stored his words as good counsel as I decided I would try my best not to provoke his hidden anger that could so quickly and violently explode at me. I vowed never to wake him from one of his nightmares. As for the sex, our lovemaking amounted to nothing after our first month together because of John's health problems. If it wasn't his headaches, it was his back; if not his back, his neck. I'd already sworn to him that it didn't matter, not when two people loved each other. I knew he needed me to take care of him, and by this time in the relationship I was willing to give up anything, even sex, to keep John in my life.

By now I was tired, worn down. Ready to close my eyes and put the past behind me. As I locked the front door, John called out. "I have an important lunch tomorrow. Can I use one of your other credit cards? I know what you're thinking, but I promise I'll get after Vestico to give me the commission check that's due."

I looked back at him, sitting in the rocker, serenely stroking my kitten. How could I turn him down?

"I'll leave it on the kitchen counter in the morning," I heard myself say. On the stairs I stopped midway and turned back to John. "I noticed on the phone bill that there were no charges for those calls to your family."

"Oh, that. It's because I charge all the calls to Grandmother Dannigan's phone number."

"How come you never mentioned it before?"

"Didn't think it mattered. Grandmother insisted. See, this way she knows I keep in touch with the family, no matter where I am in the world."

"Oh," I said wearily. "That makes sense."

Later, in bed, I again wondered why it was that John never kept in touch with the family when I was at home. I'd have to find out about that, I thought, but another time. I was beat.

The next six months were good, and not so good. Good: I was very happy to have an attentive, loving man in my life. Not so good: the man was incredibly irresponsible. My peace of mind had long ago abandoned me. Despite his promises, John's misuse of my credit continued.

John's evasiveness about his family continued as well. One day he presented me with a gift he said had arrived for me from Grandmother Dannigan. I discovered that it had arrived without a card or the brown mailing wrap. When I opened the gift—a sterling silver brush, comb, and mirror set—John told me proudly it had been his grandmother's. I could see from his expression that I was supposed to feel deeply honored, but I felt only confused. Not that I'd say so and risk insulting him, but if it had been his grandmother's personal set, why were *my* initials engraved into each piece? Was I expected to believe she'd had an engraver change them for me?

Most troubling of all were the finances. Just as they were about to cripple me, John presented me with his commission check. It was large and made up for the three months he'd been in arrears. It was a happy surprise, and so was what he did next...fly me again to Mexico City, this time to meet him for a long weekend. It seemed again that life was mostly good.

John's health worried me. One minute he seemed fine; the next, his leg would give out and he'd be on the floor in pain. I recall that one afternoon while he was on the stairs, his leg gave out, he tumbled down, and we spent the night at the hospital. After that, I watched him carefully. If he started to fall, I wanted to be around to catch him.

One day in spring, John and I set out for a picnic he'd planned as a surprise. I love surprises and enjoy driving, so I started out in a wonderful mood as I sat at the wheel of John's huge sixteen-passenger van.

The van came into my life not too long after John moved in. John said he'd gotten it for his school for schizophrenics, to help while he was gathering material for his thesis. He had turned control of the school over to someone else, but he would still pick students up and deliver them for their training program. I knew it was important to him...so important that I had agreed to finance it despite my better judgment. I knew my finances were already in trouble, but John pleaded that the lease was up and he couldn't afford to buy it. In a flood of words he talked me into buying the van for him, saying it could be in my name, and he'd make the payments on my credit union loan.

As much as I enjoyed the van for outings like this, the refinancing was a sore subject. I hadn't discussed it with anyone, and I didn't care to think about it now. Gobi, in the backseat beside the picnic basket, let out a bark, and John directed me west on the Delta Highway.

I had been taught at an early age that it is shameful to share feelings. In our family we didn't discuss personal problems. Our mantra was "Keep it to yourself," so this secret had to be mine alone. I also learned that love was rewarded only if I was a perfect little girl. Now I was that perfect little girl for John. I got him the van he wanted, and for that, he rewarded me with his love. For his love I was willing to stuff my apprehensions about the refinancing into my sack of secrets. It was what I had been trained to do, and I did it well. I would do whatever was necessary to make our relationship work.

"The van is great," I said, smiling, wanting to convince John, and trying to convince myself. "It's an adventure just driving this thing, and you know how much I love adventures. Like our last Caribbean trip."

He grinned and directed me north on I-680, across the Benicia Bridge, to a scenic overlook of the Suisun Bay. "I want to show you something special," he said, leading me up the path to the picnic table. "Look...out there."

He pointed to the Mothball Fleet, the floating graveyard of World War II ships tethered together, waiting their turn to become scrap iron.

"I've seen them all my life, John."

"Not the big one, out front. That's the *Glomar Explorer*."

"The big boat? The one all by itself?"

"It's not a boat, Barb, it's a ship. How many times do I have to tell you they're ships?"

Flipping the red-checkered tablecloth out over the table, I said, "All right, all right. I stand corrected." We laughed.

As I set up our first course of chilled Chardonnay, Sonoma Jack cheese, and fresh strawberries, I could see by the gleam in John's eye that he was off in another world, reliving his own adventures. He began to share them with me as he opened the wine and poured it into the Austrian crystal wineglasses. He told me the CIA had asked him to command that ship back in the seventies, when they wanted to recover the Russian nuclear submarine that had sunk seven hundred miles off the coast of Hawaii.

"Did you?"

He shook his head. "Told them no. After my experience in Panama, I wasn't up for any more dangerous assignments."

I remembered the gory Panama story from the night we first met. The retelling of his exploits never ceased to amaze me. His financial irresponsibility never ceased to amaze me either. Although I knew this was hardly the time, and as much as I hated having to do it, I realized I had to get him back to the present and our financial situation. I couldn't handle this problem alone. I needed his help.

He poured me another glass of wine. I took a sip, and casually asked, "Any word about your latest commission check?" I paused before going on. "They've put you off for five months now, and things are getting pretty tight."

"I know. I know," he said, hanging his head. "I'm sorry. Just can't get Vestico to break loose. But I started looking around for some other funds. You know, like you suggested."

My ears perked up. Maybe I had finally gotten through to him and he was going to come through soon after all. "And?"

"And my cousin, Jason Green, is going to buy my Danville house for two hundred thousand dollars."

I jumped to my feet. "That's great! When do you get the money?" I didn't want to sound like a gold digger, but the bills were beginning to resemble the listing *Titanic*. I was desperate to straighten out the mess, to keep us afloat, to get us back on an even keel.

"In seven years."

"Excuse me? What was that?" I slumped back on the picnic bench, shocked. *How could you sell a house and not get any money for seven years?*

John explained that Jason couldn't afford to get a loan, couldn't make payments. In seven years he'd pay the money in one lump sum. John was not going to charge Jason interest, only taxes and upkeep. Unbelievable! My body tensed and my head pounded as I watched my hopes drift out with the breeze across the bay. We both fell silent.

John eventually spoke. "You sure know how to ruin my surprises, don't you?"

Surprises? More? I held my breath. John fumbled around in his billfold, pulled out a folded piece of paper, and handed it to me.

"Grandmother Dannigan came through," he said. "Take a look. It's a five-thousand-dollar cashier's check." Before I could wonder why she hadn't sent a personal check, he continued. "She gave one to each of my cousins as well." He waited until I read the check. "But you're right. We need a long-range plan. So I put one together."

Almost afraid to hear it, I asked softly, "What is the plan?"

He told me we could rent the Antioch house where we were now living and move over the hill to my larger home in Concord, which was in a better neighborhood. The Concord house, for which I was still paying my share of the mortgage payments, wasn't selling. Until it did, I wouldn't get my portion of the sale. Unfortunately, it didn't show well because my ex-husband, Bryan, was camping out in it like a squatter. "A little paint, better furniture, and it should sell right away," John pointed out. "That would remove a large financial drain on you, don't you see?"

I did see, and the more John talked, the more it made sense, except for one thing. "Why is it always me who bails us out?" I asked.

"Because you're so good at it."

Despite his teasing, I felt my despair lift. I relaxed and began to set out the fried chicken and potato salad. "I'll call Bryan tomorrow."

"That's my girl," John said. He poured me another glass of wine. Sipping it, I could picture my desk, and the bills getting paid that night.

FIVE

The Proposal

I paid the movers, closed the double doors, and turned back into the two-story foyer. Here I was again, back home in Concord. I called out for John.

"I'm back in the bar. Almost got the liquor put away," he said.

He's so cute, I thought, happy as a lark. But nothing could dissipate the cloud of desperation that hung over my head. Fervently I hoped our plan would work. It just had to!

"The movers are gone," I yelled back. "Let Gobi and the cats out of the sewing room."

I slipped off my shoes. The cool dark oak parquet floor refreshed my aching feet. If only it could refresh my aching soul. I turned right and sat down heavily on the step of the sunken living room. I was exhausted, not so much from the physical activity of packing and moving, but from the mental strain. Stirred emotions surfaced, bringing up the memory of problems I hadn't bargained for. Initially, Bryan had accepted our moving plan, but everything went downhill from there. John's commission checks continued to be delayed, and

Bryan asked for an additional two months. All this stretched out our move-in date and aggravated our financial situation. The stress took its toll on my body. I had fainted at the annual blood drive at work.

"You have an extra heartbeat," the doctor told me afterward. "Been under any stress lately?"

"Not really," I said. How could I divulge my secrets to a stranger? How could I reveal my worry about strained finances, Bryan's delays, John's family? No, I couldn't tell. I had become a master of denial. Besides, this was a private matter, and I was sure I could find a way to handle it myself.

Sitting there on the living room step, though, I was engulfed in the pain I had experienced in this room, this house I had helped build over seven long years, and the pain of my failed marriage. I hugged my knees to my chest and sighed. In this room I had made one of the most important decisions of my life, a hard, lifesaving decision. My eyes brimmed with tears at the memory.

"Here now, what's this?" John said as he stepped into the living room and sat down beside me. Tenderly he lifted my chin with one finger as he wiped away the tears. "Today is a happy day. Why the sad face?"

My emotional dam burst. I buried my head in John's chest and sobbed. I sobbed about the way Bryan's affairs had loomed over our marriage, even as I labored to make it work. I was a good little Catholic girl clinging to my vows. Divorce was a sin, unmentionable. But no matter what I did for him, Bryan's demons couldn't be exorcised. The schism between us magnified and opened up a chasm neither of us could bridge.

I struggled with the words as I told John how Bryan had slowly distanced himself from me, emotionally and sexually, about how our marriage turned platonic. We became business partners, cordial to each other, but apathetic, and always busy. Busy finishing the house, busy building our cabin in the Sierra foothills, busy doing anything, everything to keep from communicating.

I sat up and looked into John's blue eyes and continued.

"Intimacy vanished. Evaporated. The void devoured me. One day I put a cassette into the tape deck, turned the receiver to full volume, and sat right here, where we are now, as Donna Summers blared 'Enough Is Enough.' As I listened to the throbbing beat something happened. I joined in, defiantly belting out the words, as loud as I could. 'Enough Is Enough!' It boosted my courage. 'Enough Is Enough!' I stood and firmly planted my feet. 'Enough Is Enough!' I'm getting a divorce."

"Whew," John said. "Some pretty strong emotions got stirred up, didn't they?" I nodded as he gave me a warm smile.

"What say we try to get rid of them," he beamed. "Let's plan a party."

I love a party as much as anyone, but my mouth fell open at John's suggestion. "A party? We're not even settled in yet, and there's so much to do, to get the house ready to sell."

"I don't mean right away," he countered. "I was thinking about a barbecue and swim party on Labor Day weekend. That's a month away. This house is perfect for parties, so spacious and well laid out. It'd be a shame to let a holiday go by without one."

John bubbled over like a little boy with a new toy. He wanted to show off his new house and share his good fortune with our friends, to show them a good time. His enthusiasm was contagious, and I couldn't resist.

"I'll even do all the cooking," he bribed, enveloping me in a bear hug.

"Okay, okay. I give in." I laughed. "We won't be here long, so we may as well have one big, blowout party."

We chatted about whom we'd ask, what we'd serve, getting sillier and sillier as we concocted the lists. Tired as I was, it felt good to plan something joyful together. I had no idea that John had a plan of his own, a long-term plan that was about to unfold.

"You know, this is a great house," John said.

"Of course it is. I built it. Remember?" I teased, jutting out my chest in exaggerated pride.

"No, no, I'm serious," he continued. "It's too bad we have to sell it after we fix it up."

I started to respond, but he held his index finger to my mouth. "Shush. Before you comment, I have something important to say. Wait. I need some stuff from the kitchen first."

He struggled to get to his feet, holding on to one of the decorative poles separating the living room from the foyer, and winced.

"Damn back and neck!" he exclaimed as he shuffled off to the kitchen.

This man of mine, I mused…so mysterious, so loving, so full of surprises, and in such constant pain. It tugged at my heartstrings. I heard him ramble about, open the refrigerator, move some boxes, then a distinct *pop*.

"Need any help?"

"No, thanks. I have everything under control." John walked back through the foyer holding a bottle of champagne and two paper cups. At his side Gobi padded along, head raised, sniffing for a handout.

"Well, almost under control. I couldn't find the champagne glasses, so these will have to do." He handed me the bottle and paper cups, then hunkered down beside me. Peaches and Patches scampered into the room, investigating their new digs.

"Here, let me pour," he said, taking the bottle as I held the cups for him. He set the bottle down between us and raised his paper cup.

"I've always told you my time with you has been the happiest of my life," he said, "and I really meant it. So here's to the woman who has made me the happiest man alive."

I smiled and touched my paper cup to his. We both took a sip. Not to be outdone, I raised my cup. "And here's to the man who lights up my life." We both sipped once more, basking in the afternoon sunlight filtering in from the upper foyer window. Then, gently and with purpose, he reached over and took my right hand in his.

"You have made me very happy," he said. "There's only one

thing that could make me happier. Would you be my wife? I want to marry you and spend the rest of my days with you."

It was the declaration my heart had been aching to hear for the last six months. He wants me to be his wife. The admiral's wife!

"I don't know," I blurted out, surprising even myself. I looked down at my hands, at my feet, everywhere but into John's eyes. The proposal had caught me surprisingly off guard. Instead of triumphant joy, I tumbled into an abyss, lost in the world between good and bad, positive and negative, fighting my inner self for control of my boundaries.

What young woman in her right mind would give up sex for the rest of her life? Am I really happy? Isn't this just like last time? But no, I argued with myself, *unlike Bryan, John can't help his health problems, can he?* I was being unfair, judging him and projecting the hurt from my last relationship onto this one. It wasn't that John didn't *want* to make love. At least he wasn't cheating. Besides, he showed his love in sweet gestures, in buying me presents, in cooking dinner, in rubbing my feet as we watched TV. He was definitely affectionate with me, and I enjoyed our time together.

My finances have never been so bad. I'm constantly stressed out and embarrassed by his habitual overspending. He's too irresponsible. I countered these thoughts, too. Finances were strained at the moment, but John's sizable checks, however erratic, did appear. He promised to get Vestico under control or find another consulting job. He'd already sold his house. I knew we could count on that money, even though it was seven years away. If things got really tight, there was always his inheritance, controlled by his grandmother. Surely she would help John out by advancing some of his share if he were facing a true financial hardship? Also, we planned to sell the Concord house and move back to Antioch. The finances could be handled.

What about his angry outbursts? How long before he hauls off and hits me? What about his threats to leave? I asked myself. Those concerns hadn't reared their ugly head for some time. He hadn't hurt our pets since the night with Peaches, and he'd never, ever hit me. If we were married, he wouldn't be able to leave so easily. My whitewash brush was busy making everything clean and fresh. I was a woman in love.

How about John's arrest? Oh, yes, the arrest. The month before our move, John was arrested and booked on felony grand theft, over four Remington Rand typewriters. I was devastated and scared. It had to have been a misunderstanding, otherwise Ted would not have put up his motorhome as bond. John's explanation sounded reasonable. He had purchased the typewriters for his school for schizophrenics and was waiting for his stipend from the state to pay for them. A mistake. It was all a big mistake. He'd be able to get the charges dropped. I stopped asking questions and stuffed this in my sack of things to deal with later.

As boundaries disappeared, happy thoughts flooded in and I felt more pleasure than pain. Saturday nights were no longer lonely. Travel, one of my passions, was exciting and adventurous. Mexico. St. Croix. Where else might we go? Best of all, our relationships with my family and friends blossomed.

My denial and neediness worked overtime. *All couples have issues to work through,* I reasoned. *Ours will be financial.* I knew, beyond the shadow of a doubt, that I made John's life better. He had said already that his time with me was the happiest in his life, and it would improve once we ironed out our difficulties. My resolve strengthened. I would get him reunited with his family. I would take care of him when he was sick. I would provide him with my family and new friends. I would get him to change his spending habits, to become financially responsible. If anybody could do it, it would be me. Yes, me. I could fix anything. I just had to put my mind to it.

For the second time in my life, sitting on that living room step, I made a major decision. Unlike the first time, I wasn't feeling trapped, defiant, aching for something more. I was making a happy decision, positive, and invigorating. I felt in control of my future. I was charting a new course for my life's journey. We had been together for more than a year, and I knew all I needed to know about him. I looked into John's blue eyes.

"Yes, I will marry you, John. I can't think of anything better than being the admiral's wife."

It had been a fun day, exhausting but exhilarating. The barbecue and swim party had turned out well. The weather was sunny and warm, and the financial clouds had dissipated for the time being. The last of our guests, including Pam and George, straggled to the door.

"Thanks for the great party," Pam said as she hugged me. "I'll call you tomorrow to make the list for your bridal shower."

"Pam's such a good friend, isn't she?" John remarked as he closed the door.

"Yes, friends like Pam are few and far between. George, too. I'm glad they found each other. Just like we did."

I started picking up party remnants.

"Let's not do this now," John said as he walked into the kitchen with another load of dirty glasses. "Let's go relax in the hot tub."

"What a delicious proposal," I said. "Last one in gets to finish the cleanup." We both laughed.

"I'll pour us some champagne," John called as I went to get dry beach towels.

The warm, circulating water relaxed my aching muscles. I laid my head back and closed my eyes. "This is the life," I drawled. "There's nothing like a redwood hot tub to help one communicate with nature."

We both sat in silence in the therapeutic waters, sipping our champagne, each caught up in our own thoughts. Finally, John broke the silence. "Glad we had the party?"

I opened my eyes and looked at him. "Yes. You always seem to know the right thing to do." He looked so relaxed, so happy. This seemed like the perfect time to bring up something that had been bothering me.

"John, have you told your family yet that we're getting married?"

He hesitated, as if afraid his answer would break the spell. "Turn around and I'll rub your shoulders."

"Don't use diversionary tactics on me, Mr. Military Man," I warned as I turned my back to him. "Did you talk to your family or not?"

His strong hands began to knead my neck and shoulders. "Yes, I've talked to them, all of them, one by one."

"Well?"

He repeated the same story I had heard many times. They were unhappy. I was a gold digger after their family fortune. Millions were involved. Worse, I was driving a wedge between him and his family. They were emphatic about not attending our wedding, as if that were going to keep us apart.

I knew then that I had to try harder to talk to these people, and soon. They just had to meet me and see us together. Then they couldn't deny how happy we were with each other.

"Your muscles are tensing up," John warned. "Relax. Think about this wonderful house and all it has to offer." His fingers ran up and down my spine.

"What do you mean, 'all it has to offer'?"

"It's so big, well laid out for entertaining, and in a great neighborhood. Best of all, it's close to your family and our friends. What a shame we'll be fixing it up just to sell it and move back to Antioch, over the hill."

"But that's our plan," I said. I turned around and scooted away so I could prop my feet on his lap. He obligingly grasped one foot and began to massage it.

"Plans can change," John replied. "Think how comfortable we feel here."

"This house is cursed," I blurted. "It has bad memories for me, of hard labor, joyless days, a cheating heart. I can't forget that. How can you?"

"Those are memories from the past. This is the present. You're with me. We can create our own future here, make our own memories, like today's wonderful party with family and friends."

"Minus *your* family," I snipped. John winced. He dropped my foot and I quickly apologized. It wasn't his fault that his kids lived on the other side of the country.

"My third cousins, Sarah and George, were here," he whimpered as he lowered his quivering chin. Sarah and George Green were "kissin' cousins"; at least that's what John had called them when he first introduced us. They were Jason's parents, a sweet, elderly couple from Danville who never contradicted John's relationship claim. In later years I would wonder why, but this was now and I had to squelch this latest idea of John's. I ignored his cousin comment and returned to the subject at hand—staying in my Concord house.

"We can't afford it, plain and simple," I insisted. "We need to sell it to get ourselves on an even keel. Remember? Besides, I own it jointly with Bryan."

"I've thought hard about that, calculated things, and I think I found a way for us to stay here. That is, if you really want to."

John slowly, cautiously laid out his strategy. He outlined, in full detail, how we could get a second mortgage on the house and buy Bryan out. Then, if we still wanted to sell, we could wait until the real estate market perked up. We could even get extra money to pay for the improvements. He baited me and it worked. I grabbed the hook and admitted it sounded like a reasonable thing to do.

"The problem is, I don't think I'll qualify for a second mortgage," I said.

Then it came. With all the finesse of a well-seasoned fisherman, he began to reel me in. "I'll cosign on the loan," he offered. "We'll work to get it paid off as soon as possible." It didn't dawn on me at the time, but by doing this, John would get his name on the title of my house. For now, I was only paying attention to the adventure of it all.

"Sounds logical. Promise me we'll work hard to get rid of the second mortgage."

"Nothing would suit me better."

We began at once to make plans about how I would approach Bryan, what our offer would be, and how soon we thought we could get it done. "Hey, I'm turning into a prune," I said, looking at my wrinkled hands and standing up. "We'd better get out."

"Just one more thing," John said, reaching out and putting his hand on my arm. "It's about the grand theft charge."

I froze and didn't say a word. I had stuffed that episode into my little bag of unresolved problems and given it no thought for more than a month. Now here it was in front of me. I was afraid of what might come next, afraid it might blow our new plans out of the water. Could I marry someone right before he headed off to jail?

"Don't look so worried," John said. "It's good news. I heard from my attorney, Max Rosberg. He says he can get the charges dropped."

"Dropped? How?" I sat back down. This *was* good news.

"Remington Rand will drop the charges if I pay for the typewriters."

"How much will that cost?"

"Only four thousand dollars," John said blithely, "but…"

I grabbed the side of the tub with my free hand, bracing for whatever was to come next.

"But what?"

"I also have to pay Rosberg's fee, another four thousand."

"That's eight thousand dollars," I sputtered. "You don't have that kind of money. *We* don't have that kind of money. Oh, my God, what are we going to do?" Fear made my legs weak. I dropped onto the edge of the hot tub. My perfect day was sinking.

"Now that we plan to get a second mortgage, I figured we could add that eight thousand to the amount we were going to get. There's plenty of equity in the house to cover it."

"I don't think so," I snapped. "That's *your* obligation. Why don't you call your grandmother if she's got so much money?"

"You know I can't right now. The family is upset as it is. I need you to help me."

"I'm not going to merrily hand you over eight thousand dollars, especially since I don't have it!" I jerked my arm from his grasp and climbed out of the tub. Grabbing my towel, I headed across the deck toward the house. John was quick to follow and blocked the door before I could get in. "Wow, you move pretty fast for someone always in pain," I said. "Get out of my way."

"Please, Barbara," he implored. "Listen to me. I don't expect you to just give me the money, I want to borrow it. I'm asking for a loan."

"Loan?" He had my attention. He was a master at getting my attention.

"Yes. I will pay you back. I swear. We need to get this over with and move on with our life together. Don't you see how it muddies up the water if it's still hanging out there?"

He did have a point. He always had a point. He was able to make whatever he suggested sound like the perfect solution. Once more I lowered my boundaries and became the good little girl. "Okay. But remember, it's a loan, l-o-a-n. And you will pay it back."

He put his arm around me and gave me a tender squeeze. "Of course. You're my gal. I love you so much."

I relaxed into his embrace as we went inside, and my thoughts drifted to my upcoming bridal shower and a vision of our wedding day: white chapel, John in dress uniform, trumpets blaring as we emerged under an aisle of crossed swords, smiling, ready to spend the rest of our lives together. Too soon I would discover that dreams don't create reality.

S I X

The Wedding

A month later, on a sunny October afternoon, John and I checked into the Westgate Hotel in San Diego.

"Here on vacation?" the desk clerk queried.

Definitely not, I thought. *No, we're on an exciting secret mission, like undercover agents...unmarried ones.* But not for long. Our clandestine wedding was only hours away. I giggled when John asked for the bridal suite.

"Isn't this place as palatial as I promised?" John asked as we passed the curve of the sweeping brass staircase and stepped into the mirrored elevator.

I nodded. One thing about John, he had good taste. *Expensive* taste. This fancy hotel was definitely living up to his earlier descriptions. Seeing it took my breath away. When the bellhop opened the door to the bridal suite, I pinched myself to make sure I wasn't dreaming. Gilded baroque glistened everywhere...on the white paneled walls, the elegant French period furnishings, the framed mirror above the marble fireplace, even the old-fashioned telephone.

"Well, what do you think?" John grinned as he closed the door and walked back into the living room.

"It's everything you said, and more." I ran to John, put my arms around his neck, and tiptoed to reach his lips. "Thank you," I whispered.

We quickly settled into our love nest. While I unpacked what few things we had brought, John telephoned the Clays to let them know we had arrived.

"They'll be over in an hour," John said as he put the receiver back in its cradle. He glanced at me perched on the king-size bed. "Unpacked already?"

"Didn't have much. Don't forget, this is a one-night stand."

"Well, I'd hardly call it that." John laughed, as he made his way into the bathroom and closed the door.

In the silence of the room, left alone for the first time that day, I felt somehow lost. Maybe I hadn't done the right thing, planning a wedding without family and friends. Was the decision to run away and get married as romantic as it had originally sounded? Then John emerged from the bathroom, stripped to his underwear, and my heart flipflopped back to the excitement and my need to share it.

"Can I call my mother now?" I pleaded, trying hard not to let my doubts show. I didn't want to ruin this day, of all days.

"Okay, but don't take too long," he said. "The Clays will be here any minute." He came over and put his arm around me, swaying as he sang, "because we're going to the chapel and we're gonna get ma-a-arried."

I smiled and dialed my parents' telephone number. John went off to get dressed.

"Mom, guess what?" I chirped. "We're in San Diego, getting ready to go down to Tijuana and get married!"

Dead silence on the other end of the phone told me at once what my mother's reaction was. "Last week at the shower you said that you hadn't set a date," she said. "Why so sudden? You're not pregnant, are you?"

"No, Mom." I explained that John had come home on Thursday, excited about finding a deal with the airlines. If we bought two coach tickets to a destination at least five hundred miles away, we'd get two tickets to Hawaii for only $50 each. "So let's run away and get married," John had said, making it sound crazy romantic, yet practical, too. "You know our funds are tight."

He was right, again. We really couldn't afford a big wedding. Oh, we were flush with the second mortgage money we'd received the day before, but that money was earmarked for Bryan, Max Rosberg, and Remington Rand.

"We'll surprise everyone," John continued. "We won't tell a soul. And," he winked, "the Hawaii trip will be our honeymoon."

Hawaii, beautiful Hawaii. I could feel the warmth of the trade winds, hear the soft *plink* of the ukuleles, taste the cool piña coladas. We could go to Maui, Molokai, and the Big Island and enjoy the bridal suite at a fancy hotel. John instinctively knew how to play to my weaknesses....exotic travel, a great bargain, and what sounded like a fairy-tale wedding.

As I talked to my mom, my chest tightened. I hadn't been up for the elopement idea at first; it sounded too bizarre for adults our age. But for every obstacle I mentioned, John had an equally sound reason to overcome it, offering up something exciting in its place. As he talked, I could actually believe that running away to get married in a foreign country, without telling family, made all the sense in the world. As for friends, he'd get one of his customers to stand up for us. The Clays lived in San Diego, and could meet us at the hotel. Now, here I was in that hotel, getting closer and closer to being the admiral's wife, and trying to make my mom believe the fantasy too.

"Mom, I thought you and Daddy liked John."

"We do. He's a nice man, but..." Her voice trailed off. I knew what she would say next....words of disappointment and disapproval to guilt me because we were not marrying in a Catholic church. "Don't throw away your upbringing," she pleaded.

"I'm not. You know how I feel about the Church, how I was

treated as a divorced Catholic. Like a leper. Worse! At least they minister to lepers. Anyway, John said if I want, we can have a church wedding later this year, in Mexico City. Today is the first step, the prerequisite civil ceremony."

My show of independence gave me a lift, and my earlier doubts began to dissipate. I was my own woman, quite capable of living my own life, thank you very much.

"I'll call you when we get home, Mom," I said. We ended our conversation politely and briskly. Not on the best of terms, but at least not on the worst.

I picked up the telephone once more. Pam would surely share my joy. I felt hurt when she, too, sounded cool and distant.

"Running off to Mexico is no different than when you and George went up to Reno to get married," I challenged.

"Yes, it is. We had the date planned and several couples went with us."

"Well, I have to admit I thought my second wedding would be fancy, with friends and family around. But, what the heck! It's so romantic this way."

"If you say so," she replied, and diplomatically ended our conversation.

"Why are they such wet blankets?" I whined as I set the receiver down. "You'd think they'd be happy for me."

"They're just jealous," John said as he put the final knot in his blue-and-gold striped tie—colors of the naval academy, as he'd pointed out to me more than once. "Don't let it get you down. They'll be okay when we get back. Trust me. We'll show them true happiness." He glanced at his wristwatch. "You'd better get dressed; the Clays will be here any minute."

I disappeared into the dressing area. When I emerged several minutes later, John let out a low whistle. I twirled, feeling the soft white chiffon circle my legs, and remembered the romantic evening when John first declared his interest in me, speaking French, the night Jenna wore this dress. Practical me, I made it my "something old" at a time when I couldn't afford the "something new." Even if I could have splurged on a bridal gown, I hadn't had the time to shop.

The doorbell rang. The Clays had arrived. John introduced the Clays as J.R. and Carrie, explaining that J.R.'s name was really John, but when there was more than one John in the crowd he'd go by J.R., the initials of his first and middle name.

"How about a toast?" J.R. said, handing John a cold bottle of champagne.

"And a wedding present," Carrie smiled, presenting me with a silver-and-white box.

We settled into the living room as John went into the kitchen. "Look what I found," John announced as he emerged. "Champagne glasses. They thought of everything for this suite."

Like a little kid at Christmas, I tore into the wrapping paper. I held up a crystal-and-silver salad bowl. "It even has a silver serving set," I beamed. "Isn't it grand?" John nodded and popped the cork. We drank a toast to a beautiful wedding and a long life together.

The Clays were a warm, gracious couple from England and Malta. I was pleased with John's choice and amazed that he had done it again. I was caught up in the moment, enjoying the excitement of the day: my pretty dress, great new friends, a wedding present, champagne, and best of all, my admiral who loved me, only me! I crammed the disparaging phone calls to my mother and Pam into my "I don't want to think about it" sack. I refused to let their reactions spoil my happiness.

"Folks, look at the time," John said. "We'd better get going. Don't want to be late for the chief of police. He might throw us in the hoosegow."

Twenty minutes later, J.R. drove us through the border check and we entered another world: Tijuana. As we crossed over the dry riverbed, I cringed at the sight of hundreds of shanties made from corrugated steel, plastic, cardboard, and whatever could be found to try to keep out the summer heat and the winter cold.

I tried not to stare as we made our way through the outskirts of town, but couldn't help myself. Men in torn, dirty T-shirts stood outside cluttered automobile upholstery shops, drank beer, and puffed on cigarettes. Music blared from crackling radios. Colorful signs plastered on the dusty windows of the local bars advertised MARGARITA GRANDE. Everyone waited for the gringos. Were they waiting for me? Why was I here?

I moved to the edge of my seat, ready to call the whole thing off, to say we'd do it later, somewhere else. Out the window I could see we were entering a more affluent area. There were attractive shops, banks, restaurants, pharmacies, trees and benches, and strolling shoppers. I slumped back into my seat.

"Where's the chapel?" I asked, scrutinizing each street we passed.

"I don't know," John said. "The police chief set everything up."

John had used his Mexican friend in Los Angeles to facilitate getting a minister and a marriage license. The police chief was the go-between.

J.R. pulled into a parking place between two police cars and John hopped out. "Stay here while I go in," he said. He disappeared up the steps, past guards armed with machine guns. Within minutes he was back in the car. "We missed the chief. He had an emergency and left his apologies." John waved a tattered piece of paper. "But he did make the arrangements. Here's where we need to go, J.R. Fast. He closes in ten minutes."

John turned toward me. "It's not the chapel like we thought. It's the office of a justice of the peace." He looked at the paper again. "Señor Pepe Sanchez."

"What about the ring? And flowers?" I cried. "We were supposed to stop and get them before the ceremony."

"Don't have time. We'll get them afterward."

I cringed, and fought back the disappointment. Then, as if these developments weren't enough, the car edged back into the industrial part of the city, and I grimaced at the poverty and blight that appeared once more out my window. My head began to swirl, my heart pounded, I felt queasy, and when the car stopped in front of a dilapidated former store, I just about passed out. John leaned over and whispered in my ear.

"Come on, Barbara. We love each other. That's all that matters."

I bit my lip to hold back the tears. Thankfully, J.R. and Carrie kept looking away. *Is it all that matters?* I thought. *Is love enough?* If he loved me, why would he expect me to continually accept less than we had originally planned for our wedding? Looking back, I now see these words as a powerful tool of verbal abusers.

"No ring, no flowers, no nice chapel, no family, no friends, no police chief?" I moaned.

John took my hands in his. "I love you and soon we'll be married, if that's what you want."

"Of course it's what I want. But here? Like this? It takes away from everything I thought would be beautiful."

"We can call it off," John interjected sharply, sitting up straight in his best military way. "Real easy. But, you know, we'll have put a lot of people out."

"Okay, okay," I relented. That responsible part of me reared up, ready to protect everyone's feelings but my own. "Let's do it."

I climbed out of the backseat. A middle-aged man appeared in the store's doorway, adjusting the collar of his multicolored, open-neck shirt. "Señor Perry?"

"*Sí.*" John extended his hand as he walked around the back of the car. "Señor Sanchez?"

"*Sí,*" the man answered, vigorously shaking John's hand as he put one arm around him. The two became engrossed in a conversation in Spanish and disappeared into the storefront. I caught Carrie's eye as we walked in behind them. I shrugged my shoulders and flashed a halfhearted smile. She gently squeezed my hand, as if to say everything would be fine. But when I looked around inside, there was no way she could erase the dismal setting. I viewed with distaste the dark paneled walls, the avocado open-weave drapes, the worn linoleum, the gray metal desk, the street noise, and the justice—who, it appeared, did not speak English.

"We have to fill out these papers," John said, walking over to a small Formica table next to the front window. I sat down gingerly on one of the orange plastic chairs. John handed me the legal-size pages and sat down opposite me.

"Where's that camera of yours?" J.R. said.

I felt in my purse as I read the papers in front of me.

"This is all in Spanish!" I exclaimed, handing the retrieved camera to J.R.

"Don't worry," John said. "All you have to do is sign here...and here...and here."

If there's one thing I try to be careful about, it's signing any kind of legal document. I make sure I read every word. In this case, with my one semester of Spanish, I knew that was impossible. I could make out that it was a certificate of matrimony and that it had my name and my mother's name typed into the text. I would just have to trust John that everything was on the up-and-up. I signed where directed.

"Smile," J.R. said as he posed us for our first photograph in that dismal setting. I responded with one of my happiest grins, reflecting that, after all, this was my wedding day.

Señor Sanchez positioned us in front of the gray desk, the groom to his right, bride to his left. *Well, at least something about today is traditional,* I thought. John stood in true military form—back erect, chest out, chin up, his naval aviator's wings pinned to his lapel. I was proud to be standing next to him, about to become his wife.

Without flowers or rings, John and I intertwined our hands. Señor Sanchez read, in Spanish, from a small, worn book. Soon he came to a part where he paused and nodded at John, who looked over at me lovingly and firmly pronounced, "I do."

The Justice continued a bit, then paused and looked up at me. Figuring this was my part, I gazed up into John's eyes and smiled, saying "I do."

After more words, Señor Sanchez closed his book. He grinned and motioned for us to kiss. We didn't unclasp our hands, no groom embracing his bride, no longing kiss, just a quick grazing of lips with me tiptoeing up to meet John's, as if this contributed to the seriousness of the step we had just taken. We released our hands and turned toward J.R. and Carrie.

"Congratulations, Mr. and Mrs. Perry," they chimed.

Mrs. Perry. The sound of that pleased me. *Mrs. Perry.*

"Now let's go get a ring, and some flowers," my husband said.

We left the ugly office and climbed into the backseat. I snuggled into John's embrace. *Mrs. Perry.* What a beautiful sound. Disappointing as the wedding ceremony had been, I was *Mrs. Perry.* I was at last the admiral's wife.

But at what cost, I now ask myself. What led me to accept such a dismal situation that was awful in every way? I believe deep inside I felt unlovable, and out of desperation and fear of rejection, I accepted marriage at any price. I needed John. I needed him to rescue me from the stark loneliness that existed before he came into my life. I was an intelligent woman who was emotionally insecure, and John knew just how to manipulate me to get what he wanted—I was his golden goose who would provide him with the lifestyle he wanted to live, the consummate goal of any card-carrying psychopath. So although the wedding was far from what I had wanted, I put aside my fairy-tale wishes and deferred to John's plans—all with a smile on my face.

At a small jewelry store back in town I chose a petite, dark blue sapphire set in a twisted knot of gold. It was one of the few rings in our price range—inexpensive. John paid for it and slipped it into his pocket. A clock on the wall rang out five chimes.

"We have reservations at La Escondido for five thirty," John said. "Let's go, Cinderella." He ushered me out the door. "We'll get flowers at the restaurant."

Despite the friendly banter in the car, I couldn't help feeling lost. The events of the day kept running through my mind. I tried to push away thoughts of the distasteful building and the little man speaking in Spanish, but when we drove into an empty parking lot of the restaurant, I couldn't help myself. "If this place is so popular, where are all the cars?"

We waited in the car, under a large portico covered with bright red bougainvillea, while John went inside. Several minutes later he bounced back to the car, grinning from ear to ear. "They open in ten minutes. We're early, but they said for the bride and groom to come in and have a drink." He winked at me.

I always try to make the best of a situation. So far, today's events made it a challenge. The event this evening was our wedding dinner. I was determined it would be okay.

On the way to our table, my positive attitude started paying off. We were in an upscale dinner club with burgundy leather–upholstered booths, flickering candles, white linen–covered tables, and fresh flowers. I needed this romantic ambience more than I realized.

"I asked to be near the band," John grinned. "We want to have our wedding dance, don't we? And I ordered us a bottle of champagne."

The evening was looking up. Once we were settled with the champagne in our glasses, J.R. announced, "I believe it's appropriate for the best man to give the first toast."

"Oh, wait a minute," I said, digging into my purse. Out came my camera and I set it on the table. "We must have our pictures." We all chuckled and raised our glasses. *Click, click.*

"Here's to Barbara and John—for richer, for poorer, in sickness and health, until death do them part."

John and I intertwined our right arms and sipped from our glasses. The camera flashed. "Well, let's not talk about the death part," I grimaced. "That's a long way off."

John set his glass down and fumbled around in his coat pocket.

"I think you've waited long enough for this," he said. "It's time for the ring ceremony." He took my left hand. "It's a little out of sequence but, what the heck, better late than never." He chuckled, amused at himself. I hadn't had enough champagne yet to laugh, but I did manage a smile.

John spoke at length of his love for me, and finished by saying, "With this ring I thee wed." He slipped the ring on my finger, and the camera flashed once more. I glowed. This time it wasn't the champagne. I felt deeply loved by this man...my husband.

The restaurant quickly filled with well-dressed patrons enjoying themselves for a Saturday night on the town. When the flower girl approached us with her wicker basket, John picked out the two largest orchid corsages.

"A white one for the bride and a purple one for the matron of honor," he grinned, laying them on the table. Once he had pinned my corsage on me, we put our heads together, forehead to forehead, looking into each other's eyes and smiling, as only two people in love can do. The camera flashed and captured that moment forever. J.R. was doing a great job recording our special day. The band started playing the "Wedding March." How did they know? John gave me a quizzical look, shrugged his shoulders, and smiled.

"A little bird must have told them," he said. We stood, at the insistence of the bandleader, who announced that the next song would be for our wedding dance. As we twirled around the dance floor, my spirits lifted. The audience applauded. All eyes were on us. The earlier experiences of the day evaporated. I was the fairy-tale princess at the ball, and I had just married my prince.

Later, back in the bridal suite, I put on the white negligee Debbie had given me at the wedding shower. I posed, looking into the mirror above the fireplace, to show off the low-cut back. The camera flashed for the last time that evening.

I have always been tenacious. If something gets stuck in my mind I will not rest until it is sorted out, no matter how long it takes. What I kept looking for in my relationship with John was some proof, *any* proof that would validate his stories about himself or his absentee family. On the way back to the Los Angeles Airport we stopped at the mission in San Juan Capistrano, and I saw an opportunity to shed some light on at least one of John's stories, the one I thought of as the "Three Arch Bay House" story. By now I had begun to name his stories. He had many, and he told them often.

As we walked around the inner courtyard of the mission, past the ancient cacti, making our way to the old bell tower to see the swallows, I hatched my plan.

"Isn't your house at Three Arch Bay near here?" I asked, even though I had already checked out the map in the gas station when we filled up before leaving San Diego. "I think it's a direct hop to the ocean from here, only a couple of miles."

"Yeah," John said. "It's Spanish, just like this mission." Without any more prompting, he reminisced once more about how his father had bought the land in the 1930s for next to nothing and built a home on the point with an unobstructed view of the ocean. He had barely moved in when Uncle Sam transferred him, so he leased the home to the Hollywood couple Anne Jeffreys and Bob Sterling, who still lived there.

"I'd love to see the house, John. Do you think we could go by it for just a minute?"

Without hesitation he replied, "What a great idea!"

If he didn't own it, I would have expected him to stammer, to back-pedal, and to find some reason not to go to Three Arch Bay. When he didn't, my spirits lifted. Finally, I was going to get some tangible proof that he was who he said he was, that he owned what he said he owned. I followed John's instructions and turned where he directed, but we found the street closed off by a guarded wrought-iron gate.

"I didn't know they put this up," John said. "I guess we can't go by the house."

"Why not go up to the guard and tell him who you are?" I asked. "Tell him you own the big house on the point."

"No."

"Why not? It's your house."

"I'm not going to disturb the renters," he said coldly. "Besides, I don't have any proof with me. The guard won't let us in without that."

No matter how much I prodded and pleaded, he was adamant. We were not going into that development that day. I pulled the car around and headed up the coast. John must have sensed my disappointment.

"Pull off the road, right there," he said pointing to a dirt turnoff. "We'll be able to see the roof of the house from there."

So to appease my need for something concrete, something tangible, I parked the car, and pulled out my camera. I took a picture of the house, or at least the roof of a house that I believed belonged to John and his sister, Lydia. I secretly wished John's stories would not be so difficult to validate.

We continued up the coast, talking, as newlyweds do, of the future and all the great experiences ahead of us. "Just more thing," I teased as we sat on the plane, its engines whirring, ready for takeoff. "Now that we're married, you can get my spouse card so we can shop at the naval base commissary, and I can officially prove I'm the admiral's wife."

John grabbed my right hand and kissed it.

"Anything for my new bride," John said as the plane lifted off from the runway, heading northward toward home and our new life together.

PART TWO

Patience

SEVEN

The Bliss

The sun slipped lower and created intense orange splashes and purple streaks in the Mexico City sky, but I couldn't enjoy its beauty. Not now. Not on this street, in the historic but run-down part of the city. Not in front of a locked, dilapidated colonial church, with John pounding on the heavy timber-and-iron front doors. No, definitely not now, with our religious wedding plans rapidly disintegrating right before my eyes, as our civil ceremony had done two months earlier in Tijuana.

It was déjà vu. I was miserable then. I was miserable now. Why had I let John talk me into joining him at the end of his business trip? We should have done this in the United States. As the tears welled up, I valiantly fought them back.

I craved a religious ceremony, a blessing from God, essential so I could feel truly married. I needed something more than a piece of paper with Spanish writing and vows in that crummy office in Tijuana. Even though I was no longer a practicing Catholic, God's presence in my life was very important. Was this blessing worth it if it caused this much pain?

We were a ridiculous sight, a wedding party of eight, dressed in fancy clothes, standing around on a darkening street, whispering like conspirators. Adamo and Sophia, John's Mexican business partners, agreed to stand up for us. They brought along their two children and two business associates when their last meeting of the day ran late.

"I don't know what happened," John said. "I called two days ago and made all the arrangements with the minister."

"The lights are on inside the church," Adamo said.

"I hear voices," Sophia added. "Somebody's in there."

The lump in my throat kept me silent.

John started pounding again and yelling in Spanish. Adamo joined in. The doors didn't open. They pounded harder. The ruckus attracted the locals and a young policeman walking his beat. He strutted up to John and demanded to know what was going on. I cringed. Policemen intimidate me, no matter what nationality.

John quickly explained. The policeman glanced at me, and a smile spread across his pockmarked face. I returned the smile and relaxed a little. He banged the ancient door with his nightstick and yelled, "*Policía! Abre la puerta!*" Nothing happened. He banged on the door again and repeated himself, even louder. Finally, the ancient door creaked and an old man with sparse white hair stuck his head out.

The policeman jabbered at him, and the door opened even wider. We shuffled in and the policeman went on his way. John continued to argue with the old man as the rest of the wedding party slid into the last pew and waited. The old man shook his head and shrugged his shoulders, then waddled across the chipped tile floor up the main aisle toward the vestibule.

"He's going to get the minister," John said. "We'll have this straightened out in no time, and we'll have our religious wedding." He gave me one of his everything-is-going-to-be-all-right grins. It didn't help.

The dimly lit church reeked of passing time, a time when the rich built what today's poor could not maintain. Faded paint peeled from the ceiling. Votive candles flickered in bent iron holders, and ragged red curtains covered the carved confessional doorways. Disappointment crept over me, and I struggled to breathe. The walls closed in on me. I needed to get out of there at once. I needed fresh air. I needed to be alone.

I bolted outside and stood near the corner, under the dim streetlight, and looked back at the old church. The wedding bouquet dangled sadly by my side. My free hand wiped away the river of tears that rolled down my cheeks. I was the crying bride, a pathetic vision dressed in a long-sleeved, floor-length ivory voile dress, with ivory lace at the collar, wrists, and hem. Men and women stared. Children stared. Dogs stared. I didn't care.

I should have paid attention to the warning signs that appeared earlier in the day. First, the hotel power went out. Then the flowers didn't show up and we had to scramble to find a florist for last-minute bouquets and boutonnieres.

Sophia emerged from the church, followed by the rest of the party. John strode over and put his arm around me. He was not smiling. "I talked to the minister," he said. "He's had a change of heart about marrying us, so he called it off. He said he left a message at the hotel this morning."

"If he did, we never got it. Why did he renege?"

John hugged me even tighter. It felt good to be in his arms. I relaxed into his chest.

"He said he had second thoughts about marrying a divorced woman."

"What!" My body tensed and I withdrew from John's caress. "How could he? We have the letter from the Concord pastor to cover that."

I grabbed my purse from Sophia and dug around until I pulled out a tattered envelope. I slapped it into the air. "What about this? Doesn't it count for anything?"

Before we left for this latest business trip to Mexico City, Sophia had cautioned us that we might need a letter from a minister in the States, giving an approval of why I, as a divorced person, should be married in a religious ceremony. Fortunately, we found the pastor of the First Presbyterian Church in Clayton. He understood why my first marriage had failed; my first husband's infidelities had put a rift between us that could no longer be tolerated. So he wrote the letter.

"I told him about the letter," John said. "He doesn't care. He said he didn't want to be party to a union made in sin."

"Sin? I'm not sinful." I paused to let the words sink in. "Oh my, it's my fault we can't do this in Mexico," I wailed. "I feel like a fallen woman."

The teachings of the Catholic Church, ingrained in me as a youngster, flooded my consciousness and produced big-time guilt. The Church had denied me access to the sacraments at home, so a church wedding was not possible there. Here, now, it was happening all over again.

I was inconsolable as we all piled into the two taxis that had been patiently waiting for our fiasco to finish. Back at the Hotel Chapultepec, as we gathered in the bar my dark mood continued to lay a pall of gloom on everyone. I decided to drown my sorrows in drink.

"I'll have two double margaritas," I said. "On the rocks."

With drinks delivered, John raised his for a toast.

"To my bride," he said as he smiled. He raised his glass again and toasted the two businessmen and Adamo, who were still with us. Finally, he looked at me. "We will have our religious ceremony before we go home." He leaned down and kissed my salty, tear-stained lips. I drained my first drink without coming up for air.

"I want a picture of this moment," I said. "Where's my camera?" That's me. No matter what's happening in my life, I like to record it on film even if it's not at the happiest of times, as it was now.

"Oh, my God." John gasped. "You told me to take care of it. I

set it down in the pew at the church. With all the commotion I forgot to pick it up. Be right back."

He jumped up and ran outside for a taxi. Normally I would
have been angry at such thoughtless treatment of one of my prized
belongings. Now I just smiled, settled back into the caress of the
soft bar chair, sipped my second drink, and slipped into oblivion,
hoping that somewhere, sometime soon, we would create a happy
memory of a religious ceremony in Mexico City.

Several days after we returned from Mexico City we hosted a party
for our family and friends. What they expected as an afternoon
Christmas party was, in fact, our wedding reception, planned discreetly so no one would feel obligated to bring a gift.

We had created the "Mexico City Wedding" story, and John
regaled the guests with how we finally found an English-speaking
minister who married us in the Union Evangelical Church. The ceremony appeased me. The church, in an upscale part of the city, had
been romantically embellished with fresh pine Christmas wreaths,
red bows, poinsettias, and tall white flickering candles.

John held up my left hand to show off the ring he had slipped
on my finger at the religious ceremony. I thought the ring, with its
semiprecious green stones, looked far too masculine. But because
John's cousin had supposedly made it, I kept my thoughts to myself.

"This marriage is bound to last," John said with a twinkle in his
eye. "We've been married three times now."

That brought the house down with laughter. We ate Chinese food
brought from San Francisco, cut a large three-tiered wedding cake,
and watched George and Ted blow out candles on a joint birthday
cake. After the last guests shuffled out the door, I grabbed the bag
with the mail that had accumulated while we were gone. With all
the last-minute preparations for the party, it was my first opportunity to look at it.

"Here, give me that," John said. "You relax while I sort."

I sat on the brick hearth, next to the crackling fire, and watched John quickly creating piles on the coffee table. Bills, advertisements, Christmas cards, and…six returned wedding announcements. We had sent them out in the middle of November to announce our Tijuana wedding. I reached over, quickly grabbed the pile, and read the names of John's children, his grandmother, and his sister beneath the NO SUCH PERSON AT THIS ADDRESS stamp. Pain pinched my face into a frown.

"John, what happened? Did you get all the addresses wrong?" He got up from the couch, sat down beside me on the hearth, and grabbed the envelopes from my trembling hands.

"No, the addresses are fine." He sighed. "Yesterday I briefly scratched through the mail. When I saw the envelopes, I called my grandmother. It's the same old story. She said the whole family is upset about us getting married. You know, the you're-a-gold-digger-and-out-of-my-class routine."

I shook my head. "I wish they were here, John, to assess the situation fairly. Why can't they accept me the way my family and friends have accepted you?"

He shrugged his broad shoulders. What could he say that hadn't been said before during one of our why-don't-they-like-me conversations? But we were married now. Why couldn't they be happy for us? I knew I must be missing something, but I couldn't imagine what. Perhaps I feared the truth, afraid it might change the happiness I thought I had found, or that it would irrevocably change my relationship with John. I could not take that chance. So I let it alone to gnaw away slowly at my peace of mind.

John placed his hands on my shoulders and looked me in the eye. "Someday, they will know the wonderful person that you are. We'll just have to be patient."

Three weeks later we left for Hawaii to enjoy our delayed honeymoon. We flew first class, and it got even better when we checked into the recently renovated Moana Hotel, one of the first hotels on Waikiki Beach. The hotel looked like its original image on the black-and-white postcards in the lobby. It didn't have air conditioning, but we didn't need it. We were in love, glowing with that everything-is-wonderful aura of newlyweds, despite our ages. The ceiling paddle fans stirred the tropical ocean breeze. It was deliciously romantic.

On Sunday afternoon we strolled down the beach boulevard, hand in hand, drifting in and out of gift shops and art galleries. At the window of the Center Art Gallery we paused. "Oh, look at the original Red Skelton painting," I said. "Let's go inside. I love Red's clowns."

Red Skelton was a comedic icon of the twentieth century. He started his vaudeville career in 1928 and eventually carried his talent into movie theaters and television. When my dad finally broke down and got a TV set in 1957, the family would gather in front of it and watch Red deliver good, clean comedy. It set the standard for comedy for the next twenty years.

We were barely two steps inside the gallery door when a tall, thin man with curly gray hair approached. His open shirt revealed several gold chains around his neck. He introduced himself as Isaac Rosen, a customer representative there. When John introduced himself as "Admiral Perry," Isaac's eyes lit up, his smile got even wider, and he vigorously shook John's hand. I felt like a fish being circled by a shark. I wanted to escape.

"We were looking at the Skelton oil in the window," John said.

"Good choice," Isaac said. "It's a real bargain at sixty thousand dollars."

I moved in close to John and poked his ribs with my elbow.

"Well, it's a little out of our price range," I said, laughing. John started to speak, and I let my elbow do the talking once more.

"Let me show you some of his pastels," Isaac said without skipping a beat. We walked farther into the opulent gallery, past several more of Skelton's original oils, to a side room. "Here's one he did on an airplane napkin last year, his hobo clown. It's only seventy-five hundred."

I gulped, embarrassed to say even that was more than we could afford. Unfazed, John jumped right in. "Not bad," he said, as I discreetly elbowed his side once more. He ignored my signal. "It really is unique, and what a fantastic story, being on the napkin and all."

John put his arm around my shoulders and gave me a loving squeeze. "Barbara, it would look great in the living room. Just think, you'd own an original Red Skelton."

I tried to graciously decline by alluding to the fact that we were newlyweds, struggling to make ends meet. Of course I couldn't tell Isaac the truth, that the credit cards were once more near their limits and we hardly had enough cash to cover the minimum payments. John's commission check was late again. It was going to be a stretch to pay for the honeymoon. At least the airline tickets were almost free, from the deal offered when we had flown to San Diego the previous October. Isaac wasn't listening, or he was ignoring me.

"Don't worry," he said. "You can put fifteen hundred down and make payments as you can. We'll mail it to you when it's paid off."

"That's my man," John said, "someone who thinks on his feet. We can swing that."

I grimaced and slowly drew in my breath. Isaac caught the sign.

"I'll leave you two alone," he said. "I'll be in the office when you're ready."

We stood there in the Center Art Gallery, whispering about our financial situation. I tried to convince John that the grand theft charges settlement had strained our finances. No luck. He tried to convince me we could swing the payments. I tried to make John understand it was because of the grand theft fiasco that Vestico was delaying his checks, as he had been telling me for six months. John countered that he had a new position with Gemina and that his checks would start coming in from his sales there.

I turned my back to him. I was getting nowhere and worried the discussion would end badly, with him raising his voice and threatening to leave me again. Where was that independent woman I once was? Fear crept in like the fog and clouded my vision. Perhaps more frightening was that John's twisted persuasions sounded more and more logical. I relented. I reached into my purse, turned around, and handed John my credit card.

"You won't be sorry," John said, giving me a loving pat on my butt.

While we sat in the office signing papers, John shared several of his favorite escapade stories. Soon he started to brag to Isaac about the next part of our honeymoon, on Molokai. "I'm going to show Barbara my beach," he said.

My jaw dropped. "What beach?"

"A little surprise I was keeping until we got over there."

"You have beach property on Molokai?" Isaac perked up, "with a view of Oahu? Very nice." He leaned forward in his chair and rested his arms on the desk. "Tell me more."

John sat back in the tropical rattan chair, stretched his legs out with ankles crossed, and with exaggerated hand gestures expounded on his "Father Purchasing the Molokai Beach" story. He told us that his father, Rear Admiral Perry, purchased it when he was stationed in Hawaii, right before Pearl Harbor. At that time only someone with native Hawaiian blood could buy property and his blood was one-eighth Hawaiian. (I never did quite understand how.) When his dad passed away, John inherited the beach and his sister, Lydia, inherited another property.

"This is the first time I heard that story," I said.

"Well, I can't tell you everything, now can I?" John smirked.

"Wow, our own beach. We could build a retirement house, with a huge front porch. Can't you just see it?" I said, and widened my hands. "On one side of the porch, John, you can write your life story and on the other I could do my painting, all to the sound of the waves crashing on the beach." I could hardly sit still thinking about it. It was a dream I would hold on to tightly.

"You need to write a book, Admiral," Isaac said. "It sounds like you've lived a very rich, colorful life."

"Yeah, a lot of people tell me that," John said, folding his hands on his stomach.

"Hmm. Maybe I could add something to your book," Isaac said. "Why not come back on Easter weekend and meet Red Skelton? He'll be here for a special gallery show."

"Meet Red Skelton?" I stuttered. I couldn't believe my ears. A famous celebrity; someone I admired. Reality quickly jerked me back. "We'd love to, but...."

"I'd be honored if you'd stay with me," Isaac said. "That way it'd save you some money, and we could get to know each other better. The house is only a restored cottage on Kahala Avenue, past Diamondhead, but the beach is just across the road."

Did Isaac sense I was about to make another financial objection, or that my admiration of Red would win me over? He sweetened the offer and it worked.

"Wow, a chance to meet Red Skelton," I giggled. "I'm a princess and this is my real-life fairy tale."

"We accept," John said. "It sounds like a fun weekend."

As we left the office, I dug into my purse.

"Isaac, can you take a picture of us by our painting on our way out?"

EIGHT

Glitter

Three months later we were back in the Center Art Gallery, looking for our pastel on a napkin among all of Red's art that hung on the walls of the upper floor. Meeting Red Skelton was only moments away. The stage was set. Two red canvas director's chairs were in a corner. On one, the name RED SKELTON was printed in white, on the other, MRS. SKELTON.

I could hardly contain my excitement. "Do you think I look okay?" I asked John for at least the hundredth time.

I had fretted for months over what to wear to the two receptions at which we would meet Red Skelton. Frugality was part of my blue-collar upbringing. Ultimately, casting money concerns aside, I went to a store where I would not otherwise shop, a store that carried expensive clothes. Tonight I hoped my fancy black cocktail dress and gold accessories were appropriate.

"You're the best looker here," John said.

"You're not bad yourself," I replied, and I meant it. He was tall and erect, with a sophisticated and worldly air. Just looking at him stirred me, but today it also brought out my sympathy. John was wearing his neck brace once more, still suffering from the accident that happened before we met. Doctors weren't able to help. Pain pills and the neck brace were his comforts. As he looked around, every now and then he would wince, and I could see that neither was helping today.

"I found it," John said. "Over there, on the side wall." We trotted over eagerly, like two little kids hurrying to get into Disneyland.

"Oh, my," I said. "Look. There's a card next to it that says FROM THE PRIVATE COLLECTION OF REAR ADMIRAL AND MRS. JOHN PERRY. It's so...so..."

I could feel tears trying to well in my eyes. I'm a very emotional person. I cry at weddings. I cry at funerals. I get choked up, whether it's happy times or sad, and this was definitely one of the most exciting times of my life.

"I didn't know we'd get public acknowledgment," John said, putting his arm around my shoulders. "Tell me, aren't you glad we put the money down to get it?"

I nodded in agreement as Isaac Rosen made his way over to us, smiling, the ultimate host. He was so nice to let us stay with him, and he went out of his way to make us feel special.

"Told you I had a little surprise," he said. "I thought you might like the sign. By the way, your friends came in not long ago and asked for you. I think they're still downstairs." He excused himself to mingle with the other guests who might want to purchase something.

"Don't forget, anything without a sign next to it is for sale," he added with a smile. We started to go look for Francine and Patrick and discovered them as they walked off the elevator.

Pam had introduced me to Francine fourteen years earlier. They were childhood friends and best buds. When Francine married Patrick, they moved to Oahu. The day before, we had looked them up and bubbled on about the art show and meeting Red. It piqued their interest, so I called Isaac, and he seemed delighted to include them.

"Thanks again for the invite," Francine said. "We don't usually come down to Waikiki functions. They're too touristy."

We wandered around, sometimes together, sometimes separately, admiring the many clowns Red had painted. Happy clowns. Funny clowns. Sad clowns. Some detailed in brilliant colors, others more sedate with white backgrounds. Red's imagination stirred me. It also stirred John. He halted in front of a large painting of a whimsical clown whose arms caressed a fluffy gray kitten and a wooden, red clown puppet.

"Looks like Freddy the Freeloader," I said. "I love it." Freddy was one of Red's pantomime characters, a lovable hobo who always got lots of laughs.

"I think you're right," John said, moving in closer. "It says FREDDY, KITTY, AND JACK on the brass plate. He looks similar to the clown in our painting."

"But a lot more expensive," I gulped. "It's eighty-five thousand dollars."

We continued strolling through the gallery. "I like this one of Clem Kadiddlehopper," John said, pointing to one of the few non-clown paintings in the room. Red had created a treasure trove of characters, and Clem was his bumbling hayseed.

"Look closer, John. It almost looks like a self-portrait of Red. And it's *only* seventy-five thousand. Gee, let's buy three." I laughed.

We rejoined Francine and Patrick. They had fallen in love with a large colored-pencil sketch of a hobo and were overwhelmed when Isaac said that because they were our friends, they could get the same deal we had for our airplane napkin...pay some down and make installment payments.

"We've seen a couple of oils we'd like to get," John said.

I almost choked. "Oh, you mean the eighty-five-thousand-dollar Freddy and the seventy-five-thousand-dollar Clem? Sure, John, we'll write the check today. We have some spare cash around."

"I know it sounds crazy, but I think I figured out a way we can manage it. I've already spoken to Isaac about it."

In any marriage, there will be times when one spouse goes off the deep end and wants something ridiculously extravagant—a $75,000 painting, for example. That's when the other spouse needs to be the anchor, maintain sanity, and get a firm hold on the checkbook. That was my job. However, if the sane spouse weakens, even for a moment, there's bound to be trouble. I tried to be the anchor now, but the admiral was off and away, creating his convoluted financial scheme. "I'll ask Jeremy, the CEO of Gemina, to lease the paintings from us. With that money we can make the payments and later buy out the lease. I can even ask my grandmother for an advance on my inheritance, if need be."

"You mean the grandmother I've never met or talked to?"

"Don't be nasty. Let's go talk with Isaac." John grabbed my arm and led me toward the office. When we were out of sight of Francine and Patrick, I planted my feet and refused to move any farther. "I love the paintings, John. You know I do, but we're still struggling with our finances."

"Let me worry about that. You obviously have not purchased fine art before. It's an investment that will appreciate. Even if we can't afford to keep it, we won't lose any money. We can resell and make a profit." That made sense, sort of. I wasn't a wealthy woman from the art gallery set. What did I know? John was the one who had purchased fine art before. Maybe there was no danger in an art lease; Gemina would be responsible if something went wrong. When we found Isaac, I reluctantly followed the two men into the office.

We emerged triumphant. Gemina agreed to the lease. The preliminary papers were signed. Final arrangements would not be made until we got home because Gemina wanted an independent appraisal before the paintings were shipped. I must admit I was excited. Two beautiful Red Skelton oil paintings would hang in our home. Not for a while, but someday.

Isaac called out to a distinguished gentleman with thinning gray hair, wearing a light blue blazer. He came over and Isaac introduced him as the gallery owner.

"They purchased two Skelton oils," Isaac said, smiling.

It sounded impressive and made me feel I was running in a different circle now, a higher one, and it wasn't even going to cost me any money. That was a good thing. It was enough of a struggle to get some money ahead to pay toward the napkin painting we already had.

The gallery owner enthusiastically shook our hands and said he had just received a call that Mr. Skelton was on his way up. We hurried off to find Francine and Patrick, and all of us positioned ourselves so we would get a clear view of the comedy master.

Red came in with a Hawaiian bodyguard on each side. They seemed to be holding him up as they escorted him to his director's chair. Once settled, Red started telling jokes. His distinct voice thrilled me. He was only ten feet away. It was the closest I had ever been to a celebrity. I swallowed past the lump in my throat and fought back happy tears.

The gallery owner announced, "If you have purchased a Skelton painting you need to find it now, bring it with you, and get in line to meet Red Skelton." People scurried about. I went one way, John another, and Francine and Patrick another. We regrouped with our paintings in hand, snaked our way forward, and finally made it to the head of the line.

Francine and Patrick went up first. She stood to Red's left and both of them held the painting. I snapped a photo with my new, purse-size 35-mm camera bought specifically for this occasion.

The gallery owner called for John and me and introduced John as "the admiral." Red smiled. I moved to Red's right, John to his left. The gallery owner placed the Freddy the Freeloader painting on an easel next to John and held the Clem Kadiddlehopper painting next to me. While we chatted with Red, Francine snapped two photos, a favor in return.

Suddenly, Red motioned the gallery owner to him and whispered in his ear. The security guards rushed over, assisted Red out of his chair, and walked him to the elevator. We were stunned.

"Red's feeling a little jet-lagged," the gallery owner announced. "Photo opportunities will continue tomorrow at the scheduled private reception for owners and collectors of Red's paintings. He'll also be signing the art. Thank you."

The crowd began to thin out, but our party didn't end. We had made dinner plans with Isaac, his roommate, and their girlfriends. Eight of us ate and drank our way through the evening. When it was time to pay the bill, Isaac's credit card was declined, so John generously pulled out his wallet and presented our credit card. "It's on us," he said.

I slumped into the back of my large wooden chair.

At the reception the next afternoon, we met once more with Francine and Patrick and their daughter. It was Easter Sunday and I felt like one of the beautiful people. We walked around and saw our paintings hanging back in their original places as we passed by a long table filled with a delicious array of appetizers.

"It hurts my stomach to look at this food," I said. We had just eaten brunch in the tropical gardens at the Kahala Hilton Hotel, down the road from where we were staying with Isaac. It was touted as an idyllic getaway for celebrities, and sure enough, we saw Jim Nabors and Karen Valentine.

We continued to meander through the gallery. There was a larger group in attendance today and a long line to meet Red Skelton. This time his wife, Lothian, sat in her chair at a discreet distance, her red hair pulled back. She had a white orchid lei around her neck that matched the one Red was wearing. Lothian occasionally lifted her head from her book and smiled at her husband's antics and his laughter at himself. I sensed love shadowed by concern.

I have never been afraid of speaking up, but what possessed me to approach her and chat, I don't know. We had a wonderful discussion. She shared personal stories of meeting Red and how she married him in 1976, even though he was much older, and became his third wife. I shared stories of the admiral and me and how we came to be in Hawaii. We were like old friends, chatting and laughing, having a grand old time.

When Francine, Patrick, and their daughter made it to the front of the line, I excused myself for photo duty. Francine flipped her picture over, and Red grabbed his fistful of pens and pencils. First he drew a little bear, and then he signed the painting. They left, smiling.

This time, instead of a picture, the next admirer handed Red a copy of his 1971 book *Gertrude & Heathcliffe*. Red signed the inside cover, then tousled up his long graying red hair and slipped into his Heathcliffe and Gertrude act, acting like two silly cross-eyed seagulls lisping one-liners. The crowd roared. The more pleased we were, the more animated he became. He was in his element, and loving it. Just like me. I was in the presence of a living legend, thanks to the admiral.

Red finished his impromptu act and went back to signing autographs. I realized John and I hadn't gotten his autograph yet. I went off to find John, but before we could gather our paintings Red seemed ready to faint. Lothian jumped from her chair, and the security guards immediately helped him to the elevator. Within a minute, they were gone. Isaac read the disappointment on my face.

"Don't worry," he said. "I'll set up a private signing at the Skeltons' hotel tomorrow."

"I guess it pays to be staying with a gallery associate." I laughed.

As Isaac walked us toward the door, he showed us some of the latest Anthony Quinn sculptures. Before we left, we had agreed to add a $15,000 ebony woman to the Gemina lease. I didn't even blink. I was caught up in a whole new world of make-believe, a world where money was no object.

The following morning on the veranda of the Royal Hawaiian Hotel, we met with Red and Lothian as if we were longtime friends.

Isaac had brought our two oil paintings from the gallery. We got the signing out of the way, then sat and chatted informally. Red pulled a box out of his travel bag and showed us jewelry he had designed.

"You know, right before we came, we picked up Willie McCovey's lease on his Mercedes 450SL," John said.

Red and Lothian looked puzzled. My jaw sagged.

"Willie McCovey, the famous San Francisco Giants baseball player," he added.

"Don't follow the Giants," Lothian said. "We're fans of the Angels."

"Oh, I have something for you two," Red said. He dug around in his travel bag and pulled out a copy of *Gertrude & Heathcliffe*. He signed it "John and Barbara. My thanks. Red Skelton" and handed it to me. With both hands, I clutched it to my breast. "I will treasure this, always," I said. And I still do.

Before we parted, Lothian and I shared our addresses. For a couple of years we exchanged a few letters and Christmas cards. Eventually, like many good things, it came to an end. But for now the friendship burned brightly, and I was floating on clouds.

Isaac, John, and I started to walk back the short distance to the Center Art Gallery when Isaac surprised us once more. "You're invited to an Anthony Quinn reception at the end of May," he said. "It'll be at Marina del Rey in California. Would you like to meet him?"

"Anthony Quinn? Anthony Quinn?" I was still flying high, and Isaac offered another fabulous experience, another dream. But John had said something earlier that bothered me and I wouldn't commit right then.

We left Isaac at the gallery and strolled back to our rental car. It was time to explore what had nagged at me for at least an hour. "John, what was this about the 450SL? I told you when you brought it home for me to see, we couldn't afford it."

"It was too good a deal to pass up," John said. "Plus, the MAC44 plates come with it. McCovey's jersey number was forty-four."

"We can't afford it. You'll have to return it." I struggled with my feelings and felt trapped by his cavalier financial attitude.

"See, you did it again," he pouted. "You spoiled the surprise. I can't do anything right. I can't please you."

He turned and strode off in the opposite direction, tall and erect, taking long strides as if he were still in the Navy. I ran to catch up with him and grabbed his arm. "John, let's talk about this. Let's lay out the dollars and cents before all of this gets out of hand."

He stared at me, his eyes cold and menacing. Twinkling blue had turned steel gray. "Why? It's the same old story. You don't want me to have nice things. I need that car for business to impress my clients and keep up with my admiral status." He turned and hobbled away from me.

I stood on the sidewalk, bewildered. We had just negotiated for three pieces of expensive art. Wasn't that nice enough? Why did he always have to stick the knife in and twist it?

Stress exaggerated his limp. He looked pathetic going down the street. Sad tears begged to flow, but I wouldn't let them. Not now. My heart overruled my head and my aching soul. I needed to catch up with John and tell him he could have his 450SL. We would find some way to make the payments. I had to ensure the success of his business ventures.

I also had to be sure John still loved me. My self-worth was at stake. At work it wasn't lacking—I was recognized for my excellent job performance. But at home I morphed into a different person, dependent on trying to help John live his life instead of living my own. If John failed in his business escapades, I reasoned that it was a reflection on me, and I feared the humiliation of his impending failure. I felt guilty spending money on myself because John's spending was out of control. In my perverted thinking I could be considered a success in my marriage only if I changed John and set him on a fiscally responsible path. Who else loved him enough to do the job? But the only way I could boost my domestic self-worth was to remain with John, and to remain with John I had to make sure he still loved me. I felt compelled to hold on to the relationship no matter how much it hurt.

I quickened my step to catch up with him.

NINE

The Blues

Five months later, on a crisp, clear fall afternoon, I maneuvered our sporty dark gray 450SL into the parking lot of the Oakland Airport Hilton. I was glad John hadn't listened to me, even if it was a stretch to make the lease payments each month. Gobi liked it too, especially when we removed the hard top. He'd sit erect in the back and look regal as his ears flapped in the wind.

Gobi wasn't with us today. This was not a fun trip, and the top was on. John sat in the passenger seat, wearing a white Stetson hat, his new trademark. "My Texas background," he said when he came home with it one day. On his lap rested his Hartmann briefcase, the pricey leather-and-brown-tweed one he insisted he needed to support his image as a successful businessman. John had expensive taste. Unfortunately he didn't have the salary to match it.

The mood was somber. John's relationship with Gemina had deteriorated shortly after it began. His commission checks were either late or nonexistent, and they didn't even cover his travel expenses.

I couldn't understand why he had so much difficulty collecting what was due him. Financial stress was now my constant companion.

We arrived fifteen minutes early. I turned off the ignition and looked at John. "Does Gemina realize how much trouble they caused us on our cruise to Alaska last month?" I said. John stared forward, and did not answer.

I was still bitter that their inability to provide prompt payment for services overshadowed our Alaska cruise, though it didn't seem to bother John. He was Mr. Congeniality. Our shipmates laughed and cried as John spun his stories. We were popular aboard ship, and now I wished we were that popular with Gemina. "John, we have to get this sorted out," I pleaded.

He turned to me, frowning. "I told you it's not my fault. There's internal fighting going on, some kind of in-house politics. Abigail was removed from the executive committee. I'm caught in the middle."

It was never John's fault. Not when he was arrested for grand theft. Not when he was let go by Vestico in March. Not ever, it seemed. "Let's go," John growled. "It's four o'clock. Let me handle it with Abigail."

Abigail Caruthers was a vice president of Gemina Corporation, a company started in 1978 by Jeremy Stewart, an outstandingly successful black entrepreneur. John, as a retired rear admiral, was tapped to help get contracts in the government arena, and for a while he served on Gemina's board. That's what he told me.

It was not unusual for either Jeremy or Abigail to stay overnight with us in Concord whenever they were in California. It was John's way. "Treat 'em like friends," he said more than once. Consequently, we opened our home to many business associates through the years.

I stepped out of the car and shivered. It wasn't just the crisp air. I felt a premonition that sent chills through my body. We walked into the foyer. Abigail was waiting for us in the reception area. From the moment we settled into a small conference room I sensed trouble.

She was not as friendly as the last time I saw her. "Let's get right to the point," she said, pulling out a copy of a letter from her briefcase and sliding it over to John. "You've become a legal liability," she said, staring purposefully at him.

I was shocked. I leaned toward John and saw that the letter was addressed to Jeremy, from an attorney in Ridgecrest, California. It accused John of uttering false and defamatory statements, impugning his client in his trade, profession, or occupation. That didn't sound like the John I knew, and I had never heard of the client. Yet John always told me everything, or so he said.

"I explained that to Jeremy," John said. "It was a total misunderstanding." He laughed and pushed the letter back to Abigail. She pushed it back and looked him directly in the eye.

"This is serious, John."

"What's serious, Abigail," I interjected, "is that Gemina hasn't paid John his commission, nor covered his expenses." I was adamant. This was my agenda for the meeting. Abigail had a different agenda.

"Don't pay attention to her," John scoffed. "I told her it was probably connected to the infighting. I wrote Jeremy about that, too."

Abigail rummaged around in her briefcase and extracted another piece of paper. "You mean *this* letter," she said, waving it in the air, "with all its superfluous words that say nothing?" She read the following:

Forays in your own direction
I. Isolation of capability by overloading (Frequent Criticism)
II. Criticism without constructive suggestion
    A. Verbose planning on borrowed written authority
    B. Supercilious negation of capabilities
    C. Destructive spotlighting of error

A poet I'm not but: A pox on poisoned posturing pomposity,
the poet who pondered his pocket as to what portion to pop for

the poker pot as he poo-pooed (sic) the policy of power versus poverty with a pox on pouring his possible portion.

She glared at John. "What the hell does it mean? Is this how you communicate with our customers?" Neither she nor I recognized at the time that these poorly connected words and thoughts, along with the logically inconsistent statements, were possible indications of a psychopath's ramblings.

"Can't Jeremy take a joke?" John laughed. "Besides, I can't help it. It's my doctorate training coming out; you know, my psychology degree. I'm trained to use supercilious words with inveterate pomposity."

"He didn't think it a joke when you closed the letter accusing him of plagiarism in some of the recent manuals."

My ears rang, my heart pounded, and my head spun. I couldn't understand why she was challenging John. Did this mean Gemina was going to renege on its contract? Surely they understood this was the way he always wrote, and sometimes even spoke. He was highly educated, after all.

"We no longer require your services," Abigail said crisply. "Your contract is being called, per the severance provision."

"What about the monies due him?" I sputtered. I could hardly get the words out of my dry mouth.

Negotiations started. Abigail said the company position was that John had overbilled and was not due anything. John countered he would get a lawyer; he had receipts to prove his expenses. I added that we had copies of completed contracts with customers, *his* customers. Back and forth we went until we finally reached a settlement. Gemina would honor billings totaling slightly more than $11,000, but it came at a high price. John would have to resign, and my hopes for the future fizzled into despair.

"Sign this," Abigail said. She slid a prepared resignation statement over to John. "By the way," she added, "you can forget about the lease on the Red Skelton paintings. We don't have a place to hang them. We're just glad you never got an independent appraisal."

I gulped, my stomach cramped, and my breathing went shallow. I wanted to throw up. I didn't say a word; I didn't dare.

The meeting was over. Back in the car I sniffled, fighting back tears of disappointment and humiliation. What would I say to Lothian? "John, you'll have to call Center Art," I said. "There's absolutely no way we can afford the paintings now, and we need to get our money back on the pastel."

"Hey, we don't need Gemina. That's why I started our company, Autograph Technological Systems," John said. "I knew we shouldn't have all our eggs in one basket. Maybe I can work something out about the art lease with our Santa Clara client, Claymark Computers."

"Claymark Computers? The upstart company that can't seem to get itself off the ground, let alone pay you?"

"It's just taking them time to get established. That's why they hired ATS to be their marketing arm. Their recent computer trial with Bechtel was quite impressive. Claymark computers are faster than IBM's."

My hands gripped the steering wheel, and I turned to John. "Promises don't pay the bills. We're behind in the car's lease payment again. We don't have a choice. You have to call Isaac at the gallery and cancel the paintings."

"All right, all right," he said. "I give up. I'll call him in the morning." John slouched into his seat, laid his head back, and closed his eyes.

On the way home, through the Caldecott Tunnel, past the luxurious homes in the green-and-brown hills of Orinda and Lafayette, my organizational mind began to work on how to use John's talents to get him into an earning situation. I was desperate to solve our burgeoning financial problems, desperate to keep our financial ship from sinking. Then it came to me. "John, why don't you use your

psychology doctorate and work in education? You always tell me
your thesis could help schizophrenics."

He slowly opened his eyes and sat erect. "I told you," he snapped,
"they won't give me the piece of paper until I do the seminars. Without the diploma I can't get a job, and to get it they want me to teach
one hundred hours for *free*."

"But...but..."

"I won't do it. I won't play their game. I won't be their slave. I
have a different idea. I'll contact the guy who leased the Mercedes to
me. I think he'll help with my plan to lease Claymark Computers to
the government."

I cringed, and gripped the wheel tighter. *Here he goes with
another wild idea*, I thought, *another one of his back-alley deals
that never are one hundred percent kosher—nothing illegal but
always a little far-fetched*. And somehow they never seemed to work
out—whether it was a job with an upstart company or with his
grandmother or children, who still had not spoken to me. It always
amazed me how he could flippantly go from one idea to another
without so much as a second thought. Looking back now, I see this
as another behavior on the psychopath's checklist.

Fortunately John didn't notice my apprehension. I wasn't up for
an argument about money tonight, especially because we finally had
the promise of the Gemina check. "What should we have for dinner?" I asked as we turned up to our house.

If my life with John were as painful as the financial part of it, I knew
I wouldn't be with him, but there were compensations that balanced
things out. John was helpful around the house. When he wasn't traveling, he was a good sport and fixed dinner and cleaned the kitchen
afterward. I needed this treat. My hours were crammed with work
and school. John loved grocery shopping. I hated it. He indulged
my passion for traveling and entertaining. Our photo albums were
stuffed with smiling faces from birthday parties, camping and boat-

ing trips, bridge dinners with family and friends, and cocktail parties with Red Skelton and Anthony Quinn.

We also bonded over John's health problems, which frightened us both. The previous September he had been transported by ambulance to the emergency room when he passed out at a John Denver concert. Recently he had precipitated a code blue at the hospital while he was having physical therapy. That incident kept him in intensive care for a couple of days. Overall, life was good, except when it came time to pay the bills. Four months later I sat with John at the barrel-top oak desk, trying to come up with a plan to increase his earnings. I grabbed a blank piece of paper and a pen.

"Let's make a plan," I said. "Where do you expect to get money from in the near future?" I wrote down John's response: Gemina, Beneficial Leasing Corporation, Claymark Computers, ATS contract bid to U.S. Army Support Command, and Fort Shaftner, Hawaii. I knew this was not enough. I had to find a way to produce enough funds to take care of the current burgeoning financial obligations. "Can't you get some cash now to pay off the current bills?" I asked. "Every card is at its limit and we're behind two months on the house mortgage."

I suggested adding to his Texas bank loan, where he said his military checks were automatically deposited, or getting a loan from his millionaire friend in Florida. I brought up having Judge Sullivan reverse the living trust on John's Coconut Grove home so he could get a loan, or John trading interests in the houses he co-owned with his sister in Chevy Chase and Three Arch Bay. I mentioned that he could call his Grandmother Dannigan and negotiate something from the will with millions in it. With each proffer, he countered with reasons why it wouldn't work, pointing out that the family proposals were definitely out because he still was getting resistance from them for having married me.

I slumped in defeat. I knew that the resistance from his family was real. Only last month I had felt their vicious sting once more. We had portraits taken of ourselves, John wearing a tweed coat with his naval aviator wings, and me in my tailored camel-hair jacket. I put several poses in envelopes and had sent them proudly to his grandmother and his four children as a peace offering. All came back within the month, marked NO SUCH PERSON AT THIS ADDRESS.

"Hey," John said, brightening up. He reached over and grabbed my hand. "We can refinance the second mortgage on this house. Then when Jason pays me for the Danville house in nineteen eighty-nine, we can pay the whole thing off. That's only five years off."

"I don't know. Our credit is extended now."

"Don't you remember when we got the second mortgage to buy Bryan out almost two years ago? The credit union said you could increase the loan at any time. All you have to do is quitclaim a fifty percent interest to me. That way we can use my holdings as collateral. We can make the loan for fifty-five thousand dollars, pay off all our bills, bring the house payments current, and pay off the second mortgage from nineteen eighty-two."

I hesitated. How could holdings secure a loan when they were inaccessible? My throbbing head felt as if it were being squeezed in a vise. But I could see no other way out. "I'll call the credit union tomorrow." I sighed. "But only if you promise we'll pay if off in nineteen eighty-nine."

He turned around, smiling. "I promise."

He was my husband now. I guess it didn't matter if his name was on the mortgage.

"I have a surprise for you," John said. "I was going to tell you later, over champagne, but I'll spill the beans now. I'm starting a consulting firm...our own corporation. I'll be the CEO and you'll be the treasurer."

"Just like that, a corporation?"

"I've met some folks knowledgeable about all branches of the military who can easily get government contracts. In fact, one is the rear admiral in charge of Treasure Island."

With that, John was ready to move on: from Gemina, from Claymark Computers, from getting his psychology degree, from his family. John had no remorse. He immediately looked ahead, working out his next adventure. I didn't realize what was happening at the time—he was being a typical psychopath with his lack of responsibility and his need for living on the edge. It was all a crazymaking puzzle to me. I kept trying to fit the pieces together and get John to be fiscally responsible, but I didn't understand that some of the pieces were missing, and they would never be found.

"I hope this corporation thing works out," I said. "We'll need two admirals on board. Our ship's beginning to sink."

John looked at me and smiled. "I love it when you talk Navy," he said.

TEN

The Admiral's Wife

Six months later John and I waited near the military barricade at the entrance to the San Francisco Aquatic Park pier, next to Fisherman's Wharf. It was Fleet Week. Excitement filled the air. A large crowd circulated, looking for the optimal spot to view the impending parade of ships and the Blue Angels' exhilarating fly-by performance. I watched, feeling smug and privileged. For the second year in a row, we had been accorded an invitation to join the officers-only viewing stands at the end of the curving pier.

Late-morning sun warmed the cool October breeze and sucked the fog bank back under the Golden Gate Bridge and out to the Pacific Ocean. I was relieved. The show would not be canceled, as it had been in previous years.

As I soaked it all in, I reflected on how the Navy had slowly seeped into my blood, bringing me the excitement of a new life, one that exposed me to events far beyond my previous imaginings. It didn't happen all at once, but grew gradually as John became more comfortable with being accorded his admiral status.

When I first met him, John referred to himself as Captain Perry and, surprising to me, seemed uncomfortable with the title Rear Admiral. I was proud of my man and what he had gone through in the service of our country. Hadn't he lost a lung? Didn't he have nightmares? Hadn't he been awarded the Purple Heart and the Congressional Medal of Honor? So I encouraged him, prodded him, and cajoled him to use the rank he had earned. It made him seem more illustrious to me.

Now John introduced himself as Rear Admiral Perry; signed hotel registers and charge receipts as Admiral Perry; gained access to military bases as Admiral Perry. Our house had taken on a nautical theme. We acquired a WELCOME ABOARD doormat and an eight-foot-wide blue flag with the motto DON'T GIVE UP THE SHIP in large white block letters. "Made famous by my relative, Oliver Hazard Perry, in the War of 1812," he'd boast when asked about the flag. "I'm like him, in many ways. I've had to overcome a lot of adversities in my life."

We were a Navy family. I enjoyed it, and I enjoyed seeing John enjoy it. Today, again, the Navy was in our life. One by one, our party straggled up to us…my parents with my sister Julie, and ten of our closest friends.

"Should be a hell of a show," John said as he herded our group toward the MP at the barricade, who gave a crisp salute to John when he handed him the tickets.

"Guess what?" I announced with a big grin on my face, as we started to weave through the crowd. "We got to meet the Blue Angels at a reception on Treasure Island last night."

"Really?" asked Marie Passini, a friend since high school.

"It was great," I said. "We even got a framed photograph of the planes in flight autographed to Rear Admiral John Perry and signed by the guys who are flying today."

I was bragging and didn't care. I was just so proud of my admiral, of being the admiral's wife. The event last night offered me proof that John was indeed who he said he was.

We meandered to the middle of the pier, selected a bleacher, and climbed to the top for a bridge-to-bridge view. Large, colorful signal flags draped the back of the bleachers and flapped in the breeze; military brass and public dignitaries mingled around the podium, and music from the nearby small Navy band filled the air. It was festive and exhilarating.

"I've a surprise for you all," John yelled above the din. "After the Blue Angels perform, we're going to take a cruise under the Golden Gate on a Navy ship."

"We wondered if you were going to be able to top last year," Marie's husband, Mark, said.

"What happened?" my dad asked.

Mark leaned past me to talk to my dad more directly. "Last year, we were in a long line waiting to tour the *O'Brien,* and John marches up to the ensign and tells them who he is. Next thing we know, we're walking past everyone, and they're staring at us with that who-do-you-think-you-are look. When we got to the top of the gangway, the deck mate snapped to attention, pulled out his signal whistle, and blew it to indicate an officer was boarding. You should have seen the salutes."

"We got to see some parts of the ship that were off-limits to the general public," Mark's dad said. "Being on board reminded me of my World War II service aboard a Navy ship."

"Sorry I missed it," my dad commented. "It would have been something, to see you all piped aboard ship as an admiral and his party."

I caught the point. Fortunately no one else seemed to. No matter how much John proved his connection to the military, Dad always had reservations about John's former career. Why couldn't he take Mark's lead? Mark had served in the Navy and saw action in the Vietnam War, and he didn't needle John about his military career.

The band picked up in volume to signal the start of the activities. Several dignitaries spoke at the podium. A lone plane flew overhead, and paratroopers with colorful chutes fluttered out to announce the parade of ships. A majestic aircraft carrier cruised under the

Golden Gate Bridge and into San Francisco Bay. "Look! The *Enterprise* is in the lead," John said. "I was the executive officer on her years ago."

One by one, other large ships slipped in behind her, past the review stands, under the Bay Bridge and on to the Alameda naval base. John described each ship in detail. After the last one, smaller boats suddenly appeared, bouncing in the choppy water as they crisscrossed through each other's wakes. They fired one volley after another, and soon they disappeared in the ensuing smoke.

"It's the black boats, the black boats!" John cried, almost jumping out of his seat. "That's what I commanded in Vietnam, where I lost my lung." He almost tipped over backward from excitement, like a boy who has hit his first home run or caught his first fish.

The Blue Angels soared over the spraying fireboats. A loud roar filled the air as the six F/A-18 Hornets made their first pass and dipped their wings right in front of our bleachers. I covered my ears. Goose bumps rippled my arms.

In the middle of the excitement, I suddenly felt a pang of sadness. John and I would never have a child who would share his exciting history and feel the rush of the Blue Angels as John pointed out that he had belonged to the elite flyers not once, but *twice* during his tours of duty. We had tried to conceive, but John's continued physical deterioration eventually made sex impossible. He was in too much pain from his back and neck to find a comfortable position. We discussed the effect this had on an objective important to both of us. More than once he hung his head and said, "Having a child with you would be the most wonderful thing in my life."

We tried artificial insemination, but John's sperm was not motile. The doctor said it could be his age or the excessive amount of medication he took, and he suggested we use an anonymous donor who closely matched John's physical characteristics. I selfishly refused. I wanted John's child. I was childless from my first marriage, glad there were no little Bryans to remind me of that mistake. Maybe that was selfish, too. With children out of the question, we filled our void with plans for Gobi to sire a litter of golden retriever puppies. We took the first step and brought home a bouncing bundle of fur that we promptly named Gidget. Gobi was delighted.

The Blue Angels show concluded, and the stands emptied much faster than they had filled. We gathered up our coolers, coats, and cameras and shuffled to the bottom of the bleachers. "Wait here while I find out where we need to go for the cruise," John said. He approached an officer near the podium; they exchanged salutes and shook hands. A young officer and his family walked past me and mentioned a stop at the commissary on the way home.

John returned. "I sure made a mess of this one," he said. "I blew it. I misunderstood about the day and conditions of the sail. It's tomorrow, and only officers and their immediate family will be on board." We all expressed our disappointment.

At the end of the pier, we said our good-byes and parted. Near our car, I put my hand on John's arm. "What ever happened to the military IDs you were going to get for us so we could shop at the commissary?"

"Haven't been able to get it done."

"It's been two years now. You promised when we got married."

"I've been trying, did again last week, in fact. But the issuing clerk at the Alameda naval base was on vacation."

"It's always some excuse," I said, realizing as the words slipped from my mouth that I had not chosen the right time to bring it up.

John tensed and abruptly stopped. He turned to me with glaring eyes and hissed under his breath, "Are you trying to embarrass me? I told you I'd get them. You don't believe me, and that really hurts. You've seen how the Navy treats us with respect, so get off my back."

Once again my aspirations of having tangible proof that I was indeed the admiral's wife were dashed by his evasive words. Once again I felt guilty, as if my persistence were wrong. How could I not trust my admiral? Still, deep inside, it nagged at me that he had not come through.

*   *   *

On July 24, 1985, Gobi and Gidget presented us with a litter of eight squirming puppies. The first one was born in our bed, in the middle of the night. We quickly hustled Gidget to the birthing area we had set up in my downstairs office and as each wet head popped into the world, we proudly selected a name from our list of male and female names that started with the letter "G." (Ironically, we had had to use artificial insemination. Either Gobi couldn't quite figure out how to connect with Gidget, or she was playing hard to get. She kept sitting down.)

We sent out birth announcements with a photo of the new family and received visitors with gifts and good wishes. As the pups neared nine weeks old, we took applications for "adoption" and promised a pup only if the new family met our strict criteria for a loving environment. Departure days were heart wrenching. When the first car drove away with Gatsby, I stood on the curb and broke into tears. John hugged me but he did not cry. However, when Gigi left a couple of days later with our friends the Passinis, John joined me with big crocodile tears flowing down his cheeks and, as each successive puppy left, he sobbed right along with me. I took his tears as a measure of his love for the puppies. Now I have to wonder. I have since learned that psychopaths do not feel emotion and that they watch the reactions of others in order to mimic the feeling. Psychopaths are like magicians. They grab our attention and hold it by pulling whatever emotional prop they need out of the proverbial top hat.

Almost a year later, in 1986, John and I stood in our garage, packing up salmon-colored floral arrangements that would decorate the tables at my graduation party that evening. After seven long years of dragging myself into the city, my day of reward had arrived. When John glanced at me and grinned, I grabbed my camera and clicked. I captured him in his well-worn fleece bathrobe, leather moccasins, and black felt beret. He looked comfortable. And he was mine. I sidled up to him and put my arms around his waist.

"I couldn't have done it without you," I said. "You've been my encouragement and my rock."

"Now don't get all mushy on me. You've got to get ready for the limousine. Remember, you have it for the whole day."

I smiled as I remembered my first limousine ride the year before, for my fortieth birthday. We cruised around Fisherman's Wharf three times, then dined at the exclusive Big Four restaurant on Nob Hill. It was special then. It would be special now.

"It's a good thing we can afford limousines." I laughed. John finished putting the artificial flowers into the back of our van as I continued, "I just wish..."

"Wish what?"

"Well, I wish your family were going to attend."

"You know how they are," John said, shaking his head.

"I know. But my family and friends will be there."

"Hey, don't ruin your graduation day," John admonished.

"I know the invitations came back, like everything else we've ever mailed them, but I was hoping...just hoping that..."

"...that the impossible would happen? Look at the positive side; we don't need Grandmother's money any more."

We were on an even keel, for a change. John's salary was somewhat constant, and during the last two years the finances had remained in check, even if John's spending had not. John had signed a contract with Westinghouse as a consultant. Then we formed our own company, Two Star Incorporated. John assured me everything would be fine; there wouldn't be much to it. We'd keep our business spending separate, and our lawyer would help us with any legal issues. We received our own corporate stamp to use on official company business. The business cards I ordered were printed with two gold stars above the name *Rear Admiral John F. Perry,* to match his personalized license plate, TWO STAR.

The main financial stabilizer during this two-year period was a settlement for John's injuries from the baggage cart accident before we had met. I had watched him deteriorate during our courtship and marriage. John was constantly in pain from excruciating headaches and neck spasms, and in a state of discomfort from the numbness in his right arm. He still intermittingly wore a foam neck brace, especially when we traveled in a car. His leg crumpled beneath him without notice. His debilitating back pain still precluded sex.

With the settlement came the relief of a check to help fill the financial gaps. We brought our creditors up to date. We contracted for needed renovations to the Concord house to help ease John's afflictions—a therapeutic Jacuzzi tub and resloped stairs.

"That's the last of the graduation flowers," John said as he shut the back door of the van. "The officers' club at Treasure Island will look better than it ever has when we're done decorating." He put his arm around me as we walked back into the house.

"I still can't believe you arranged it," I said.

"My rank provides some privileges." He laughed. "Also, it doesn't hurt that we're friends with the rear admiral who heads the base."

During the last two years, I learned that being the admiral's wife did have advantages. When the USS *Missouri* was decommissioned in San Francisco, we were there. When John arranged to take several of our friends on a personal tour of the USS *Enterprise,* we lunched in the Alameda officers' club. When John escorted a couple of male friends on an overnight excursion aboard a Navy ship, they had observed the respect given to him. When the Coast Guard Commander for District 12 hosted a luncheon for retired admirals and their wives, we were among the honored guests. If I ever had doubts about John's status, I had none now.

Today I was about to graduate with a bachelor of science degree in marketing from Golden Gate University, summa cum laude, and receive the Outstanding Student of the Undergraduate Business School Award. With hard work and sacrifice I had met the challenge and reached my goal. I would have preferred to complete my higher education right out of high school, but I was the oldest of five children, and my siblings then were all under age eight. We were a one-salary machinist's family. My parents would have been happy to give me a four-year ride, but the money wasn't there. So I settled for Diablo Valley Junior College, catching a bus every day to go fifteen miles over the hill to get there.

I suffered from OCS (Oldest Child Syndrome), as I called it. Ask anyone who's an oldest child. It's hard. Parents are extra strict. They overreact. They're afraid the baby will break or get in trouble, and they err on the side of caution while trying to figure out how to do their job.

The oldest child is the trial run. My case was no different. I tried to be the good little girl, to help out in the house and with my siblings and still keep up my grades, but my parents' attitudes affected my studies. I felt like I was being squeezed in a vise, and I didn't know how to escape. Finally, when they balked at my taking the car to a nighttime lecture back at the college, I went to see a school counselor.

I wanted out. She offered a way and I made a choice. I accepted a live-in babysitter and housekeeper position for a family in upscale Alamo, with full use of their car to help me keep up my studies. Within a year I confronted yet another life-changing choice. When the family's husband got promoted, entailing a move to Ohio, they asked me to come with them; they even offered to send me to Ohio State University. I was astonished by their generous offer, but was too scared of the unknown to do it. Instead, I moved back home and took a job as a lab technician at the same chemical plant where my dad worked.

That was in the past. Today my biggest choice centered on who should ride with me in the limousine. I wanted to share my good fortune and make people happy. It was ingrained in me. Later, when I was called across the stage, the audience in the Masonic Memorial Temple broke into applause, and many of them stood up for me.

After the ceremony I proudly showed my diploma to my dad so he could see I had included my maiden name on it. "Hmm," he said and handed it back.

"I thought you would be pleased to see your name on my diploma," I said.

This was my day. It was important to me to please Dad and make him feel honored. Why didn't he? Because today was no different than any other. I had always tried to please him, hoping to hear him say three simple words…"I love you." It was too much to expect. I never heard him tell anyone he loved them, not even my mother. His Germanic background forced his feelings into hiding and left his loved ones yearning.

My father was an honorable man who worked hard for his family. He was strong, steady, and always there. He helped guide me in my schoolwork. He toiled in a chemical factory to provide a decent home, food, and clothes, even though his health suffered. He took us on exciting camping vacations to national and state parks. No matter how much I told myself that actions speak louder than words, a simple whisper of "I love you" would have resonated as loud as if it had been bellowed from a mountaintop.

"I don't know why you did it," Dad said. "It's no longer your name."

Even his negative reaction couldn't bring me down, not today, with its beautiful weather, my award, and my upcoming party, where all our friends would have a grand time.

The sun dipped behind the Golden Gate Bridge, and the white lights of San Francisco twinkled to life. The guests stuffed themselves with crab and prime rib. When I cut the cake, after the drum roll from the band, I announced, "We've got the booze, the food, the cake, the band, and the presents. But where's the bride and groom?"

The room rang with laughter.

On the way home that night, at my godson's request I opened the moonroof of the limousine. It was his first ride in such a luxurious vehicle. He grinned from ear to ear, stood up, and waved his arms into the warm air. Inside, I snuggled onto the chest of my admiral.

ELEVEN

The Admiral's Family

Two months later, I accompanied John on an August business trip to the East Coast. I didn't mind sharing business with pleasure when it came to travel; I had done it since I'd met John five years earlier. For this trip, when John hinted at seeing some of his family's history, my heart skipped a beat. Today our first stop was the U.S. Naval Academy in Annapolis, to visit the grave of John's father. The academy was a key ingredient to John's family history. His father had gone to school there, graduating with the Class of 1923; taught there in 1946 and 1947; and been buried there in 1955.

We sat in the visitors' parking lot, with the engine running, as John scratched through his briefcase. "I know my security pass is in here somewhere," John said. "I wouldn't have left it in the hotel room. It's too valuable."

John's security pass was always a mystery to me. It was the magic wand he waved that opened gates to military bases and government facilities, both here and abroad. I witnessed its power many times.

The enigma of the hardbound black leather identification wallet was that it contained a photograph that was not John Francis Perry, nor was the name typed under it—Robert Lee Stuart. I queried John the first time I noticed the discrepancy. He immediately shut me down and ranted about it being a high-level security issue. I let it drop, but still wondered.

"A-ha! Here it is. It was hiding behind your photograph."

"That tattered photo from the Mexico trip?" I laughed. "I should get you a new one."

"Not on your life. I like this one." He leaned over and kissed me.

The overcast sky suited a visit to a cemetery. The wipers cleared the light mist on the windshield; I put the rental car in gear and maneuvered from the parking lot to Gate One. John flashed his magic ID card; the guard immediately saluted, then gave me a day pass. I drove onto the academy grounds.

"Turn left at the next intersection," John instructed. "The cemetery's that way, toward the water."

"Of course," I said. "We saw the cemetery last weekend, from the river."

I have always had a good sense of direction, a trait that has served me well on more than one occasion. Two days earlier, we'd sailed down the Severn River with our friends in their forty-eight-foot sloop. We slowed near the academy, and John pointed out its significant buildings and the cemetery, on the small peninsula that overlooked the river.

As I drove into the cemetery we had to make an immediate choice, Cushing Road to the right or McCandless Road to the left. "Turn right," John directed, but as we slowly moved along he seemed disoriented. "It's been a long time since I was here," he mumbled apologetically. "The trees have grown, things look different. I remember my dad's buried on a small knoll, near a tree."

"It looks like there's more than one knoll, and more than one tree," I said as I scanned the grounds.

"I thought I'd remember," John said. His lower lip began to tremble.

We circled the cemetery, and when Cushing intersected McCandless we took a left and ended up back where we started. "Let's go down Sigsbee Road," John suggested. "I saw it to the left, up ahead. It may help me remember."

It was the only other road in the cemetery, and it was short. We made another circle and ended up back at the entrance. I was beginning to wonder if there really was a grave. But why would John lie about his father's final resting place? Was this going to be another episode in the missing-family saga we had lived with for the last five years? What was the truth?

The truth was that John's relatives were still phantoms. It had almost ruined our summer business/vacation trip to the Miami area the year before. I had been stubborn and relentless. "We will be right in your family's neighborhood," I said. "And they'll see that I'm not a gold digger." I was still intent on proving it, even after five years.

In Key West we checked into a white-shuttered, historic bed-and-breakfast, with no telephone in the room. After lunch, John called his grandmother from a pay phone at the wharf, to set up a time to meet them in Coconut Grove. He looked debonair and relaxed, leaning against the booth, in his white shorts and shirt, straw hat and sunglasses. Suddenly he became visibly angry and tense, and slammed the receiver onto the hook. "No answer," he mumbled. "I'll have to try again."

Later that evening, John went down to the foyer, to a closet under the stairs designated as the phone booth. He told me to stay in our room, and I acquiesced for a moment, but I wanted to hear his conversation. So shortly after he left, I crept down the stairs and sidled up to the phone closet. Its door was ajar, but not a word was being spoken. John was just sitting silently with the receiver to his ear. I felt a cough come on and managed to stifle it to some extent, but the noise tipped him off that I was near, and he immediately started speaking Spanish in a louder and louder voice. Then he slammed the receiver down and emerged. His ruddy complexion had changed to deep red, and the veins in his neck bulged. "I told you to stay in the room," he growled.

"What's the matter?" I said, ignoring his condemnation.

"The maid says the family took my grandmother to the Ocean Reef Club, near Key Largo. They don't want her to talk to me."

"We have to go back through Key Largo. Let's stop in and pay them a surprise visit." I was always looking for a way to put faces to the names of John's family.

"You don't understand. Ocean Reef Club is private and exclusive. We can't just drive in. You have to have your name on a list to get past the guard, and ours won't be on it. It's the kind of place frequented by presidents and movie stars."

"And elusive grandmothers with lots of money." I was stubborn and on a mission. Later, when we drove north through Key Largo, I insisted that John show me the entrance to the Ocean Reef Club. At least *it* was real. But no matter how much I whined and pleaded, he would not allow me to drive up to the guarded entrance. We were so close, I couldn't understand his hesitation. Maybe he didn't want to confront his grandmother. To me, John's family was a mirage that disappeared whenever we got too near.

Now it was going to happen again. The dead father's grave would somehow turn up missing. What excuse would John give? Where could the dead go? Just as I was beginning to doubt him, John came through for me and quieted that nagging voice inside.

"I think I see it," he whispered. "Park here."

He was out of the car as soon as I turned the engine off. I reached into the backseat, grabbed the two carnation bouquets we had picked up earlier, and followed him as he started up the small rise. He stopped, stood erect in front of a large granite headstone, and saluted. When I finally caught up with him, he was quietly crying. I said nothing as I read the inscription:

JOHN RICHARD PERRY

REAR ADMIRAL CIVIL ENGINEER CORPS
UNITED STATES NAVY
1899–1955

What John said was true. His father was buried in the U.S. Naval Academy cemetery. I handed John the flowers. He bent over and gently placed one bouquet of the pink, red, and white carnations to the right of the tombstone. As he straightened up, he winced in pain and grabbed the headstone for support. He wiped the tears from his eyes with the back of his hand and said, "I always tried to be a good son, but I could never be the man my father wanted me to be. He was strict, with his military background and all."

"I'm sure he loved you very much."

"Maybe. It was hard for him to show it, and my brothers and I needed him to show it. Mom died when I was seven, when Dad was at the Naval Training Station in Great Lakes, Illinois. My dad didn't know how to take care of five sons, and he took out his sadness on us. It wasn't our fault that Mom died so young."

"I'm sure it just looked that way. You were sad, too."

"I guess," he sniffed, fighting back the next onslaught of tears. He moved to the other side of the stone and placed the second bouquet of carnations against the base. He struggled up with a deep sigh, came over, and put his arm around me.

"My time with you has been the happiest of my life," he said. "I never lived in one place so long. I never had a family as loving as yours, or the friendship of so many wonderful people."

We both stood there for a few moments, in silence, looking at his dad's grave. I let him be. "I couldn't attend the funeral. I was the black sheep of the family. I was the only son left, and I couldn't even see my dad off."

"Surely you must have misunderstood."

"No. My stepmother sent word that I was not to show up. I don't know what I did to deserve that kind of treatment."

"Seems like they're still doing it," I said, shaking my head.

John had told me many stories about his family. He provided detailed stories every now and then, and updated me on their latest exploits.

John's family continued to remain resistant and missing. I couldn't stand it. I couldn't stand seeing John cry when his birthday slipped by unacknowledged, or Father's Day was ignored. I couldn't stand his pain when he saw a FOR SALE sign on his Coconut Grove home the previous year.

The Christmas before, I wrote his children a letter explaining what John had been through over the last four years...emotionally, physically, and financially. All the letters came back to me, marked with NO SUCH PERSON AT THIS ADDRESS. I wasn't surprised. Not any more.

"Come on," John said, "Enough of this maudlin stuff. I want to show you more of the academy, where my dad lived, and where John Paul Jones is buried."

I recorded my visit in photographs, including several of John at his father's grave. I had finally met someone in John's immediate family, even if he was dead.

TWELVE

The Admiral's Decorations

By the following July, John and I had been together for six years, and we both found it hard to believe that time had passed so quickly since our first date at the Drexels', when I had consented to be the "fourth" for dinner. It was 1987, and the past six years were full of dreams come true for me. Fantasies continued to become realities. John's admiral status took us on exotic trips and opened up naval facilities like the officers' club on Treasure Island for my graduation party. Family and friends validated my relationship with John by participating in our lives for all types of social occasions. Even my father, who had been suspicious of John when they first met, never again said another disparaging remark. We still struggled with finances, but what married couple didn't? The euphoria of fantasies becoming realities far outweighed my distress over the financial strains as I was caught up in John's world and could not imagine it any other way.

When John's fifty-ninth birthday approached, we decided to go to the Fairmont Hotel on Nob Hill. Normally we would have held one of our annual backyard Fourth of July birthday parties, where our friends and family would splash in the pool, chow down on barbecued steak, listen to my dad give a cornet concert, or laugh at the serenading gorilla wearing a pink tutu and carrying balloons and flags.

This year we weren't in the big party mood. Our friend Ted Drexel had died from congestive heart failure two months before. It wouldn't have been the same without his husky voice and perpetual grin. We wanted quiet. We also wanted to continue our relationship with his widow, Debbie, so we asked her to dinner at the Tonga Room in San Francisco. I even enticed her with the story of the first time I went there.

It was for my thirty-sixth birthday. We were seated next to the waterfall with our friends Pam and George when, midway through dinner, John jumped up from his chair and hurried through the door. We were puzzled, but I figured it was an emergency bathroom call. Fifteen minutes passed and John still wasn't back. I was concerned and about to go after him when he reappeared and leaned over the table. In a conspiratorial whisper he told us he had just seen a fugitive Colombian drug dealer, so he had called the CIA.

"Watch," he said. "Two couples are coming in. They're agents. They'll sweep the room, making it look like they're trying to choose a table. But I think they're too late."

I thought it was quite exciting. Many years later, after John was no longer in my life, Pam and George would tell me that they thought it mighty strange. But their silence at the time validated that we were all having an intriguing time. What I didn't recognize then was the ploy used by psychopaths—that of having stories of somehow being involved with the CIA or the FBI.

"So you've just got to come, Debbie. You need to get out."

"I suppose, but only if you let me fix the cocktails and appetizers before we go."

It was set. We sat in Debbie's elegant living room, munching wontons and sipping rum and Cokes. "It's almost like the night I came to dinner, when you and Ted introduced me to John. Except that the big kahuna isn't here."

Ted's dark complexion had allowed him to pass for Hawaiian on many occasions. We raised our glasses. "To the big kahuna!"

Debbie noticed the Rolex on John's wrist. She had impeccable taste in jewelry and a quick eye.

"Yes, twenty-five hundred dollars' worth," I said testily. "Lately, whenever I come back from a business trip, I find John has bought something new and expensive."

"Barbara's such a worrywart," John said with a laugh, giving my knee a pat.

The timer in the kitchen dinged. Debbie rose. "Got to get the egg rolls out of the oven."

John stood up and excused himself, saying he had to get something from the trunk of the car. I shrugged my shoulders at Debbie's glance. "Mystery man," I said. "We know that by now."

I picked up the empty appetizer plate and followed Debbie into the kitchen. The trunk slammed and we heard the rustle of plastic coming up the back steps. John emerged into the kitchen, with a grin from ear to ear. "Come on, I've got to show you this. It's the best birthday present I ever received."

We settled back in the living room, drinks and hot egg rolls refreshed on the coffee table. John grabbed his mystery bag from the floor and put it in his lap.

"You know I've been trying to get the kids to come around, accept Barbara and all that. Well, it's happened."

"Good or bad?" I interrupted. "The kids' track records have been anything but exemplary so far."

"The best," John beamed. He clutched the bag closer. "Sonny sent me something very special...my service medals."

John explained that his medals had been kept in a safe-deposit box at Riggs National Bank in Washington, D.C., waiting for him to settle in one place. Sonny was the only one who had access. I thought it strange but plausible, like so many of the things John said. When John moved in with me, Sonny resisted sending them along. Now he had relented. He had decided that because John and I had been together for six years, John should have the medals earned from his distinguished military service in three wars.

"Let's see them," Debbie commanded.

John turned the sack upside down, over the couch. Thirteen boxes of various sizes, textures, and colors tumbled to the cushion. One by one, he opened them. "This one is the Purple Heart," he whispered, fighting back a tear. "I got it in Korea when my plane went down." He handed the box to me and I passed it along to Debbie.

"When you lost your best friend?" I said. I was proud of myself. I had tied the Purple Heart to one of the horrible stories that still gave John nightmares. Little did I know at the time that a psychopath uses pity to keep his victim engaged in the relationship.

"Here's the Navy Cross." John took it out of its case and clutched it tightly to his breast. "This is from World War II, for a dangerous mission when I was in the Navy SEALs. I lied about my age to get into the Navy, to make my dad proud. The best way to do that, I figured, was to sign up for the underwater demolition team."

John continued to open each box: the Air Medal, the Distinguished Service Medal, the Legion of Merit Legionnaire, the Distinguished Flying Cross, the Silver Star, the Bronze Star, the Navy/Marine Corps Medal, the Joint Service Commendation Medal, the French Croix de Guerre, and the Australian Military Cross. When he came to the last box, the largest of them all, his hand paused over it before picking it up.

"This is it. My most prized of all. It's my Congressional Medal of Honor, for valor in action against an enemy force."

"From the battle where you lost your lung?" I whispered.

"Yes," he said, placing his hand on his shirt, right where his scar was. I doubt Debbie caught the symbolism. I got a lump in my throat.

John left the medal in its rectangular box and passed it to me.

I wasn't raised in the military. I didn't know what service medals were supposed to look like. I had heard about the Congressional Medal of Honor, probably from the World War II movies I watched as a kid and more recently from John's stories, but now I was holding one. I felt proud of John, and of my country. I ran my finger along the blue satin ribbon that fastened around the neck, along the square fabric knot in the middle with its thirteen white stars, and down along the inverted five-pointed star that hung from an anchor below the knot.

"I never knew there was so much detail in one of these," Debbie said. "Ted would have liked to see it."

"He's seeing it now," I said. "I can feel he's right here with us in spirit."

"To the big kahuna," we said in unison, raising our glasses again.

John collected his boxes and put them back in the plastic sack. What irony, I thought, to have so much valor stuffed into inconspicuous plastic. They deserved better. "I just had an idea," I cried. "Let's get your medals framed, maybe group them around the Medal of Honor. We can hang them in the family room, above your chair, alongside the naval prints and the Stiha painting."

"The Stiha painting?" Debbie said.

I reminded Debbie about my moment of weakness that past April in Santa Fe, New Mexico, when I let John purchase an oil painting from the artist V. Stiha. We were in town visiting my sister Meredith, playing tourist in the historic square.

In all fairness, I have to say I loved the painting at first sight. It sat in the front window of the La Fonda hotel. Brilliant ducks on a river called to both of us, and when I was the one who eventually figured out where we could hang it, John's Spanish came in handy. He was able to bargain the artist down to $12,000. I must have been crazy to give him the go-ahead, but we put $1,000 down on *Country Living* and had it shipped home.

We were back in the collectible art world. I thought we could afford it. It wasn't like the time we tried to purchase the Red Skelton paintings. John had a new contract with Foxboro, and commission checks were coming in regularly, so I felt we could make the payments. That would prove to be a mistake.

"Are you going to wear one tonight?" I asked, excited for him.

"No, I think not."

I didn't pursue it. I didn't understand Navy protocol or the rules for wearing medals, and I figured John knew best. I didn't understand that he now had another avenue to put his admiral status on display, nor did I understand that medals are not worn nonchalantly in public. A true hero doesn't want the attention. I turned to Debbie and changed the subject. "I'm so glad you and Ted got to go to Mexico with us in February."

"Who would have guessed it would be our last trip together?" Debbie sighed. "But it was a good one."

We reminisced about the truck that lost its brakes and almost plowed our VW bus over the cliff, and about Debbie getting so sick in Mexico City that she had to be hospitalized.

"I was just lucky you had the thousand dollars to pay my hospital bill when they wouldn't take our credit card," Debbie responded. "I can say I literally owe you my life."

After a delicious dinner at the Tonga Room, we said our goodnights to Debbie in Walnut Creek and headed home to Concord. I was getting undressed when John came into the bedroom, looking worried.

"Your mother left a message on the answering machine. She got a call that your grandmother is dying."

I rushed to the phone. Mom and I agreed that we both would fly to Arkansas. John, in the marvelous way he was able to pull things together, secured the ticket and made rental car arrangements. We made it to Hot Springs just in time; Grandma Shirley passed away one hour after we got to the hospital and told her how much we loved her. I believe she waited for us to say good-bye.

* * *

Almost three months later John and I were sitting in the bar of the 25th Floor Restaurant on the twenty-fifth floor of the Sydney Boulevard Hotel in Australia, where we were staying. The world kept opening up to me, and it was all because of John. We were doing a three-week tour Down Under with eleven pieces of luggage and a full itinerary.

The sunset cast warm shadows over the harbor as the city lights sporadically flickered on. "Breathtaking," I said as I sipped my wine.

"Wonder where Joe and Paula are," John said, looking at his Rolex.

We had met Joe and Paula only six days before on Dunk Island, off the Queensland coast. When we discovered we would all be in Sydney at the same time, we made plans for dinner at our hotel. "They'll show up," I said, ever the optimist. Then, to keep the conversation going, I asked "Who was on the phone when I was in the shower?"

"The front desk. Said the credit card I gave them was overextended, so I gave them another card."

I cringed. We were running close to empty in the money department again. We had planned the trip when there was more in the coffers, but when John's commission checks from Foxboro didn't show up, I saved the trip with my $2,000 inheritance from my grandmother and a $700 advance on my paycheck. My mother didn't approve. I felt it was very resourceful of me when, in fact, I didn't recognize at the time that I was sucked up once more into the glory and glamour of John's plans. I changed the topic.

"You look very distinguished wearing your Medal of Honor tonight," I beamed. "It's the first time you've worn it since you revealed it to Debbie and me."

"Australians are patriotic. They always say if the U.S. hadn't been here in World War II, they'd be speaking Japanese now." It didn't occur to me to ask why he chose a foreign country for the premiere display of his medal.

We made our way to our table. A few minutes later Joe and Paula joined us.

"Sorry we're...." Joe froze and stood at attention. "Honored to be in your presence, sir."

"Thanks," John blushed. "Now sit down before we make a spectacle of ourselves."

"I've never known anyone who had one," Joe said, following orders. "I feel privileged to be sharing your table."

The waiter came over, explained the nightly specials, and asked for our drink order. "Champagne," John said. "It's a night for celebrating."

"Celebrating what?" Paula asked.

"In two days, it will be our fifth wedding anniversary."

Later, while we were having dessert, John told the story of how, in January, he had been offered the post of undersecretary of defense. He had turned it down. "Too political," he laughed. "I think Ted Kennedy had it out for me. Something to do with his family and my father."

A man and woman on their way out crossed over to our table. The man extended his hand to John. "I recognize the medal, sir. I'd like to shake the hand of someone who was brave enough to have won the Congressional Medal of Honor and lived to tell about it."

John blushed and whispered, "Thank you."

Later, in Perth, at the end of our trip, John wore his Australian Military Cross to an upscale restaurant. "Awarded when I served with some Australian mates in the Pacific during World War II," he reminded me, when I couldn't figure out why John would get a medal from Australia. At the restaurant, the Australian Military Cross commanded recognition and respect from those customers who knew its significance. John was a hero, even on this side of the world.

THIRTEEN

The Inaugural Ball

For the past seven years, life with John had been like a long-distance flight; most of the time it was long stretches of clear skies and smooth sailing. Occasionally we'd hit financial turbulence. Then I'd hold on tightly until we found some means to once more move into stable air, by refinancing or John's acquiring new contracts. Now my dream to be debt free was close at hand. Jason's future payment was due in three months. Debt free? Would it ever happen? My soul ached for it to be true. The payment was the only thing that had kept me from totally losing it these last seven years. It was the carrot John always dangled. That, and his grandmother, each time we played the refinancing game.

At least John had secured a job with Cremcon, a Silicon Valley company run by Bruce Wenden, a pioneer in color copier and fax machine technology. John was on the board. As a signing bonus he received 250,000 shares of stock and was part of the marketing team. We even looked at houses in upscale Saratoga, just in case we needed to move. Cremcon fed my appetite for travel. This time it was to France and Spain as John looked for production facilities for the company.

One evening in our family room we discussed Cremcon and the fact that they, too, were slow in paying John's consulting expenses. John knew how to play me, distract and entice me to move beyond the subject at hand. "Right now Cremcon is small peanuts when it comes to electronic companies," he said, "but we'll make it big when the stock takes off."

I was noncommittal. "I'm ready for another drink."

"I think you're going to need it."

What was coming now, I wondered?

John retrieved a large white envelope from under the bar and handed it to me, with an expectant grin. It was addressed, in formal script, to Admiral and Mrs. John F. Perry. The presidential seal adorned the left-hand corner.

"We've been invited to attend the inauguration and inaugural ball for George Herbert Walker Bush!"

"I'll take that drink now," I choked.

The following month we exited the Capitol South Metro Station and looked for the Capitol. I still couldn't believe I was going to attend the inauguration of the forty-first president of the United States, but the closer we got, the more real it felt. The excitement in the air was palpable. Crowds blocked the sidewalks and spilled out into the streets. Barricades blocked cars. Police directed confused pedestrians. The skies were gray, the chill wind invigorating, but at least it wasn't raining or snowing. We had bundled up for the weather.

"Our orange ticket says we are to enter by the Independence Avenue gate," I said.

"It's this way, to the left," Alec Baxter said.

John and Alec were business associates, a relationship that had developed into a friendship. When I insisted that we couldn't afford to accept the inaugural invitation, John worked it out so we could stay with the Baxters in McLean, Virginia. On the day of the inauguration, we had opted to get there by Metro and squeezed into a car with standing room only.

We made our way to security, showed our tickets for the orange section, and eventually reached our seats. "John, how did you get such great seats?" Noreen Baxter asked.

"I called up several Democratic congressmen. They get tickets, but since a Republican was being sworn in, I figured one of them wouldn't want to go."

"At least we get to sit," I said. "A lot of people are standing." A man in the row ahead turned our way. "May I shake your hand, sir," he said to John. "It's an honor to meet someone who has won the Congressional Medal of Honor." John fingered the medal hanging around his neck, said thanks, and offered his hand.

"Do you see Calvin Coolidge?" I asked John.

"In this crowd? You can't be serious."

We had met Calvin Coolidge, his real name, on the red-eye flight from San Francisco, which we boarded with free mileage tickets. Calvin told us he was named after his distant cousin, the thirtieth president of the United States, and he explained that he was on his way to a luncheon hosted by the Calvin Coolidge Foundation at George Washington University. He asked if we would be interested in coming as his guests. History piled upon history. My life with John had exposed me to many new and exciting adventures, and now historical ones. Of course we said yes.

The United States Marine Band started the program. I choked back tears as the president gave his oath. I felt goose bumps when he said, "A new breeze is blowing—and a nation refreshed by freedom stands ready to push on: There is new ground to be broken and new action to be taken." Then it was over. The new president disappeared from the podium.

"What now?" I yelled above the din of the band.

"We have to make our way to the Medal of Honor stands for the inaugural parade," John said.

"That'll be a problem," Alec said. "Look at this crowd."

"You mean we're going to have to walk fifteen blocks?" I complained.

Three hundred thousand people crammed the streets, all inching their way toward Pennsylvania Avenue, unable to walk faster than a shuffle. I'd never seen anything like it, hoped never to do so again, and made a vow never to go to any event with a large crowd. We were squeezed and jostled. It was a nightmare, but we trudged on.

By now the sun had come out, too weak to dispel the chill in the air. We braced ourselves against the cold. I looked at my watch. It would be a miracle if we got to the Medal of Honor stands before the parade started. When we reached Freedom Plaza, John checked us in.

As we climbed to the top bench for the best view, John received more than one salute. I was proud of my man and proud of his Medal of Honor hanging around his neck. I didn't notice whether anyone else was wearing one. We all did notice that the parade started an hour late.

"We're lucky we know the right guy." Alec laughed. "This is perfect. We'll be able to see the parade coming from the Capitol, and then it turns, right in front of us."

"Not only that," John said, "each band, float, car, whatever, will stop in front of the stand and salute us."

"Including the president?" I gasped.

"Including the president," John smiled.

And, sure enough, everyone did. It was just as John had said it would be. I was impressed, and in my glory.

The inaugural ball had sounded romantic and sophisticated. At eight p.m. we were almost there. Alec crossed the Theodore Roosevelt Bridge and followed the limousines to the drop-off point for the Kennedy Center.

"I'll be back at midnight," he said.

"I'll try not to lose my glass slipper." I laughed. "We wouldn't want to find you in a pumpkin, turned into a mouse!"

A young Marine opened my door and offered his white-gloved hand. My black-gloved hand accepted, and he helped me out of the car. I felt like Cinderella. My Prince Charming got out the other side and came around. "Love your dress and diamond necklace," John whispered into my ear.

"I feel like a princess, a beautiful but financially strapped princess."

John had insisted I needed diamonds for the ball. I had never worn anything but costume jewelry. I thought his suggestion outlandish, and I refused. In the end John got his way as he always did.

"You're dazzling," he said. "The prettiest woman here." I did feel elegant.

We entered the Hall of States, checked in, and got our inaugural plate. "Most expensive plate I own," I said, taking it out of its box. "I figure it's worth almost five thousand dollars."

"How do you figure that?"

"Do the math. It cost three hundred fifty dollars for our tickets to the ball. Add clothes and accessories and what do you get?"

"A five-thousand-dollar plate." John laughed.

We made our way down the crowded hall to the Grand Foyer, and my notion of what the inaugural ball would look like vanished…poof…just like that. It was so disappointing. The Grand Foyer was as packed as the Metro car we rode in that morning. People in formal dress stood shoulder to shoulder, trying to find a spot to stand, holding their two-dollar-fifty-cent drinks in plastic cups. Tacky. I scanned the room and saw folding chairs in some areas cordoned off with ribbon. Each area had a paper ice bucket on a stand.

"Let's go this way," I said. "My feet are already screaming from these dress shoes." We maneuvered to the chairs, but immediately a Marine came over and asked to see our reservation. We didn't have one. He explained that patrons had donated a couple of thousand dollars for the privilege of sitting on the bare, cold, folding chairs.

I realized that the round tables with white cloths and candles I expected were only in my mind, as was waltzing around the dance floor with my prince. Not a chance. The dance floor was one small area at the end of the foyer, and it soon disappeared as the mass of standing bodies challenged the posted room limit. A military dance band was playing, but the music was lost in the buzz of conversation.

We soon learned there were seven balls going on all over Washington, and the president would be visiting ours at the south end of the foyer. We were at the north end. My feet threatened to go on strike. "How are we going to get there, John? There must be a thousand people crammed in here. No one is moving."

"Take my hand, and don't let go."

John wedged through the crowd, smiling and excusing himself as he did. It helped that he was so tall. It also helped that he was wearing his Medal of Honor. Like Moses parting the water, John's medal was soon clearing a small path for us to squeeze through the mob. We arrived at the south end of the foyer and scoped out a spot, back by the windows overlooking the Potomac River. It wasn't ideal, but it would do. At least we could hear the band assigned to this end of the room.

An older gentleman, his chest festooned with medals, came over to John, extended his hand, and introduced himself. John shook it eagerly. "Sir, my mates and I served with President Bush in World War II, in his flight squadron," he said. "We're in that reserved roped-off area, next to the press stage. Some of us noticed you're wearing the Medal of Honor. My mates and I would be honored if you'd join us."

I looked over. People there had elbow room; it was an oasis in a hot desert. And it was directly opposite where the president would be appearing, on one of the balconies to the concert hall. We immediately took him up on his offer.

Inside the area, we made our way to the edge of the press stage and leaned out, but the view was not much better. How was I going to get good photographs standing behind people a lot taller than I? I examined the stage. There was some room next to a man in a gray pin-striped suit, who was intently watching the crowd. I concluded he was Secret Service. I'm not shy, no matter who's around. I nudged John. "I'm going to get up on the stage," I said.

"You're what? Don't be silly. They won't let you."

"Watch me. All they can do is tell me to get down." I hiked up my gown and John gave me a boost. The man in the suit bent over and offered his hand. I climbed onto the stage. He smiled. I smiled. We chatted. I was right; he was a Secret Service agent. John handed me my camera. No one asked me to get down.

The trumpets in the orchestra blared. A hush swept over the crowd. Charlton Heston walked out to the center of the balcony and said a few words, and when he introduced the new president and his wife, the orchestra played "Hail to the Chief." George and Barbara Bush appeared. George said a few words, then called for Bob and Dolores Hope and Neil Bush and his wife to join him on stage.

I was starstruck. It was all happening in a blur. I couldn't take pictures fast enough. I fielded other cameras from the floor, offering to take pictures for those stuck without a view.

Quickly, as fast as they appeared, the presidential party disappeared. They had other balls to attend, other speeches to give. Neil and his wife were left behind as the official hosts for the Kennedy Center Ball. I was transfixed by what I had just witnessed.

Moments later, it got even better. Neil approached the press platform and climbed up on it to give an interview with a newspaper reporter. "John, get our program out. Now! Get his autograph."

When the reporter was finished, Neil jumped back down. John approached him. Neil signed. It seemed the thing to do, even if he wasn't an important dignitary.

Later, in the car, as Alec drove along the George Washington Parkway, I looked across the Potomac River. The lights from the

Kennedy Center danced on the water; the chandeliers glistened through the windows. I was proud to be part of this historic day.

"It was interesting," I told Noreen when we arrived home, "but not what I had imagined and I definitely would never do it again. It's too political. I'm not into politics. Let the lawmakers play their little games."

FOURTEEN

The Storm

Five months after the inaugural ball, I sat in the San Francisco International Airport at American Airlines gate 65 and waited for John to return from a two-week business trip in Europe. I was still the romantic, and in love. On a whim I bought a bouquet of white gladiolas and a Mylar balloon saying YOU'RE THE GREATEST. I was happy my man was coming home, and I had insisted on picking him up.

John's business was going strong. He held contracts with well-known companies and several smaller businesses as well; he was finally bringing in enough money to cover his expenses and make a meager salary. But I was disturbed. The $200,000 payment Jason had promised to John, the one we had been awaiting for more than seven years, did not arrive in February, nor in March, April, or May. I was beside myself. I begged and pleaded, but John refused to press his cousin for the money. By June I insisted that John meet with Jason before he left on his business trip. John relented, but by his departure date, he had yet to see him. "I can never get hold of Jason," he said. "I'll do it when I get back from Spain."

I made a mental note to make sure he did.

"Hey, good-lookin', what's this?" John said as he emerged from the gate. I handed him the bouquet and balloon and took his briefcase. He flashed a sexy grin.

"I missed you," I said. It was true. He was my other half, and the house was empty without him. He was my best friend, my partner, my travel buddy. We had many happy memories, as long as bill paying wasn't part of them. Stretching on tiptoes, I kissed him passionately.

Back home, John made our favorite drinks and we settled on the deck outside, overlooking the swimming pool. I was just about to ask him when he planned to meet with his cousin when he surprised me with a delicious diversion.

"How about celebrating your birthday in Lyon, France, with Bruce and Laura Wenden?" John said. "And don't bring up the money issue. Bruce is paying. Part of the time it will be business."

How could I say no? I had the travel bug, and John continued to make my travel dreams come true. The previous year we had connected with London friends for three days in Paris, then took a day trip by train to Dijon and toured Burgundy's charming towns, wineries, and cobblestone lanes. Next, we'd flown to Malaga and driven through Granada, Cordoba, and Toledo before ending up in Madrid. There John had donned his Navy dress whites and Medal of Honor for a visit to the American embassy while he sent me off to the Museo Nacional del Prado to enjoy the art of El Greco, Goya, Rubens, Titian, Rembrandt, and others. Say *travel* and I'm ready to pack.

"Here's to more of France and Spain," I said, holding my drink in the air. John's glass clinked into mine. I looked at my watch. "We're expected at the Rammells' in about twenty minutes for dinner. I can't wait to tell them about our next trip." I decided to wait until another time to press John on the overdue loan situation with his cousin.

I've always considered myself an intelligent woman. My university diploma and long-term employment attested to it. But somewhere along the way, my emotional needs blindsided me. I developed flawed thinking when it came to John. My naïveté, gullibility, and neediness allowed me to compromise, to reach erroneous conclusions, to subjugate my very soul to make him happy and make him stay in my life. I convinced myself that John could change his spendthrift ways. When he didn't, I told myself everything would be fine when we paid off the mortgages with the sale of John's house, or with the advancement on John's inheritance. This was my focus. He was so convincing that I came to accept as true whatever he said. It was a situation the French call a *folie à deux*...a folly in which two people participate, one person (John) setting up a false reality, and the other (me) joining him in it. I had been dancing with the devil for eight years.

I should have walked out, but love bound me and fear paralyzed me. I was happy at work, but with each successive mile on the ride home I would slip deeper and deeper into depression. By the time I pulled into the driveway, I would be exhausted, wondering what twist of fate would be revealed that evening to complicate my life further.

It didn't help that our beloved dog Gidget had died in September from an aggressive brain cancer and that my father's health had rapidly declined from August to October, with two shunt surgeries and a stroke that left him an invalid, in a wheelchair, dependent on my mother and sister Julie to hoist him in and out of bed and feed and bathe him. I could see fear and shame in his eyes when he could no longer shift himself onto the toilet, and his frustration manifested itself into clamping his teeth into the arms of his caretakers. My father was but a shell of his former self. This compounded my gloom.

The one bright spot during this time was the acquisition of a female golden retriever puppy. Devastated at the loss of Gidget, we did not plan to bring another puppy into our household, especially since Gobi was a geriatric nine years old. But the vet convinced us that a puppy would keep Gobi active and prolong his life, so several weeks later, John and I chose a wiggling pile of soft blond fur that we christened Gaby. We bonded with the puppy immediately. This was during one of my father's hospital stays, and on the way back home with Gaby, we pulled into the hospital parking lot. I emptied my large purse, stuffed the fluffy pup inside, and with the bag held snuggly under my arms, John and I snuck through the lobby and up the elevator to my father's room. There, I closed the privacy curtain and placed Gaby next to him on the bed. The smile on my father's face was worth the effort.

One afternoon, at the start of December, I pulled into the garage and noted that John's car was not there. Inside the house I found a note attached to the refrigerator. "Have an emergency trip to San Jose. Back late this afternoon."

I started the teakettle and was pulling out a tea bag when the doorbell rang. I clicked the security lock and opened the door about five inches. Two stern-looking faces peered at me.

"Can I help you?" I asked.

"FBI, ma'am," the taller one said as he flashed his badge and handed me two business cards. My hand trembled. The cards looked official enough, but I still didn't open the door. "We're looking for Mr. Perry. Is he home?"

"No."

The shorter agent reached into his jacket, pulled out a white legal-size envelope, and thrust it through the crack. "We have something for him. Will you accept it?"

I've always felt in awe of and inferior to the police. Now the FBI was at my door. I was nervous, confused, and evasive as my heart pounded in my chest.

"No. You'll have to come back another day."

I slammed the door. It reminded me too much of a couple of months back, when I had accepted an envelope for John at the door. It was a summons from a bill collector. John got angry with me and told me never to accept anything from someone I didn't know.

I needed a drink. I made my way to the bar, fixed a rum and Coke, and relaxed on one of the stools. I spun around to look into the room, at all of John's Navy nostalgia hanging on the wall...seven historical Navy prints, the DON'T GIVE UP THE SHIP flag, the porthole mirror, John's medals.... John's medals? I couldn't believe my eyes. The case with John's military medals was gone.

Maybe he'd put them on the floor. I slid off the stool to look behind his chair. They weren't there. I looked next to the Wurlitzer jukebox and into our liquor closet. Not there either. I gave up, grabbed my drink, and sat down on the couch to watch the evening news. Gobi and Gaby joined me, one on each side, and laid their heads in my lap. About half an hour later, I heard the back door open. "I'm home," John called out. The dogs barked as they ran into the foyer.

"I'm in the family room."

"How's my gal?" he drawled as he sauntered over and kissed me on the forehead.

"Not good," I said. I grabbed the remote and turned the TV off. "Look at the cards on the bar."

John picked them up, scanned them, and flipped them back on the bar. "Don't worry about it," he said nonchalantly. "It might have something to do with Bruce Wenden. The FBI is investigating him on securities fraud. I told him he had to be careful when looking for investment capital."

"Is that where you were?"

"Yeah, he called me, all upset, so I went down to talk with him."

"Why didn't you let me know?"

"It happened so fast. I had to get down there. Sorry, I just didn't have time to call. At least I wrote a note."

His explanation seemed reasonable enough, and he was home safe and sound. I remembered what else bothered me. "Where are your framed medals?"

"They're gone?" He walked over to the empty spot on the wall. "Must have been one of your godson's friends at the surprise sixteenth birthday party we gave him last week. He said he wanted to borrow them for a school project or something."

John slipped into his recliner chair, hoisted his feet into the air, and clicked the remote to turn on the television. Strange, I was more upset about the missing medals than John seemed to be. Why would he lend them out and not say anything to me about it? I went into the kitchen and called my godson. "He said no one borrowed your medals," I reported, walking back into the family room. "I'm worried about what happened to them."

"Oh, I just remembered. Guess my brain is fuzzy from the long drive home. I took them to the frame shop to have the frame fixed. It was coming apart at one corner."

"Why would you leave all your medals in it?"

"Don't be a worrywart. They'll be fine. Come on, let's fix dinner. Do you want grilled steak tonight?"

We walked into the kitchen and started dinner together. My world was spinning out of control and I couldn't find the button to shut it off. The payment from Jason was now nine months late. I still had not met John's family. John continued spending. He had cancelled his appearance as the guest speaker at the Navy ball during Fleet Week. The medals disappeared and the FBI appeared. For each instance, John had an explanation, with enough of a kernel of truth inside to make it seem plausible. Still, I felt unsettled; although I couldn't pinpoint the uneasiness, I knew it was there, a small voice whispering in my ear. For the second time in a month the voice had broken through. Once more, without thinking, the words tumbled from my mouth. "John, who are you?"

"What!" He slammed the refrigerator and stared at me.

"Who are you?" I repeated.

"You asked me that in October," he said, "when I was in Madrid on business, and you called to let me know you were okay after the Loma Prieta earthquake." John walked to the sink and set the package of steak on the blue tile counter. I put my hand on his arm. He recoiled at my touch. I looked him in the eye. He glanced away. But I would not give up.

"You told me you would answer my question when you got home, but you never have. Some days I feel I don't know you anymore," I said, grabbing the romaine to fix the salad. "Coupled with my dad's illness, it's draining me emotionally."

"You know who I am." He laughed. "Don't be so dramatic."

I tore the lettuce into tiny bits into the plastic bowl, harder, faster, then froze and glared at John. "No, I don't believe I do. I've never talked to your family. Jason hasn't paid the two hundred thousand dollars. After eight years of marriage I still don't have my military ID. Now the FBI shows up at our door."

"You know there's a good explanation for each one, don't you?" he snapped. "Lady, you're something else."

"But you promised and..."

"I don't think I'm hungry anymore." He turned away abruptly and strode toward the foyer, but at the door he yelled in pain and crumpled to the floor, his knees landing hard on the oak parquet. "Damn leg!"

I ran to help him up.

"Get away from me," he commanded as he crawled toward the brick planter. "You don't care about me." He righted himself and limped upstairs. John's health had continued to worsen. Didn't he know I cared for him? After all, I was the one who'd insisted on getting the new spa to soothe his back and legs. I would just have to be careful how hard I pushed him. I set the salad bowl in the refrigerator, made us both a drink, and went upstairs to smooth things over. It was what I did best.

That evening, I didn't realize that the FBI standing on my porch was the beginning of what I now call my Crazy Year, a time when unusual events gnawed away at my sanity, leaving me feeling confused and unsure of myself, when all I wanted was a loving and financially stable marriage. I had no reason to suspect that the FBI visit had anything to do with John. And the missing medals? Why would I think they might be connected to an official investigation? I don't know what I expected John to tell me—but never in my wildest dreams would I have imagined that John was a lying, devious psychopath with a different agenda for our marriage. So I ignored the whispers in my ear. That evening, as I soothed the situation over once more with John in our office, I made a mental note that I had to try harder to change John's nonchalant attitude toward our finances. When I did, everything would be fine. I disregarded the warning signs as the storm gathered momentum.

Looking back, I now see that my outlandish behavior with John developed as it did over the years because I had been caught in the crazymaking web of a master psychopath. I had lost my sense of self. Although I realized deep inside that I was drowning in a turbulent storm, I didn't know how or where to yell for help. So I did the only thing I knew. I relied on my planning skills and organizational ability to try to change John; an impossible task, I know now, because no one can change another person, let alone a psychopath with no conscience.

As stressful as my life had been with John up to now, it paled in comparison with what was to follow during the next year.

Nearly a month later, near midnight on New Year's Eve, we slipped into the steaming spa in our backyard. John poured champagne into our Waterford hocks, and I gazed at the clear winter sky while I melted into the warm water.

"It's almost the new year. Here," John said, handing me a glass.

Neighborhood firecrackers popped in the air. "Happy New Year," we chimed together as our glasses clinked. John bent over and gave me a long, passionate kiss.

My lips quivered as I remembered the past month. John and I had plunged into the holiday spirit and the traditions we created together. We elaborately decorated our two artificial trees and set out the collector Christmas village. We bought and wrapped presents for each other and family and friends, bustling about and keeping busy. I hoped the activity would quell my continued uneasiness. I could blame it on holiday stress. It didn't work.

Deep down I understood the source of my depression. John had continued to be evasive. He had not answered my question but did offer a ray of hope. On the night we returned from my father's birthday celebration, I was feeling upset after seeing how crippled my dad had become since his stroke. John sensed my pain. He promised he would reveal who he was on New Year's Eve, in the spa. A special time for a new beginning, he said.

Now, as our lips separated, I waited for John to begin. The frosty winter air hung silently between us. I wanted to break the ice. *Patience, Barbara, patience*, I admonished myself. I knew I had to be careful, so I decided to jump-start our conversation with something that had been developing over the past several months but which I had only recognized in the last several weeks.

"John, you're not going to Silicon Valley anymore, or talking to the East Coast. Is it getting to be too much for you? Do you want to retire?"

John hung his head. "I don't know." He sighed. "I just don't have the stomach for all the political games with our different customers anymore."

"We can plan around it, if you want to stop working. We could sell this house and move back to Antioch. With our profit here, we could be comfortable. We'd just have to cut back our spending."

"I don't want to talk about moving."

"Well, what gives?"

John told me that clients of our Two Star Incorporated no longer needed John's services. The news hit me hard. "Is that why you started playing so many sweepstakes?" I gasped.

"Yeah, I thought I could get lucky and bring in some money that way."

"That's gambling! You'll never get ahead that way. Besides, we don't have the extra money to buy ten magazines, let alone find the time to read them all, and you need to stop buying that stuff from the United States Purchasing Exchange."

"You have to make a purchase to be entered in their sweepstakes."

"John, it's all crap. No quality, and definitely not anything we need. What we do need is a feasible plan, not a plan based on Lady Luck."

"Back off. We have some money due. It should make you happy that I still have a commission check coming from the sale of some surplus equipment for Foxboro."

I dropped back into silence and gulped down the last of my champagne. John quickly refilled my glass. "It'll be okay," he said. "Just wait and see."

"Just wait and see? Like tonight, when you were going to tell me who you are?"

"You're right. I made a promise. Now don't interrupt me," he said, putting his finger to my lips. Words spilled out of his mouth and I couldn't believe my ears. I became nauseated, then angry. It was the same old story of being born in Costa Rica on his family's finca, of being the black sheep. On and on, through his marriages, and children, and military exploits, he tried to cast his spell, but this time I wasn't buying. My delight at a new beginning vanished into disgust.

"Same old shit," I spat when he finally stopped. "I'm getting out." He grabbed my arm and held me. I didn't move.

"I'm sorry, but I've told the truth all along. I don't know why you don't believe me."

"I guess because you've never proved any of it. There's never any family to talk to. There's no military ID. There's no money from Jason. You name it, you haven't come through."

"Please be patient, Barbara. I love you very much. You're the best thing that ever happened to me. It will all work out. I'll think of something."

"With all your assets, you should have been able to do something by now," I ranted. "And, speaking of assets, we don't even have a comprehensive list of what they are. What would happen if you died?"

"If I get the list together, will you be happy?"

"I wouldn't call it happy, but it would be a step forward."

"My attorney from Long Beach is coming to San Francisco in a couple of weeks. I'll get together with him and put it all down. I promise."

He put his arm around my shoulders and gave a gentle squeeze. Then he kissed me on the top of my head. I wanted everything to be all right. I was desperate. I felt I was slowly going crazy. So I made a plan.

"Okay, I'll go with you when he comes." I had to try to direct the outcome, to get John to finalize a commitment, even if getting him to commit was like trying to catch the wind. Somewhere deep inside me a little voice had rumbled, but I failed to follow through. Right now, once more, I felt in control. Or was it just the effervescence of the champagne? Either way, I chose to ignore the dark clouds that continued to swirl around our marriage.

In hindsight, I should have bolted from the hot tub and not looked back. I had given John plenty of chances to change, to prove his elusive stories, to come through with the money to sweep away our debt. Why would I stay? What anchored me to a situation where my exasperation made me feel like I was going crazy? I didn't recognize at the time that I was a victim of domestic abuse or the mark of a psychopath. I believe now that it was the fear and shame of a domestic abuse victim combined with the psyche of a practicing codependent (me) who had the misfortune to hook up with a psychopath (John). Subconsciously I feared the unknown of what would happen to me if John were no longer available to help extricate us from our financial mess. With another divorce, I was ashamed my family and friends would see me as a second-time loser. I still believed in "happily ever after, until death do us part." The challenge for me was to make it be happy, a burden many codependents carry. So that New Year's Eve, while I was intent on moving our marriage forward, I failed to connect John's lack of work with the FBI visit, and I placated my inner stirrings with getting a list of John's elusive property. The approaching storm intensified, but I didn't notice.

FIFTEEN

Deceitful Winds

Four months later, on Easter Sunday, we were in Hot Springs, Arkansas, at my grandfather's house. By the time we finished dinner, dark ominous clouds had rolled over the setting sun and the crickets began their nightly serenade. "Looks like rain," John announced as he scoured the last of the pans.

"Yup. I can feel it in my bones," Grandpa Jonas added, "and sniff it in the air."

"It can't rain until tomorrow afternoon," I said, as if I could control the weather. "We all have flights in the morning."

I dried the dishes while my sister Meredith tidied up the table. I was sad and Meredith and Grandpa Jonas were, too. He sat hunched over the table, nursing his lukewarm cup of coffee, on this, the last night of our four-day visit. "It's going to be mighty lonely," Grandpa mourned. It had been three years since Grandma passed away.

"We'll be back, Jonas. I promise," John said, drying his hands. We all sat down and joined Grandpa.

"I just wish you had gone to the baths with us, Grandpa," Meredith said, reaching over and giving his wrinkled hand a tender squeeze.

"Been here all my life and never saw a need to do it," he drawled.

I had visited my mother's family in Hot Springs many times, but had never soaked in the thermal waters of Bathhouse Row. This trip was different. I desperately needed the hot water and the massage. My soul ached more than my body, but I had hoped the distraction would take that pain away, too.

I had slipped into the New Year mentally exhausted. John was an enigma—a mysterious, somber, jobless man dedicated to sweepstakes and spending splurges...a man who would not collect money due him. "I'll do it my way," he insisted over and over again when pressed for answers.

I would have lost my sanity had I not clung to my career. Only one person looked out for my work success and satisfaction. Me. *Want to go up the ladder, Barbara? Get a degree.* I planned and worked hard, holding down the job and going to school at night. I capitalized on my skills and determination, and it paid off with respect and new responsibilities. Four years after earning my bachelor's degree, I had moved up the career ladder from an hourly lab technician to an exempt quality assurance coordinator.

The job stirred my imagination and sated my soul. Even better, it allowed me to travel. I tacked weekend stays onto business trips and drastically lowered the airfare. It was a win-win situation. I got to see the sights and my family, and the company got to save money. When a mid-April trip popped up, I called my sister Meredith in Santa Fe, New Mexico. Sixteen years younger than I, she had blossomed in her computer career. She agreed to spend Easter with me at Grandpa Jonas's in Hot Springs, Arkansas.

Three days before I was to fly out, John announced he had great news. He had a job interview in New York, two days after Easter. So, per his logic, it only made sense that he go to Hot Springs with me.

I didn't know if this was good news or bad. John desperately needed a job, but I had learned not to count on what he told me. Too often his promises vanished like a mirage in a desert, leaving my soul more parched than ever. I needed my space and would have preferred to go alone, but as always, John prevailed. My gloomy premonitions about his presence proved wrong. John's spirits were up, and it spilled over into four adventurous days with Grandpa. Meredith's antics and sharp wit provided a buffer. She kept us all laughing. On our last night we sat at the Formica kitchen table, bemoaning our next-day departure. I glanced at the old red clock above the stove. "We'd better get ready for bed or we won't be able to rouse ourselves when the alarm rings at four a.m."

"Why so early?" Meredith yawned.

"It's my fault," John said. "My flight leaves at six thirty in the morning. The shuttle for Little Rock is coming at five a.m."

I went off to the bathroom, and the rest of the family settled in the living room. Grandpa Jonas stoked the wood-burning stove. "Going to be a cold one tonight," Grandpa warned as he slid the floor-length curtain separating the living room from the bedroom across the antique iron rod.

I emerged and set my clothes out for the morning—black wool skirt, white knit top, black high heels. I dressed for success and when I arrived in Midland, Michigan, I wanted to look professional. Meredith went into the bathroom.

"How do you feel?" John called out. I pushed the curtain apart. "I'm a little tired. I dread the long travel day tomorrow."

"I know just the thing," John said. He stood, and winced as his knee almost caused him to fall. He rambled into the bedroom, dug around in his suitcase, and pulled out one of his medications. He twisted the lid and tapped two pills into his hand. "Here, take these," he said. "They'll help you sleep."

I pushed his hand away. "I don't like pills, and I don't take someone else's prescription."

"I know what's best for my gal," he said, putting his free arm around my shoulder. "Do as the doctor says."

I resisted; John persisted, twisting his words to make sense out of the senseless. I opened my hand. He dropped the pink pills into it, and I went into the kitchen for a glass of water. He followed me and stood by until I swallowed them. "Good girl," he said, taking the empty glass and setting it on the counter. "Now let's go back in and visit with your grandpa until you feel relaxed."

Half an hour later, John said he needed to check his briefcase and make sure our tickets were there. He sauntered into the bedroom, grabbed the case, tossed it onto the bed, and clicked it open. The rest of us began to say our good-nights while he flipped through his papers. "Damn!" John yelled. "Damn!"

"What's wrong?" I asked.

"Goddamn it! What a stupid ass I am. Look what I found." He withdrew a manila envelope and waved it in the air. "It's our federal income tax forms and payments."

Fear and anger came over me. I am more afraid of the IRS than I am of the police. Though I had nothing to hide, stories of unwarranted audits with their scramble for receipts and devastating fines were enough to petrify me. "What do you mean?" I yelled as I stomped up to him and grabbed the envelope. "You told me you mailed them several weeks ago."

"I guess I forgot," John said softly, hanging his head.

"Forgot? You forgot? Then you lied? That doesn't make sense. We always mail before the deadline."

I clutched the envelope, dropped onto the bed next to John's open briefcase, and began thumbing through its contents. What else could he have forgotten to do? I found out. He hadn't mailed the five legal-size envelopes, addressed and stamped by me. I grabbed them and shoved them toward John. "What about these?" I seethed. "You were to have mailed them, too."

In January we had met with our Long Beach friend and attorney.

He agreed to do John's will, but said John needed to provide exact details of accounts and property deeds. John said he would, but kept putting it off. When he didn't take action, I did. We went to the library and found whatever addresses were needed in their collection of phone books. I typed the letters; John signed them and licked the envelopes. Here they were, two months later, lying in his briefcase. John made it very difficult for me to help him keep his promises. "This is a fine mess," I wailed. "First the taxes, then the letters to help finalize your will."

"Hey," John said, "I just remembered. Today is April fifteenth."

"So?"

"We can drop off the envelope at the main post office. As long as it's postmarked today, we're safe."

"That's right," Meredith added. "I remember a newscast saying that because the fifteenth was on a Sunday, a postmark of the sixteenth would be accepted."

"Let's go." I snapped, slipping into my high heels because my sneakers were already packed. "The sooner we get it mailed, the sooner I'll feel relieved and the sooner we can get to bed."

"You can't drive," John said.

"Why not? I always drive." I grabbed my coat and put it on over my nightgown; time was of the essence, and there was no reason for me to change as long as I had my coat.

"The pills. You took the muscle relaxant," Meredith reminded me.

"I feel fine."

"Give me the car keys," John commanded. "You're on a business trip and you don't need an accident on company time."

"I'm not on company time until tomorrow, when I'm on my way to the meeting."

"Give me the car keys. Now! Besides, you need to go with me to show me the way."

I grabbed my purse, retrieved the keys, and threw them at him. It wasn't worth a fight at this hour. "Let's go," he said. "You can be copilot."

I reasoned that at least I would be with John to make sure the taxes got mailed. We got into the car. "Take a left, go over the tracks, then take another left," I directed. "Then turn right on Ridgecrest."

In the middle of town, near the post office, the traffic turned insane. John grabbed a parking spot from someone pulling out. I opened my door to get out. "Give me the damn envelopes," John said. "You're in your nightgown. You don't want to give a show to the other late birds."

I handed them to him, slumped into my seat, and watched as he marched into the building. "Mission accomplished," he said as he slid back into the driver's seat. He rubbed his hands together. "It's getting cold and wet out there."

It had started to drizzle. John put the car in gear, turned on the windshield wipers, and retraced our route. I stared at the passing dilapidated brick buildings. Only the mechanical sounds of the car broke the silence. The car turned left onto Ridgecrest Drive and quickly passed through the older, working-class neighborhood. When the road flattened out, John accelerated. I panicked. I braced my right foot on the floorboard and gripped the seat and the door rest. "Slow down," I ordered. "You're not used to driving this road."

"It's a country road. It's straight for at least a mile."

"The pavement is wet. Slow down!"

He backed off, but as soon as we approached the creek bridge his foot got heavy again. "Slow down!" I yelled as we flew across the bridge. "Our left turn is just ahead. You won't make it at this speed."

The right tires left the pavement and crunched on the gravel shoulder. "John, *SLOW DOWN!* What are you doing?"

"There's something wrong with the car. I can't control it."

"Look out! There's a telephone pole on my side."

John jerked the steering wheel hard to the right, toward the pole.

"What the hell are you doing?" I screamed.

"Can't control it."

The car passed the pole, left the road, and crashed into a vacant field. We began to fishtail through the wet weeds. Low brush and saplings snapped under the weight of the car. We careened from tree to tree. Branches slapped the windshield. Glass shattered. I shielded my face with my arms, and a vision engulfed me. "Oh God, it's the creek!" I yelled hysterically. "We're headed for the swollen creek. We're going to drown."

"Can't control it," John wailed.

"Brake! Cut the engine! Do something!"

Then it was over, as quickly as it had begun. The car came to an abrupt stop in a thicket, its headlights dancing on the broken branches. The mist had turned to rain. At first I was only aware of silence as I tried to gather my thoughts. Then I heard the hiss. "John, we've got to get out of here. The gasoline. It could explode."

"I don't smell any, do you?"

I sniffed. He was right, there was no gasoline smell, only the hissing sound from the steam that rose from the hot engine as it rested on the wet grass. My panic subsided and became anger. "Goddamn it, John. I told you to slow down. Now we're stuck out here in a deserted field, with no one around."

"Help me," he moaned. "I can't move. Get help."

I grabbed my door handle and pushed, and met resistance. Then I felt an adrenaline rush. I thought my heart was going to burst right out of my chest. I couldn't climb out the window; it was a gaping hole with jagged glass at the perimeter. I had to get the door open. I put my shoulder against the door frame, closed my eyes to protect them, and pushed. The door gave two inches.

Tears welled in my eyes. *Not now*, I thought. I scooted toward the middle of the car and levered my high-heeled feet against the door. *On three, Barbara*, I told myself. On three I pushed with all my might. The door yielded another three inches. I slid back and maneuvered my shoulder against the doorjamb. One more push and

I had enough room to escape. "Don't try to move, John." I said. "I'll be back as soon as I can."

I squeezed out the narrow opening, pushed it shut, and struggled through the knee-high weeds toward the road. My high heels slipped through the wet grass and sank into the mud with each step. Brambles and stickers clawed at my bare legs. *Damn it, he should have let me drive. For sure, I'll never let him drive me again. Stupid, stupid, stupid!*

When I reached Ridgecrest, I frantically waved down the first passing car and was thankful it stopped. I doubted I had the energy to walk to Grandpa's house, although it was only four blocks away.

"Barbara, you look a fright!" Meredith gasped when I walked through the door.

"Call the police and an ambulance. John is stuck in the field near the bridge. We had a car wreck." My voice was stoic.

It was after midnight by the time a cousin brought us home from the hospital, scraped, cut, and bruised, but not severely injured. Per the doctor's instructions, I jumped into the shower to remove the glass fragments from my hair. Then I got on the phone and reported the accident to Avis, rebooked my flight, and arranged for an early shuttle service for Meredith and one for me later in the day. John dragged himself out of the recliner and staggered to the bathroom. I was hanging up the phone when he emerged, still unsteady on his feet. He caught himself on the dresser, his face contorted. He gasped for breath. "Must be the shot they gave me at the hospital," he said in a hoarse voice. "Help me get to a chair."

I walked over and he put his right arm on my shoulder. I almost buckled under his weight. Fortunately, the recliner was only a few steps away. My anger vanished. John's health needs once again triggered my caretaking self, and I pushed his behaviors into that little sack of things I chose to ignore.

"You need to call and rebook your trip," I said. "The agent told me I couldn't do it."

"I don't think I can go. Every bone in my body aches. I'll have to cancel."

"What about the job interview?"

"They'll understand. I'll reschedule. If it's okay with Jonas, I'll hang around here for a couple of days."

"Stay as long as you like," Grandpa said.

"Thanks," John grinned. "You know, it's a good thing for us that Barbara is on business. The company will pick up all the expenses."

"No, John," I said coldly. "I told you. I'm not on business travel until tomorrow."

"I thought if you were injured they paid a premium, double your salary."

"That's only if I die during business travel."

"Well it's a good thing you didn't die," Meredith said.

I got up and walked to the green curtain divider. "Let's try to get some sleep," I said. "I'll call Uncle Stan in the morning. We have some errands to run, and I know he won't mind ferrying us around."

We might as well not have gone to bed. None of us could fall asleep until it was almost time to get up. It was barely daylight when the shuttle whisked Meredith off to the Little Rock airport. I waited until eight before I called Uncle Stan. He came right over.

I had the stops organized. First, the insurance office to file a claim, then the hospital to get copies of the emergency treatment records in order to exchange the airline tickets without a penalty. The wrecker yard was next. We had to retrieve the rental papers, and I wanted to take photos of the car, just in case we needed them later. I was relieved that the rain had stopped and left sunny skies for our errands.

As we walked to the back of the wrecker yard and approached the car, my body tensed. I wasn't prepared for the devastation. I drew a sharp breath and framed the first picture. The driver's side door was smashed and off its hinges. *Snap.* Uncle Stan and John surveyed the damage. On both sides, major dents near the front tires bent inward. Glass was missing from the front seat doors. *Snap.* The windshield wipers were stuck in the full upright position. The car was covered in leaves and debris, as if the heavens had dropped brown-and-green snow. *Snap.* The front seat was covered with broken glass and twigs. *Snap.* Uncle Stan let out a long, slow whistle. "Lordy, it's a miracle you're both alive."

I looked at my watch. "We have one more stop to make," I said. "Let's go. My shuttle is picking me up at noon."

Uncle Stan drove down Ridgecrest and parked his truck just over the bridge, right before the telephone pole. Camera in hand, we approached the accident scene. *Snap.* Here are the tracks where the car left the road. *Snap.* Look at the broken trees. *Snap.* You can trace the tracks in the wet grass. *Snap.* Here's where the car came to rest. *Snap.* Beyond the thicket, the water in the rain-swollen creek rushed around the rocks and surged near the top of the bank. I shivered. Then I picked up a piece of the bumper that was caught in the brambles.

We walked back to where the car left the road. I examined the car tracks once more, closely. "Oh, my God." I gasped. "If John had been over a couple more inches to the right, I would have been smashed into the telephone pole."

Later that afternoon, I walked up to the car rental desk at the Little Rock airport. "I'm returning my rental car," I said.

"Where did you park it?" the attendant asked.

"Right here."

I placed a piece of bumper on the counter. The attendant's jaw dropped and her eyes grew wide. Leave it to me. Even in an almost tragic event, I had found some humor. What I hadn't found were the hints blowing in the deceitful wind: John's medicating me, his insistence on driving, and his calculation of how much he would get if I died on a business trip. As we crashed through the brush it never entered my mind that the car wreck was anything but an accident. It would take ten more months for the truth to emerge.

SIXTEEN

The Sinking

Two months later, on a warm June afternoon in Coral Gables, we crossed the lobby of the Biltmore Hotel, an immense edifice that exuded elegance and old money way beyond the Perry budget. In the elevator on the way to our room, I mentioned the cost to John. He just laughed. "We have to stay here. It's part of my plan to pry money from my grandmother."

John had sucked me into another plan. He chose the right moment to spring it on me, a moment when I was vulnerable and grateful to him for his care and concern of my father, whose illness had put him in a wheelchair. We had treated my parents, sister, and nephew to a weekend escape to see the Monterey Bay Aquarium. John took charge of the wheelchair and pushed my dad around the undulating kelp forest and next to the tidal pool, never complaining. When we got home, John proclaimed that he would force the issue of his inheritance with his family. It was music to my ears. We were in desperate need of money again, same old story of credit card debt. The New York job never materialized and John wasn't working, yet he continued to refuse to press his cousin for money. I lived in a crazymaking world that swirled around me like a tempestuous storm. I knew stress intimately. It was my middle name.

One day John told me his grandmother had agreed to meet with us. He insisted I buy three tailored outfits so I would look my best for this occasion. I had to ignore the $1,000 charge. It was part of the plan.

Now in Coral Gables, I gazed out our seventh-floor window at the sparkling Olympic-size swimming pool. It was like John to pick a grand place like this. In spite of my misgivings, I was excited by the ambience, and as usual tried to see the best in every situation.

In the distance, dark gray clouds moved in from the horizon and lightning crackled across the dark skies. The little kid in me was entranced, and I didn't leave the window. The storm moved on as fast as it had blown in. In its wake it left a glowing rainbow stretched across the landscape. "Look, John," I said, "maybe it's a sign. The end of the rainbow is touching down right outside the hotel."

John joined me at the window, placed his fingers on my shoulders, and gently massaged. I melted into his touch.

"Maybe it means your family is finally going to come through."

"I don't know. They've done a pretty good job ignoring us so far on this trip."

He was right. The original plan called for John's family to join us in Key West for a holiday. We booked three double rooms at Eaton Lodge, an 1886 mansion with tropical gardens and white wicker Southern ambience. We arrived on Saturday, but his family didn't. I was furious when we had to pay for the unused rooms for the first night on our extended credit card. It wasn't right. I insisted we cancel their remaining nights.

When the family didn't show, John revised the plan. He figured if they wouldn't come to us, we'd go to them. He called the Biltmore. We flew back to Miami. Now we were in Coral Gables, right next door to Coconut Grove and his grandmother. "Maybe you should try calling your grandmother again," I suggested.

He released his grip and sat down on the floral couch, next to the phone. I went into the bathroom to freshen up as he dialed. Through the open door, I heard him ask for his grandmother, first in English, then Spanish. "Crap!" he said as he slammed down the receiver. I peeked around the corner. "She's not there, or at least that's what the maid says. I think she's trying to renege on her promise."

I bristled, then marched into the sitting area and folded my arms over my chest. "John, it doesn't make sense. You called down to the front desk and retrieved messages from your cousins, so why can't you connect with them, or your grandmother?"

"I don't know. It's my family. They aren't always logical about their actions, especially when it comes to us."

"This is our second day here. It's lawyer time. From what we found out yesterday, the sooner you see one, the better."

The previous morning had been an eye-opener. After breakfast I insisted we go to the Dade County recorder's office and look up the deed on John's Ingraham Highway property. He resisted, but I did not give up. John finally relented, and I drove to the center of Miami. We were shocked when we pulled the records on his house and saw that John was not listed as the legal owner. To make matters worse, he didn't recognize the name on the microfiche. His face reddened, and then he blew up. "I don't believe it! They found a way to take my property away from me."

"Let's look up Grandfather Dannigan's will," I said, "so we know what we're up against." We went to the Hall of Records and ordered the will, but were told it would take four weeks to get it. We needed a shrewd lawyer.

"You're right," John said. "Something shady is going on, but I've been away from the area so long I don't know a good lawyer."

He grabbed the phone book from the end table drawer and flipped to the Yellow Pages. "I'll call Randolf Harrington, the vice president of the Coconut Grove Bank, and ask him for a recommendation. He and his father have handled the family's accounts for years. In fact, his father is the one who put everything in the trust for my grandpa. He'll stand by me, I'm sure."

Harrington wasn't available, but his assistant recommended a Miami lawyer known for getting results—Gene Janofsky. John made the next call. "We have an appointment at nine a.m. tomorrow," John said as he hung up the phone.

"Good. I can wear one of my new expensive suits. Obviously your grandmother isn't going to see it."

"Now don't be catty."

"Why not? I won't get reimbursed by your grandmother, like you said."

John immediately changed the subject. I never noticed that this was a recurring tactic in his war for my mind. "Let's go play," he said. "We'll catch the tourist trolley outside and see the Miami sights."

"We shouldn't. We splurged yesterday with the spa treatments here at the hotel."

John stretched over to the pile of brochures on the coffee table, retrieved one, and thrust it into my hand. "See for yourself...it's not that expensive. It even stops at Vizcaya, the fancy Italian villa."

I flipped through it. I did need the distraction. The gardens of Vizcaya and the grandeur of this unique home intrigued me. Still, I hesitated. So John pulled another enticement out of his arsenal. He knew I was curious about anything to do with his family, even if that person was now deceased, so he added a family tidbit. "After our tour, we can go to Miami Beach. I'll show you the hospital my grandfather bought for my Aunt Dorothy when she became the Mother Superior of her religious order."

I was hooked. The outing would give me more photographs to add to my bulging albums and pacify me until next morning and our meeting with Janofsky. Finally we would get what was rightfully John's, and we would do it by invoking the law.

* * *

The next month passed with no improvement in John's family situation or our financial crisis. We slipped back into our daily routines. I went to work each morning and John…well, I don't know what John did while I was out of the house. Some days he just disappeared. He no longer had consulting jobs, or any prospects, and it was putting a strain on our relationship.

I was caught in a quagmire. No matter how much I cajoled, explained, budgeted, or planned, John refused to rein in his spending behavior or get a job. Mentally, dealing with John was like being trapped in a Chinese finger puzzle—the more I struggled to be released from our debt, the tighter the pressure held me. I was enmeshed in a financial mess with a husband who would not cooperate, and I could not find a permanent solution; not much different, I imagined, than living with an alcoholic or a compulsive gambler. I couldn't walk away with an immense debt hanging over my head. Where would I go? How would I survive? How could I erase it without John coming through with some of his family money? I clung to this illogical prospect in order to save my life. I didn't recognize at the time that my flawed thinking was the result of years of emotional and financial abuse from a psychopath. I would have had a mental meltdown except for the balance of a job I enjoyed, our socializing with family and friends, and John's way of being helpful with chores around the house.

One hot mid-July afternoon I came home from work to an empty house. I thought nothing of it because John sometimes took the dogs for a ride or to the park for a run. I laid my purse on the kitchen counter and grabbed a Diet Coke out of the refrigerator. The cold can felt good in my hand, and I placed it on my throbbing neck.

As usual, a feeling of dread had descended on me during my ride home and remained to torment me. I popped the tab and took a long swig. It burned going down. I wished I could be brave enough to expel my demons, instead of constantly trying to fix them.

I glanced at the top of the microwave, looking for the mail. There wasn't any. John must've left before it was delivered, I guessed, so I went to the mailbox and retrieved it. Back inside, I sat down on the living room sofa and began sorting the envelopes....junk mail.... bill....junk mail. About halfway through, I paused. There was a legal-size envelope from the Miami lawyer.

The meeting with Janofsky had not turned out as well as I hoped. It had started off great. John and Gene bantered names back and forth of people they seemed to know in common, then got down to business. John scribbled out a list of his property and sketched his family tree, all the while explaining their significance. Gene listened intently and finally said he thought he could help us. I almost jumped up and clapped my hands in delight. Good thing I didn't. "I'll get right to work on it," he said. "All I need is a seventy-five-hundred-dollar retainer."

I deflated. He might as well have said a million dollars. We didn't have it. Try as hard as I could, over the past month I still had not figured out a way to get it. As I held the envelope from Janofsky, I allowed myself to hope it meant he had waived the fee. He seemed to get on with John so well and was appalled by the treatment John was getting. I ripped open the envelope.

Despair engulfed me. It was a bill for $450, and that was after a $100 discount for professional courtesy. Apparently our first meeting was not free, as John had sworn it was. I felt dizzy when I saw the bold red letters stamped across the bill: PAST DUE—SECOND BILLING. Why hadn't John told me? Instead he'd led me on with the story that he was still working with Janofsky to take the case without the retainer.

I set my jaw, stomped upstairs to John's office, and pushed at a pile of papers to make room for me to pen a note to the lawyer. Then I saw my corporate American Express statement. When had that arrived? I was well organized when it came to bills. I knew each one and when it was due, so my internal alarm had gone off when the company credit card statement didn't show up. I had told John it was missing. He must have inadvertently brought it up here. I grabbed it and slipped my finger under the flap.

I scanned the statement and almost stopped breathing. Surprise turned to disbelief, then to rage. There was a charge for $1,162.54 for the Biltmore Hotel in Coral Gables. He had somehow managed to charge the Biltmore Hotel on my company credit card.

No, it couldn't be. Our trip to Florida was for personal, not company, business. I had deliberately left my company credit card at home. My head pounded and I swallowed hard. Then I heard the garage door and the dog tags jingling as doggie paws padded across the parquet floor in the hall. "I'm home," John sang out.

I grabbed the two incriminating pieces of mail and stormed downstairs, just in time to see him disappear into the kitchen and set down two bags of groceries. "What the hell are these?" I cried, thrusting the bills at him. He snatched them from my hand.

"Whoa. Just a minute. Give a guy a break."

He limped into the breakfast room, sat down in one of the rattan chairs, flipped open the American Express statement, and smirked.

"How did you do it, John? It's my company card...in my name!" I grabbed my now-warm Coke and sat in the chair opposite him at the glass-topped table.

"You got your new card in the mail and threw the old one in the trash, but it hadn't expired yet, so I retrieved it and stuck it in my wallet, in case of an emergency. Good thing, too. Otherwise we wouldn't have been able to pay the Biltmore. Hey, it's no big deal."

"It *is* a big deal," I seethed. "I could lose my job. The company card can *never* be used for personal business. It's grounds for dismissal."

John got up, sauntered back into the kitchen, and started unbagging the groceries, seemingly oblivious to my exasperation. "You'll figure something out," he finally said. "You're good at that."

My mind whirled, trying to come up with some resolution. Finding a way out of our financial maze had become my forte. Damage control. Yes, the first step was to do damage control. I grabbed the bill John had left behind and perused it once more.

"I guess I can get in touch with American Express and explain that we mistakenly used the card, and that I'll repay them with three monthly installments."

"Fine. Do what you must."

I reached over, picked up the letter from the lawyer, and shook it in the air. "What about this bill from Janofsky?"

"What about it?"

"You said the first visit was free."

"That's what Gene told me. The office girl must have made a mistake. I'll call him in the morning and get it straightened out."

Once again John calmly explained away damaging circumstances, with no remorse for his actions or his lies. He never got upset when he was found out, and he refused to accept responsibility. He just moved on. It was driving me crazy. Years later I would find that this behavior is typical for a psychopath and that my reaction was the expected result.

John poured himself a glass of orange juice and sat back down.

"Got some good news, if you're up to hearing it," he said.

All I could do was stare at him. It was too risky to open my mouth; I couldn't trust what I might say. He said he had talked with Randolf Harrington at the Coconut Grove Bank, and the bank was funding a $15,000 second mortgage for him. The check would come in a week or two.

This should have been good news. It was exactly the amount we needed to get ourselves back to minimum-payment status on the mortgage, the utilities, and the credit card bills. But I cringed. How many other times had a check been "in the mail" and never shown up? *I'll believe it when I see it,* I thought. I didn't question how Randolf would be able to fund the loan, because the house was not in John's name. Desperation clouds rational thinking.

"Also, he's going to start a refinance on my house," John continued, "just like you suggested. He'll move it out of the trust. Wants us to come down next month, finalize the deal, and pick up the check."

"We can't afford the airline tickets, or a hotel, or a car."

John didn't miss a beat. He had a plan. "No sweat. We'll use airline mileage, and I can get a good weekend rate for a hotel in Fort Lauderdale, about half an hour from the bank. Anyway, what's to afford? We'll be picking up a check for sixty thousand dollars."

Could this really be the end of our financial nightmare, after nine long years of scraping, second mortgages, late checks, broken promises, and unfulfilled dreams? John, who had held the key for all these years, now dangled it in front of me, saying he would use his property to unlock the financial chains that bound us. Relief had been so long in coming. I desperately wanted it to be true—so not to spoil the mood, this time *I* changed the subject.

"Where were you today? I tried to call earlier."

"I went to see your dad. He enjoys my visits. Then I got some groceries. That's all."

I reached across the table and caressed John's right hand. "You've been very good to my dad and the rest of my family. Thank you."

For all the financial stress John had put me through, I still loved him, especially for how well he treated my family. When my father had a massive stroke after two shunt surgeries, John canceled a business trip and returned from the airport to sit with my mother and me during the five-hour operation. Now, whenever we traveled with my parents, John pushed Dad in his wheelchair—around Disneyland, through the Huntington Gardens, and on picnics.

John was also kind and gentle with my brother, who had schizophrenia, saying that his thesis had prepared him to respect the mentally ill when he ran his now-defunct school. And there was my young nephew, Julie's son. We were present on the day he was born, and he soon filled in as the grandchild John never had. John spoiled him with books, toys, and clothes, and many times would stop by to read him a story.

"I love your family," John said. "It's the family I never had. Being the black sheep of my family has been very lonely." He got up again, grimaced in pain, limped over to the kitchen counter, and fumbled through the groceries.

"Here, I got something for you," he said. He handed me an envelope. It was addressed to "Little Bit." I tore at the envelope and extracted a card. On the front were four Care Bears in pastel colors, playing on a seesaw. Whimsically written in green letters was the sentiment, "Thanks for being the special kind of person who always lifts me up when I'm down." Then, in John's printed script, "At my age I should know what's best for me! Love ya, me, too."

My heart fluttered. How could I stay mad at John when he was always buying special love cards, or flowers, or perfume? He knew how to touch me. I stared at the card and noticed a strong significance. I, too, was on a seesaw, just like the bears, up and down, happy and sad. At that moment, John made me happy once more.

My instinct for survival pushed me forward. I had to make my second marriage work. I couldn't be a failure. I knew that if I could put us on a strong financial footing, I could keep us from bankruptcy, and we could live happily ever after. My life had become a crazymaking jigsaw puzzle with the pieces laid out in front of me, but no picture on the box to follow. Events lay scattered, disjointed, making no sense. I couldn't find the corners or straight edges to start the frame.

My crazy year continued. On a sunny Monday morning in the middle of August 1990, I maneuvered our rental car south along Interstate 95, crawling along, stop and go, through the clogged Miami commuter traffic.

We had just come off a fun weekend in Fort Lauderdale, visiting friends, walking along the beach, and watching the idle rich play on their large luxury yachts and sleek racing boats. This morning, however, my mood was serious. We had an important meeting in Coconut Grove, and it wouldn't do to be late. "The traffic's impossible," I muttered. "I hope we make it on time."

"Relax, you're doing fine," John said.

"It will look bad if we're late. Especially since Harrington finally came through for us with the check for fifteen thousand dollars."

I said *finally* because each day for a month John told me the $15,000 check would come. It hadn't, causing me great confusion and many sleepless nights. Nothing was stress free anymore. Then, when I was due to leave on a business trip, John told me he had heard from Harrington; the money would definitely come while I was away. Thank goodness! I wrote postdated checks. John said he would mail them when the funds arrived. I trusted him that he would do so and left, feeling relieved.

When I returned home, John acted agitated and remorseful. There had been a glitch, and our money was tied up at the main branch of Wells Fargo Bank in San Francisco. Stupidly, he had already mailed the payments, but saved the day by negotiating with a bank officer to hold the checks and honor them as soon as the funding cleared. I found out the hard way that something had gone wrong. My phone started ringing at work with creditors who said no payments had arrived. It was time for damage control, once more. "They must have gotten lost in the mail," I'd say. "It does happen. Or maybe our mailbox got robbed, because all of our checks have gone missing."

Then, within a week, a $15,400 deposit appeared in our joint checking account. I had never seen the check. I promptly paid the overdue house payments and the credit card minimum balances, but my hard-won relief was short-lived. The large balances hemmed me in. Until they were removed, I would feel half dead.

Luckily, the bank approved a $60,000 mortgage on John's Florida home, and we were about to collect it. We passed through the interchange for the Palmetto Expressway and continued south on I-95.

"My wife Cindy died not far from here, on the Palmetto Expressway," John said, "while I was in Nam." He related once more the tragic story of her car accident. He always did when we were in Miami and near the expressway. I could feel his anguish.

"We're getting closer," I said, trying to divert him. "There's the sign for the MacArthur Causeway."

"I…I'm not feeling well," John complained.

"You just need to think some happy thoughts."

"No, I mean it. I didn't sleep last night, between the nightmares and the pain in my leg. I even took extra meds, but it didn't help." John grunted. He slipped a little lower in his seat and laid his head back. I glanced over at his tortured body and wished there was something I could do to help. His eyes were closed.

"Maybe it's the stress of going around your family," I said. "With the check you get today, we'll be able to hire Janofsky and get the show on the road. That's a good thing, a positive thing. It's one more step toward being solvent."

By now the interstate had turned into U.S. 1 and we were on the divided four-lane South Dixie Highway. The area looked familiar. I had driven around it a couple of months ago when we stayed at the Biltmore. Once I've driven somewhere, I file it in my internal direction finder, and it's a good thing, too, because I was about to call on that skill.

"You always cheer me up," John said. "That's why…Oh! Oh!" John clutched his chest.

"The pain. My…my…heart. Hos…pi…tal. Mer…cy Hospi…tal." He collapsed into the middle of the seat.

"John, John!" I shook him with my right hand. No response.

Looking back now, it may seem unreal that I didn't suspect that this might be another ruse to deflect me from the truth. But my ailing husband had just suffered what appeared to be a heart attack. Why would I have reacted any differently? I immediately switched into survival mode to get help for the man I loved.

Pay attention to traffic, I told myself. *Be calm. Where are you? Think! Stoplight ahead. Good, it's turning green. Major intersection. Need to go east, toward Biscayne Bay. Get in left-turn lane.*

I was now on SW 17th Avenue. At its intersection with South Miami Avenue there was a blue sign with a white H and an arrow pointing left. I followed it, and the slow truck in front of me. One block. Two blocks. "Hang in, John, we're almost there."

Finally I saw the hospital, set back from the road. I swerved into the driveway and pushed the speed limit as I followed the emergency entrance signs. John was now moaning. At least he was alive! I slammed the car into park and ran through the automatic doors, yelling at the nurse behind the desk. "Please help. My husband just had a heart attack."

The emergency staff jumped into action, and within minutes John was on a gurney and whisked away out of my sight. I stood glued to the floor. "Dear God, please let him be all right."

A security guard approached. "Ma'am, you'll have to move your car from the driveway."

I followed orders. As I walked back into Emergency, it hit me. We had missed the appointment with Harrington at the bank. I needed to call. I immediately returned to the car and looked in the backseat to get John's briefcase, but it wasn't there. I looked on the floor, then in the trunk. No luck there, either. I couldn't figure it out. John had paperwork for Randolf in it. It was another piece of the crazymaking puzzle, but it didn't register.

I returned to the nurses' station and was told they were still working on my husband. I dragged myself into the waiting room, sat next to the pay phone, and looked up the bank's phone number in the well-worn telephone book. After I fumbled through my purse for the correct change, I dialed. "Mr. Harrington, please."

I listened to scratchy music for almost two minutes that seemed like two hours. Someone finally picked up the phone. "I'm Mr. Harrington's secretary. May I help you?"

I told her about our scheduled meeting and John's emergency, and apologized for any inconvenience. "Oh my," the secretary said. "I don't see an appointment for Admiral Perry this morning, or this afternoon. In fact, I don't see anything at all for this week."

"There must be some mistake," I stammered. "We came to Florida specifically to conduct business with Mr. Harrington."

"Perhaps you should speak to Mr. Harrington. I'll get him for you."

When Randolf Harrington came on the line, I explained the situation. He seemed very confused and said he didn't know a John Perry. I told him about when he and John went to summer camp as kids. He still couldn't recall John. I explained the family crisis and the trust and the mortgage. He was perplexed, but tried to help. "Perhaps my real estate loan officer is handling it." However, when I was connected to her secretary she, too, said there was no appointment on the books. I hung up, baffled. One more puzzle piece, but out of context it meant nothing but frustration. I would have to attend to it later.

"Mrs. Perry," the doctor called from the hallway, "you can come in now." He led me into the emergency room and drew back the white curtain. John was lying there, groggy but awake, hooked up to a horde of beeping and thumping machines. I scooted close to the bed, bent over, and kissed him on the cheek. He gave me a weak half grin.

The doctor reeled off the battery of tests they had performed, things foreign to me. "We think he's had a heart attack," the doctor said. "His blood pressure is dangerously elevated. We're moving him to ICU for a couple of days."

I grabbed John's hand and squeezed. My eyes filled with tears as I relived my fear of losing John. Only this time, it was fear of his death. I was consumed with grief but didn't want to show it. "It will be okay, John," I said. "It will be okay."

Back at the Holiday Inn in Fort Lauderdale, the clerk helped me secure a room in a hotel closer to the hospital. I rushed upstairs to pack. The doctor said it would take a couple of hours to get John admitted, and I wanted to be back with him as soon as I could. When I pushed open the door, I saw John's briefcase lying on top of his bed. I assumed he had forgotten it, a not uncommon occurrence.

I gathered the bathroom toiletries, including John's eight prescription bottles, and threw them down onto one of the beds, next to the Pullman bag. I grabbed clothes off the hangers and from the bureau drawers and tossed them onto the other queen-size bed, next to the matching garment bag. We never did pack lightly. Finished, I set the two bags by the door.

I mentally checked off my "to do" list. Next I had to take care of the airline tickets. They'd be in John's briefcase. I grabbed the case and moved closer to the telephone on the nightstand. I snapped the latches, lifted the lid, and stared. There were seven more pill containers and two objects wrapped in aluminum foil. Puzzled, I moved the objects and searched around until I found the tickets. A quick call to American Airlines and our return flights were canceled, the tickets left open-ended.

As I started to place the pills back into the case, I noticed they were for drugs I had never seen John take before. I made a list of these new medications. I don't know why. Next I grabbed the odd-shaped, larger wrapped object and peeled back the foil. It was a gun! I dropped it on the bed and recoiled. I hate guns. My hands shook and hesitated over the second package before I unwrapped it. It was ammunition. I had never seen it before.

I sat frozen on the bed. Then it hit me. John had carried his briefcase through airport security and the X-ray machines. That idiot! Just like John to get us nearly detained and arrested when we were on our way to such an important meeting. I felt nauseated but forced myself not to throw up. I swallowed an aspirin to ease the pounding in my head, rewrapped the foil surprises, and drove back to the hospital.

When I entered John's room I was livid, but I waited until the nurse left to let loose. "You stupid son of a bitch, why did you have a gun in your briefcase?"

"Hey, don't fire at the patient." John chuckled. A nurse walked by and I lowered my voice, but I couldn't keep my arms from flailing in the air as I paced around John's bed. "What in God's name did you think you were doing? We could have been arrested."

"Don't be so dramatic."

"Dramatic? How am I supposed to feel when you've done something so stupid?"

"Calm down. I've had a heart attack. Remember?"

"If we had been arrested we would have been in a real mess. We don't have the money for lawyers, let alone bail. Why carry a gun?"

"For protection, little one. I brought it for protection. Miami is a rough place, and we were going to have sixty thousand on us."

"Not cash. It would have been a cashier's check." I accepted his explanation. Never in a thousand years would it have crossed my mind that he might have brought the gun along to kill me.

John grimaced and grabbed his chest with one hand and his leg with the other. "Get the nurse, quick," he cried. "Oh…the pain…the pain."

I grabbed the intercom from John's bed and called for the nurse. She came immediately, syringe in hand, and injected its contents directly into John's IV. Now I felt terrible. Here was my husband, lying in bed, having just suffered a heart attack, and I come in with both barrels blazing. I walked over to the window and waited until John's pain subsided. "I talked with Randolf Harrington today," I mumbled through my tears as I looked at the placid bay waters. "He says he doesn't know you." I turned and looked at John, pathetically hooked up to a multitude of IVs and monitors.

"He must have misunderstood the name," John whispered. "Maybe he thought you said Terry. You are quite upset."

I nodded. He was right. John understood me and knew what I needed to hear him say. "I'll call Randolf tomorrow and set everything right," he said. "Don't worry your pretty little head about it."

John's eyes slowly closed, and he drifted into a deep sleep. I felt alone and lost. I didn't know anyone in Miami. I had never met John's family and didn't know their phone numbers, even if I had wanted to call them and tell them about the heart attack. I meandered back to the ICU visitors' lounge, but the droning television was no company. I was restless and needed to talk with someone. I decided to call Gene Janofsky to say hello.

He was pleasant enough when I spoke to him, but his closing comment mystified me.

"Mrs. Perry, I recommend that you get away from John, before he hurts you."

I didn't understand why Gene gave such an ominous warning. It was another piece to my puzzle, but there was no way I could make any sense out of it. So I ignored it. I had to. Hadn't I just caused John major distress when I railed on about the gun in the briefcase? John's recovery was foremost in my mind, and I would do whatever I could to get him home safely. I decided not to mention it to him—or anyone else.

SEVENTEEN

Deep Waters

On the second Saturday in September, John was in his upstairs office checking out his latest volume of *Jane's Fighting Ships*. I insisted he take it easy after his week-long stay at Mercy Hospital in Miami, where John had split his time between the ICU and a private room. The myriad tests he underwent proved inconclusive. My fear for John's life pushed all concerns about our anemic finances to the back burner. Getting him well was priority number one.

While I was out front trimming the junipers, the postman drove up and handed me the mail. I took it over to the brick porch and sat down. The top envelope from State Farm intrigued me. I tore at the envelope. It contained a copy of a notice providing proof of insurance to a Walnut Creek loan company for a $13,400 second mortgage on August 1. I looked closer. The loan was on my house in Antioch. No! It couldn't be! I scanned it again. The loan seemed valid. Then it gradually sank in. The money we received right before the trip to Miami wasn't from a loan on John's property...it was from mine! A corner piece of the puzzle was in my hands, but I didn't recognize it at the time. I felt sick. Trembling with rage, I raced inside and ran up the stairs. Heart attack or not, John had to be held accountable. "You son of a bitch!" I screamed. "How'd you do it?"

John looked up from his book and removed his reading glasses. "What are you shrieking about?"

I rattled the notice in his face. "How dare you!"

"What are you talking about?"

"The loan…on *my* property. And it's not even for the full amount that appeared in the checking account."

"Oh, that," he said dismissively. "Someone had to do something about getting some money. So I got the loan, and a two-thousand-dollar advance from your mom to go with it."

His audacity was shameless. "You approached *my parents*? You got a loan on *my property*? How? I didn't sign any papers."

John slammed his fist on the desk. I jumped back. "Who do you think you are, second-guessing me? My loan got stalled and we needed the money, so I took charge. Don't you ever appreciate anything I do for you?"

I opened my mouth to continue questioning, but the glare in John's eyes said I was on the edge of a precipice, so I dropped the subject.

"My father is dying, John," I sobbed. "I don't have the energy for further discussion." I turned and left the room, tears streaming down my face. *Someday I'll look into this*, I told myself, *but not now*. Other problems with higher priorities besieged me. *How was I going to control this damage*? I was halfway down the stairs when the decision came. I spun around and returned to the office.

"I'm going to have an extra fifteen thousand added to the pending HFC loan. I don't want any second mortgage on the Antioch house, and I don't want to encumber my parents."

Another second mortgage for $150,000 on the Concord house was already in the works. With no other funds to count on, John had insisted, and I wasn't able to defend my position. What position? We were over our heads in debt. There was no alternative. I was forced into a corner and I hated it.

This time the funds would pay off the current second mortgage, the charge cards, and the car loans and bring the first mortgage up to date, as well as pay off the Antioch second, and my parents.

John assured me he would get his inheritance and the money from Jason. Desperate, I believed him. I had to believe in something. I wondered how we would make the high monthly payments. "Remember, John, this is the last time we're using my property to bail us out. The last time, do you hear? We can't afford any more until *you* come through with some money." I turned sharply to leave.

"It's not my fault my family found a legal way to stop me from completing the refinance with Randolf Harrington," John said.

I escaped to the backyard and dangled my feet in the pool, throwing the rubber toy in the water for the dogs to retrieve. Splash. They loved to swim, and I loved to watch them. Today their antics weren't enough to dispel my feelings of being trapped with nowhere to turn. My heart was breaking from fear and disillusionment, and no one could help mend it.

To share with anyone else would reveal I wasn't perfect. No, I had to remain silent. I would solve the problem myself. My family and friends and the outside world would only see me smile, so I would look good and be accepted. Who would like me if they knew I was in a terrible financial situation and a failure in marriage? I was bound by what the world thought of me, when I didn't even think enough of myself to get help.

It was now ten months into my Crazy Year—ten months since the FBI had shown up at my door—but at the time I did not recognize the connection between their visit and my continuing chaos amid unexplained events. All I knew was that it felt like I was drowning, just as I nearly had once when I was seven years old, settling toward the bottom of a community swimming pool in Bishop, California, watching the moving arms and legs above me in amazing silence. Drifting, drifting ever so slowly to the bottom in deep waters. It was my own fault. I didn't know how to swim, yet I had tempted fate with treacherous childhood bravery. I couldn't save myself then, and as my mind swirled with financial complications and a husband who became more of an enigma with each passing day, I didn't know how to save myself now. No matter how hard I tried to make John change, no matter how hard I thrashed about trying to get our finances under control, I was drowning, and I didn't possess the tools or knowledge to extricate myself. But deep inside me the little voice was getting stronger, more resilient, and less trusting. Deep inside me the metamorphosis had begun. I just didn't recognize it yet.

About ten minutes later, John emerged from the house with two drinks in his hand. He came down the wooden stairs and set the drinks on the patio table nearest me. "Here," he said. "I think you need this."

I didn't move. He sat down. "I'm sorry things have been a little tight lately, but I have been listening to you."

I turned and silently glared at him.

"I've talked with my professor at Berkeley and worked out a deal with him to teach at UC Davis and Cal. I'll even get paid and have it count toward my doctorate."

I perked up. His words offered to dispel my misery. "You'll actually be working again?"

"Three days a week at the Davis campus, and two days a week at the Berkeley campus. My thesis subject is in demand. My course will be about schizophrenia and the influence of electrical impulses on the brain."

I stood and walked along the submerged bench in the pool, came up the steps, and sat at the table with John. "I haven't signed the contract yet," John said, handing me my drink. "I wanted to check it out with you first."

"Go for it," I said. "It's about time."

"Yeah, I know. I haven't been the best provider. I love you for understanding, about my health, absent family and all."

"Hold on, hasn't the semester already started?"

John said it had, but this was considered a fill-in class and wouldn't start for another month. He told me his checks would be automatically deposited into our checking account, to make it easier for me to pay the bills.

John struggled to his feet, walked over to me, took my right hand in his, and kissed it. My emotional seesaw moved me from bottom to top. John picked up the rubber duck and threw it into the pool for the dogs. Splash! Splash! I smiled and relaxed a little. We looked like a typical suburban family enjoying a Saturday afternoon by the pool. Nothing could have been further from the truth.

Because I worked five days a week and John hadn't started to teach, it was more convenient for him to coordinate the details of the second mortgage with Household Finance Corporation. The papers were consolidated and ready to be signed. Late in the afternoon during the first week of October, John and I walked into the HFC office in a strip mall near our house. A blond woman in her twenties was on the telephone. She gave us a smile and a wave to come and sit down at her desk until she was finished, and pushed a fat manila folder toward me. I opened it and started reviewing the forms. "Thanks for waiting," Kirsten said as she hung up. "Would you like any coffee or tea?"

We both declined. I had too much acid in my stomach already. This was not a pleasurable event.

"Okay, let's get down to business," she said. Using her pen as a pointer, she commented on each section of the form—confirming the distribution of funds, the loan amount, annual interest, penalties. I followed along nervously. When she got to the section on life insurance, she paused and looked at John. He spoke. "Kirsten said we could get insurance that would pay off the loan if you die."

"What?" His statement caught me off guard. We had never discussed life insurance. "That doesn't make sense," I said. "You're much older than I. If we take it out on anyone, it should be you."

"Can't," John replied. "I'm an old fart, and it's too expensive. If we take it out on you it's only fifty dollars a month."

"We don't have an extra fifty dollars a month in our stretched budget," I reminded him.

We talked back and forth for several minutes. I could not understand John's insistence. He bombarded me with reasons. I resisted. I would not tolerate his nonsense, and I didn't care if we were playing out this little drama in front of a stranger. "We can't afford it and that's that," I scolded. "Please continue, Kirsten."

"This is an equity loan. You can draw money against it. Do you want to require one or two signatures?" she asked, pushing a signature card toward us. "One," John interjected immediately.

"Two," I countered. "It's safer that way."

"Not really," he returned. "What if you weren't available and we needed money right away?"

"Nothing would be that urgent."

John would not give up on this contentious point. He had lost the insurance issue, so he dug his heels in and would not surrender. His insistence wore me down. My head pounded. Butterflies danced in my stomach. I had begun to lose trust in John and was apprehensive about future financial abuse.

"If we approve one signature and change our minds, can we make it two?" I asked.

"The signature choice can be changed back to require two," Kirsten confirmed.

"In that case, make it one...for now."

After we signed the papers, I glared at John. "Remember, this is the *last* time we are doing this!"

The following morning, I sat at my desk at work, mentally and physically exhausted. I hadn't slept well the night before, racked with anxiety. It appeared John would never rein in his spending, and in nine years he had shown no remorse for his extravagance. The constant confrontations over his behavior had chipped away at my sanity and eroded my trust.

Though I had agreed to only one signature for cash advances on the equity loan, it didn't sit well with me. The nagging inner voice said that something was amiss. I listened, and reacted. I wanted to change our arrangement. I reached for the phone, but hesitated, feeling guilty for going behind John's back. Both of our names were on the loan, so his one signature could wreak havoc. No, I had to change the permission to two signatures. I called Kirsten. "I've thought it over," I said. "I want two signatures. I'll feel more comfortable that way."

"No problem," Kirsten said. "I'll mail you a new signature card. You can both sign it, and John can bring it in when the loan is funded."

I hung up the phone, relieved that I'd had the courage to follow through on my convictions. Now I had to get John to sign the card. That might not be easy.

In the middle of a cold, wet day in November, the weather mirrored my dismal mood. It was time to pay the monthly bills. I was filled with dread as I sat down at my desk to sort through the stack and decide which ones would get paid and which would not. It was difficult to concentrate on the task. My world was spinning out of control, and I was having a hard time holding on. My father had passed away a week after John and I signed the HFC loan papers, but I was allowed little time to grieve. Work responsibilities intervened; two business trips called me away. John continued to spend beyond our means. I felt I was going crazy, and I didn't know what to do about it.

I should have found some solace in the fact that John was teaching now. Several days before my father passed away, I was visiting Dad when John bounded into my parents' kitchen with a big grin.

He said he had just come from his class orientation at Davis, and he pointed to the UC Davis name tag attached to his tweed sport jacket. It had PROFESSOR JOHN PERRY hand-printed on it. John also showed us the UC Davis stamp on the inside covers of the books he had laid on the table. My dad was too far gone to care, but I was impressed, only because I appreciated the true significance of the evidence. It was critical to bridging our financial abyss.

Today, as I sat in a state of inertia and dismay, I gazed at the photograph hanging on the wall above the desk, of my dad, mother, and me. I was holding a teddy bear, a lively five-year-old with black curly hair. My parents were young and smiling. It was a happy picture. I wished I could remember when it was taken.

Snap out of it, Barbara, I told myself. Get to work. I reached for the bank statement and reconciled the checks that cleared. Next I analyzed the deposits and, to my dismay, discovered that the $920 weekly deposits for John's university salary had been made at a teller machine in Berkeley, not as direct deposits. I made a mental note to ask John about it when he came in from Davis after his class.

Next I grabbed the bills and realized the MasterCard statements were missing. I checked John's desk. No luck. I closed my eyes and took a deep breath. *Dear God, help me. What is going on?*

A sixth sense propelled me through the house, into the garage, and to the garbage can. I had never in my life considered rummaging through my garbage and felt I was operating by remote control. I pulled the trash out, piece by piece, and threw it on the ground, getting angrier and dirtier by the minute. Halfway down my persistence was rewarded. There were the missing statements, torn in half, buried where John believed they'd never be seen again.

Back inside, I cleaned them and taped them together as best I could. The first statement showed that on my first business trip after Dad passed away, John had charged $1,500 at a store in San Jose, on the same day he said he was in Davis, seventy miles away, giving one of his seminars. The next statement revealed that on my second business trip, John charged $1,000 for a hairpiece and $600 for his collectible David Winter cottages. I had put my foot down and said no more cottages. He already had more than $4,000 worth displayed in his office. We could no longer afford such indulgences, as if we ever could in the first place.

I stood up and paced, trying to keep a level head. Two more corners of the puzzle had appeared, and I began subconsciously to lay them out. If he had purchased those collectibles and they were not displayed in his office, where were they? I scurried from closet to closet and climbed into the attic over the living room, but found nothing. I looked in the liquor room, the garage cabinets, the pool house. No luck anywhere. There was only one place left: the attic above the bedrooms. I pulled the folding steps down and climbed up. I surveyed the darkness with a flashlight, back and forth, farther and farther. At the far corner, the light beam landed on a black garbage bag. I untied it, and there they were.

I grabbed the black garbage bag and set it in the entry hall, along with the taped credit card statements and deposit slips. About an hour later John sauntered in, professorially dressed, with his naval academy tie and brown tweed jacket with leather patches on the elbow, carrying his Hartmann briefcase. When he saw the accusatory pile, he froze. Unlike other altercations, this time I sat stoic on the living room couch; the book I had been reading lay in my lap. *Let him talk his way out of this one*, I thought.

And that's just what he did. For each statement, for each question, he came up with a plausible explanation. He could sweet-talk the birds out of the trees, or in this case, an irate wife out of her anger. He was depressed when I went away on my business trips, so he bought compulsively. He knew it was wrong, but he couldn't help himself. It was a sickness. His one class was canceled, so he went to San Jose. Once more I backed down. What I didn't realize at the time was that I was up against a seasoned psychopath who knew how to manipulate the conversation. There was no way I would ever win. But I gave it my best attempt.

"Look, we can work this out," I pleaded, slipping back into my pattern. "But you have to help me. I can't do it alone. You said you had a contract, but I've never seen it. Doesn't it make sense that I would wonder?"

I believed that if I could see proof that John was teaching, everything would be okay. I wanted something tangible and wouldn't let it go. John took me into his office and extracted a paper from his metal file cabinet.

"Here's a copy of my contract," he said.

I looked it over. It was a letter from the assistant vice chancellor, with the title DEPARTMENT OF PSYCHOLOGY located under the UC Berkeley letterhead. It did indeed have a schedule of classes, a time limit, and a pay scale. What it didn't have was the name of the assistant vice chancellor or his signature, nor the date the letter was written. I didn't notice at the time that the word *Psychology* was of a different font and size. Another corner piece of the puzzle passed unnoticed. "The original is on file at the university," John said when I questioned him about the signature and date.

I tried to believe him, but I yearned for more. The letter had not totally convinced me, so I came up with a plan. "I want to go with you to your next seminar," I said. "I'd like to see my professor in action."

"It's a week from today, and you'll be working."

"No problem. I'll use a vacation day. It will be fun."

"Okay. Just hope you're not disappointed," he said. "Now let's have a glass of wine."

A week later, on the day of the seminar, John woke up complaining that he didn't feel well. He lay in bed while I took my shower and dressed. "Come on. You just need to get up and get going," I said.

He groaned and sat up on the edge of the bed. I jokingly grabbed his arm and pretended to pull him up. "You'll feel fine once you take a shower."

"I had a bad night. My head is pounding."

"Some extra Motrin should do the trick. Plus you'll get to rest on the way up to Davis. You have your own personal chauffeur today."

He stood up and wobbled and almost fell down. "Since you're ready," he said weakly, "you may want to see the report I wrote for your brother's doctor. It's about your family. Look on my desk. Can you type it up for me so I can mail it?"

He straggled into the bathroom and I went into his office. The notes lay in plain sight. I read some of it. He had interviewed my sister from Washington. It was interesting, but his psychology jargon was hard for me to understand.

Twenty minutes later John came into the office, picked up his briefcase, and announced that he was ready to go. "I still don't feel well," he said as he wobbled to the top landing of the stairs. I followed right behind him. He stopped at the top of the stairs. "Help me," he moaned. "I don't think I can get down the stairs." He leaned against the corner of the wall and extended his left arm toward me. "Let me lean on you."

Normally I would have braced up against John and helped him as much as I could. But today, deep inside, my inner voice rallied and took control of my lips.

"No. Hang on to the rail, it's safer. If you slip, I can't keep you from falling."

He extended his arm once more and pleaded with his eyes.

"No," I said. "If you can't walk down, sit on your butt and slide down, one step at a time. You want to get to your seminar in one piece, don't you?"

He cried out once more, asking for help. Against my better judgment, I let him put his right arm around my shoulders. "Put your left hand on the rail to support most of your weight," I commanded.

I leaned against the wall for leverage. We took one step. John yelled in pain. His leg gave out under him. His weight pushed me from the back and I lost my footing. There was nothing for me to grab, and I tumbled down twelve steps. John fell right behind me. We lay motionless on the landing, a tangled mass of arms and legs, until we caught our breath. I struggled to get up, then limped down the last two steps to the foyer. "I told you it was dangerous," I scolded. "When are you going to start listening to me? We're lucky we weren't killed."

He crawled down the last two steps and sat up. "Are you okay?" He moaned.

"No broken bones, but the bruises will be colorful."

"I can't teach today," he panted. "I'll have to call the school and cancel."

What could I say? We were both shaken, and he definitely looked the worse for wear. He struggled to his feet and limped into the kitchen to make his call. I clung to my desire to see him in the classroom. My plan would be delayed, that's all. "Fine," I called. "I'll go to your next one. I have lots of vacation time coming."

Denial gripped my soul. It's easy to see that now, as I reflect on the most confusing and stressful time of my life, when reality blurred with fantasy. As a child I held Santa Claus and the Easter Bunny deep in my heart, but as I grew older and learned the truth, I transitioned from innocent child euphoria to adult understanding, while maintaining the spirit intended by society's deception. But there was a part of me that couldn't release my childhood fascination with fairy tales, especially with Prince Charming who would one day come and sweep me, a modern-day Cinderella, off my feet to live *happily ever after.*

My Prince Charming was John. And when all was not peaceful in the castle, I could not—or would not—acknowledge the clues to his true identity. He was an evil wolf in sheep's clothing who recognized my neediness—and when he cast his spell as only a psychopath can, with his undivided attention, gregarious and entertaining conversation, fascinating stories, and amazing credentials, I was trapped. Once I was mesmerized and under his control, John could roll lies off his tongue or perpetrate financial abuse so cleverly that

I felt crazy for doubting him. I was inside the wolf's den and could not find my way out.

With an insane sense of desperation, I continued to try to find ways to make this marriage work. In my mind, John was indispensable and vital to my life, vital to living *happily ever after*, even though it was not so at the time. I refused to awaken from my fractured fairy tale. My survival depended on my belief that one day my prince would make everything all right.

However, since the day the FBI had appeared at my door, I had become vaguely aware that something wasn't quite kosher. An internal battle was taking place between my conscious and subconscious self. At a deep level, one part of me knew that something was amiss. But when suspicions emerged, the other part of me, desperate to make the marriage work, attacked the thoughts with the mighty tool—denial. Fortunately for me, my subconscious would not surrender, and it lay in wait, gaining strength and momentum. Unbeknownst to me, my biggest combat was yet to come.

EIGHTEEN

Suspicions

On a sunny, crisp Wednesday afternoon in mid-December, I pulled my car into the Queen of Heaven Catholic Cemetery. It had been a year full of John's extreme crazymaking behavior and two months since my dad's funeral. Earlier I had marked time for each special event following his death...the first time he missed his wedding anniversary, the first Thanksgiving without him. Today was the first birthday he didn't live to see. I decided to bring flowers and talk with Dad about the strange events going on in my life. What a paradox. I felt safe talking with the dead but didn't have the courage to share my fears with the living, who might have helped.

The deserted cemetery fit my mood. I placed the flowers on Dad's grave and stood to avoid the wet grass. I started small. "Sorry John couldn't get the Army bugler for your ceremony, Dad. There are some things even a retired rear admiral can't accomplish." It was just another of those small promises John made that never came through, and it had brought a pang to my heart. "I need your help, Dad. Things are a mess and I need you to straighten them out.

I'm going to the library after this. Please guide me to what I need. Research was your strong point."

My little voice inside had grown bolder and louder. I paid attention and decided to investigate John. I was going behind his back, but I had to do it to save my marriage. Too much had transpired over the years, and over the past six months the drama had intensified. My trust in John was eroding. I didn't suspect another woman, but I sensed something was amiss. I wanted the truth. Hadn't I told John when we first met that honesty was the most important thing to me? Hadn't he assured me it was important to him, too? I didn't have the money to hire a private investigator, and the Internet was in its infancy, so I chose the main branch of the county library in which to do my research. I took a half day of vacation for my clandestine quest. The serenity of the cemetery calmed my apprehensions and feelings of dishonesty.

The library was down the hill from the cemetery. Briefcase in hand, I walked in and immediately felt overwhelmed. I stopped at the checkout desk, but the clerk was clueless. I headed past the empty research desk, turned right, and entered a room ringed with metal bookcases. Tables and cubbyhole booths filled the center of the room, divided by a waist-high metal bookcase with three shelves bulging with thick tomes. As I stood in the doorway, looking puzzled, a woman pushing a cart half full of books offered to help me.

"I'm looking for information on Rear Admiral John Perry, who started the Seabees in World War II."

"Hmmm. You might find something in *The National Encyclopedia of American Biography*. It's over here." She led me to shelves in the middle of the room and pointed to the index, a red leather volume on the bottom shelf. I pulled the thick volume out, took a seat at the closest cubicle, opened my briefcase, and set out a pad of paper and a pen. Limited sunlight shone through small windows. I wished for more brightness to warm the chill in my bones.

I fanned the pages until I got to the P names, and ran my finger along the columns until I found *Perry*. There were three listings: John F., manufacturer; John J., congressman; and—I sucked in my breath—John R., naval officer. I scribbled the volume and page number on my scratch paper, replaced the index, and pulled out volume 43. Back in my seat, I zeroed in on page 461, and stared in amazement. There was a photograph, and it looked like my John!

I started reading. Facts that John had spouted for years were in the article…Waco…Rensselaer…Seabees…Great Lakes Naval Training Station. It had to be true. This was John's father. He had served in Great Lakes from 1930 to 1933, spanning the time when John said his mother had died and been buried there.

I pondered each piece of information detailed in the career of this distinguished man. I heaved a heavy sigh as I turned the page and found the 1934 marriage to his stepmother, Janette, listed, as was his half sister, Lydia, and his father's death from a heart attack in 1955. Facts that John had told me over and over again were true.

I began to feel like a traitor until it occurred to me there was no mention of a previous marriage, or children. I reread the article from beginning to end. Nothing. It was as if John did not exist. I was confused. So much of what he told me was in the biography; why not John, or his mother and siblings, even if they were dead by the time his dad passed away? I grabbed the book and found the photocopier.

Now that I had an exact date of death for John's dad, what was my next move? *Ask the expert,* my dad whispered in my ear. I walked up to the lady at the periodicals desk. "I have a death date of September 25, 1955, for a John Richard Perry. Can you help me find his obituary?"

She directed me to the card catalog in the back. I soon returned with a triumphant smile and asked for the microfiche reading machine. It didn't take me long to find the obituary. JOHN PERRY DEAD; FOUNDED SEABEES. As grainy as it was, the accompanying photograph also closely resembled John. The article was short and to the point, listing only his widow, Janette. No daughter. No deceased first wife. No sons, living or dead. I photocopied this, as well.

I thanked the research assistant and went back into the main part of the library. What else could I look up? Something about John that would be easy to find. Oh, yes, the Congressional Medal of Honor. There must be a book about the brave men who risked and mostly lost their lives in the service of their country. I attacked the main card catalog and found a book on Congressional Medal of Honor winners from the Vietnam War. That's when John said he had earned his medal. I pulled the book and took it to a chair near the copier.

Recipients were listed with detailed explanations of their heroic deeds, but not alphabetically. That didn't help. I didn't want to read the whole book; I wanted a list of names. In the back, I found the appendix with a Register of Vietnam Medal of Honor Heroes. The men were identified alphabetically. I flipped through until I came to a page with listings from Monroe through Roark. My finger guided my eyes along the list...Penry...Perkins...Peters. I stopped. No Perry. I scanned from the beginning of the Ps to the end. Still no Perry. I grabbed my purse and fed change into the copy machine once more. Then, as an afterthought, I also copied the publication data. I would order my own book.

As I stuffed the copies into my briefcase, I glanced at the large clock behind the reception desk. It was almost four o'clock. There'd be no more research today. If I left now I'd get home at my regular time and that was absolutely necessary. I didn't want to arouse John's suspicions.

I walked back to my car, placed the briefcase on the front seat, and gave it a pat. My quest was successful, providing me with concrete facts...puzzle pieces I desperately needed to help me start putting together the whole, even though I still had no picture on the box to guide me.

My ultimate goal was to make things right between John and me. The documents I had just found would help me understand John's mysterious self. Then and only then could I help us both. I was still caught up in the fairy tale. I couldn't bear to let it go.

On the way home I decided I wouldn't tell John what I had found. Not yet. I wanted to hold my aces until I could win the jackpot. I would fill out what I had already learned by calling people and places to find the truth about John's autobiographical assertions.

Three weeks later John and I sat in a patient's room at the University of California Veterinary School at Davis, each caught up in our own thoughts about the well-being of our cat Peaches. Eight days earlier her ears had suddenly swollen so severely that the tips had compressed and flattened. She constantly scratched at them. Our veterinarian was stumped and suggested we bring her to the university. Now, after two days of tests, we waited for the head veterinarian to bring her into the room. The door opened and he came in with our pathetic little kitty.

"We can't figure out what caused this," he said. "It might be some type of allergic reaction. We're prescribing prednisone for the swelling. You can give it to her whenever her ears seem to bother her." He handed Peaches to John. He cuddled her, being careful not to crush her sensitive ears. "There are still a couple of test results to come back," the doctor continued. "We may have another prescription for her then."

"Can you call it in to our local vet hospital?" John asked. "It would save us the forty-mile trip to get here and pick it up."

"No problem. Stop at the desk on the way out and give the receptionist your vet's name and phone number. You can also settle up with her."

I looked at the bill for $330 the doctor handed me. "There must be some mistake, Doctor," I said. "John is teaching here in the psychology department. He was told he could use the vet school services at no charge as part of his benefits." The doctor looked at me, puzzled, and said he had never heard about the program. Now I was also perplexed. Well, maybe it was something new, and he had not been apprised of it yet.

We put Peaches in her carrier, thanked the doctor, and left. At the receptionist desk John wrote down our vet's information, and I talked to the receptionist about the bill. She hadn't heard about the benefit program, either. Reluctantly, I pulled out the checkbook. When we stepped outside, John broke into a furious tirade. "How dare the school not honor a promise! I'm going to talk to the dean about this. There will be hell to pay. I'll get our three hundred thirty dollars back, mark my word."

My heart ached at yet another strange happening, one of the many that had piled up over the last several months. My investigations had come to a screeching halt as I stumbled through the Christmas holidays. This unexpected bill got my mind back on track. I had to follow up on John's teaching activities to prove he was actually involved at the school. We settled Peaches on the backseat and I slipped behind the wheel.

"John, since we're here, let's drop by your office and classroom. I'd like to see where you're working, since I never made it up here after that fall down the stairs." No matter how much I persisted, John found some excuse for us to go directly home: Peaches was in the car, the office would be locked, another class was using the room. "Well, let's go to the professors' cafeteria and have lunch."

John didn't answer. I started the car and turned left out of the parking lot. "Is this the way to the cafeteria?" I asked.

"We're not going to the cafeteria," he said icily. "You have to have a reservation." I tensed at the tone of his voice, fearing my quest would fail once more. "But if you insist, we can go to the bookstore. I need to pick up some supplies. Turn left at the next corner." I did as I was told. It was not what I wanted to hear, but it was something. While in the bookstore, John pointed out the student coffee bar. "Sometimes, if my students need extra help, I meet with them there," he said.

I was silent on the way home. John's excuses infuriated me, while at the same time they snared me into acquiescence. No matter how hard I tried, John was able to worm his way out of proof of his teaching employment. My stomach growled from tension. Would this seesaw existence never end? My little voice worked hard to get me to pay attention, and I had tried to find more proof...but to no avail. John's conniving made it hard to pin him down. I needed to find out what was going on and decided that I would have to play my hand with the cards I already held.

The next evening at the dinner table we got into another spat about finances. The vet bill stuck in my mind. Where was the money from Jason, or John's inheritance? His stipend from the university didn't keep up with his spending. The pressure intensified, and I got ready to play my first ace. "Who are you, John?" I was beginning to sound like a broken record, but something deep inside told me I had to continue asking the question.

"You damn well know who I am. I've told you, many times."

"Oh, yes, your father started the Seabees." I hoped he caught the sarcasm in my voice.

"Yes, you know he did. Why bring that up again?"

"Well, it seems strange...if you were his son, why weren't you mentioned in his obituary?" John stiffened and was silent. His eyes glared at me, and I braced myself. "What do you mean by that?" he said. I explained what I found in the library.

"I want to see the articles," he demanded.

I retrieved them from my office and threw them on the table. He quickly scanned them. "It's an oversight that I wasn't mentioned. I told you, I'm the black sheep of the family. My stepmother probably didn't include any of dad's first family, out of spite."

"There's always some excuse, isn't there?"

"I can't help it if there are errors in the article. Even some of my dad's military history has been mixed up."

I played my second ace. "Okay, what about the Medal of Honor? I bought a book listing the recipients from the Vietnam War. Guess what? You're not in it!"

"Show me."

I retrieved it from my office, and opened it to the P page in the appendix. John took the book and started scanning the list. "Jack Peterson isn't mentioned." He flipped through several pages. "Neither are George Ramsey or John Reese. This book has left out at least four of us."

"Seems fishy to me," I said.

John erupted. "How dare you question my Medal of Honor? Haven't you seen me wear it? Haven't we sat in the Medal of Honor stands?"

"Yes, John. And speaking of medals, where are your medals?" I was on a roll now and not about to give up. "They've been missing for over a year."

John's eyes narrowed. He pounded his right fist on the table. "I told you. The frame shop lost them."

"Right. For such a distinguished, decorated military man, you don't seem the least bit concerned about their disappearance." I was ready to play my third ace. "I followed you this morning."

"You what? How dare you!"

"I wanted to see where you go in the mornings when you leave the house in dress clothes, with your briefcase. The teaching stories don't add up."

"What did you find out?"

"I lost you at the stoplight on Ygnacio Valley Road, so I went to the BART parking lot where you said you park the car to catch the university shuttle to Davis. The car wasn't there."

"Well, Miss Smarty Pants, that's because I had a special meeting with the professor in Berkeley, so I drove in. I really don't like your insinuations."

Tears trickled down my cheeks. "And I don't like the lies," I sniffed as I played my fourth ace. "I called Davis this morning and they couldn't find any record of you on their teacher roster. I even tried to check out your family this afternoon. I called NASA, but Sonny Perry is not listed as an astronaut. I called Juilliard. They never had a Desiree Perry as a student. I called MIT. Sandy Perry was never a student. I called the Stanhope Hotel, but Lydia Perry doesn't live there. None of your stories checked out."

John's face reddened and he clenched his teeth. He put both hands on the table and pushed himself up. "You little sneak," he hissed as he turned and marched out of the room.

My fear overtook my common sense, and I could no longer think rationally. The self-confidence I had so courageously mustered was still no match for John. But I was getting stronger.

"You have to help me believe in you," I whispered as I wiped the tears from my eyes.

Looking back now, it seems unbelievable that I would have stayed in this marriage for so long, especially with a repeating pattern that is easy to recognize now, but that was indiscernible at the time. You had to be there. John was a psychopath—a master manipulator who made it seem reasonable and plausible at the time the abuse happened, and he abused when no one else was around to be able to validate my feelings. If I had told others, they wouldn't have believed me anyway. He was too charming. He was the life of the party who went out of his way to help others.

During this time, verbal abuse wasn't even discussed as domestic violence, and because I wasn't physically beaten, I didn't think I was a victim of domestic violence. Most important, the emotional trauma was not constant. It came in spurts. Most of the time we had a happy existence that appeared normal, integrated with a close-knit social support system of family, friends, and co-workers. I don't feel embarrassed by my vulnerability at that time of my life. I now know that I stood no chance against John. Psychopaths are so clever that they can even disarm mental health professionals, who are trained to recognize and deal with their behavior.

So as strange as it sounds now, back then at the conscious level I still wanted the marriage to work. It was my subconscious that struggled to make me more aware and propelled me to try to find proof, any kind of proof, that John was who he said he was.

Unfortunately I didn't make a good poker player—I revealed my hand too soon. Even though I had four aces, I didn't win the hand; instead, I set myself up for elimination from the tournament.

The next evening I sat alone in our special booth at La Cigale and sipped my aperitif. I remembered the first time we came here, when John spoke to me in French. I wondered if he'd do it again tonight. Right after lunch, John called me at work, all bubbly and excited. He told me to meet him at six o'clock at La Cigale for a celebration. He had wonderful news, hinting that it was about a contract with the government. He'd provide details later.

I looked at my wristwatch. He was late, but that was not unusual. I ordered another drink. It had not yet arrived when John breezed into the room, looking hassled and tired, but smiling. He threw his briefcase, Stetson hat, and Burberry raincoat onto the bench seat and slid into the booth.

"Sorry I'm late. Traffic from the city was a bear tonight, but my news is worth the wait." I desperately wanted to hear good news, anything to ease my pain. My dream was to be the cheerful admiral's wife, not the morose person I had become.

The waiter arrived with two drinks and a plate of escargot on his tray. "Ordered on my way in," he said to my inquisitive look as the waiter set them on the table.

"What's the news?"

"Let's have a toast first," John said, "to our financial destiny." Our glasses clinked, and John went on to explain that he had gotten a call that morning from the Federal Government Contract Administration office in San Francisco about a special assignment.

"You said years ago you wouldn't take on any more special assignments from the FGCA."

"This one is different," he said. "Low risk. No guns, bullets, or espionage." He had been offered a job in Cairo, Egypt, for six months, as part of a team of specialists to design a peace strategy for the Middle East. They would also work in Beirut and Athens.

"The Gulf War is going on." I gasped. "Egypt isn't that far from the front."

"The fighting's not that close. Besides, I'll be working with a prestigious group from places like Stanford University."

"I don't know. It sounds risky to me."

"Well, I guess I can turn down the nine thousand dollars a month they're willing to pay me, tax free, plus a fat per diem for expenses."

I couldn't believe our good fortune. It was like winning the lottery...the financial break I had prayed for. My plans to investigate John vanished. The waiter interrupted and we placed our order.

I slipped back under John's spell, wanting to believe that he and his stories were real, our financial woes would clear up, and all would be well. Yet I felt unsure. I reached across the table, caressed John's hand, and looked directly at him. "But, dear, your health is declining."

"I'll take extra medication along with me and take it easy. Most of my work will be in meetings, not in the field."

"I don't know. I worry about your legs giving out and your headaches and..."

"One team member is a medical doctor."

"What about your teaching job at the university?"

"My Berkeley professor said that world peace is more important. He'll let me continue my program when I get back."

"This is such a big step."

"The project director, Jack Berger, said I could take you along for the first two weeks, all expenses paid. He figured you might have a problem with me going, so this way you can see where I'll be working, and also some of the Egyptian sights."

Egypt was a country I longed to see, with its mystique of pharaohs and pyramids and the Nile. My dream trip lay before me. I could not refuse. I took the bait and John reeled me in.

"How soon do you have to report?" I asked.

John explained that we had a choice, but the sooner the better. I opened my purse calendar to February. "I have a business meeting in Indianapolis on the fifth and sixth, and I'm going to visit Grandpa in Hot Springs on my way. What about the following weekend?"

We settled on Sunday, February 10. But even in the excitement of the moment, I felt nagging doubts. I wanted some proof this was real, because I had never been able to pin John down on much of anything. "I want to meet Jack Berger and see the contract." John agreed.

Throughout the meal we discussed the finances. We would use an international bank because his salary check would be issued in Cairo. I figured out monthly payments for the credit cards. "Good news," I beamed when the apple strudel and lemon tart arrived. "By the time you finish your assignment all the balances will be paid off. We'll be debt free!"

The next three weeks passed in a blur of activity. As we prepared for the trip to Egypt, the pressure on me heightened. Not only did I have to maintain my work schedule, I also had to plan for the household and for John's clothes for six months. I had other reasons for feeling apprehensive. The departure date was only two weeks away, and I still had not met Jack Berger, read a contract, or received airplane tickets.

John had set up a meeting at a restaurant in Orinda, but Berger and his wife had not shown. The diplomatic passports John said Berger would issue didn't appear either. How could a passport be issued in only two days? "You've never dealt with the FGCA," John said. To add to my stress, I had to report for jury duty and was picked for a two-day trial.

The following evening, John and I finished dinner and started to clean the kitchen. "What did you do at lunch today?" John asked. "Have lunch with another juror?"

I hesitated, and swallowed hard. Was this the time to share? Good as any, I decided. "No, I went to the county recorder's office, down the street from the courthouse."

"What?" John stood erect and stared at me.

"You heard me." I slunk back into the breakfast room, sat down at the table, and reached for my glass of wine. John followed and sat down, too. He looked genuinely puzzled. "What would possess you to do that?" he asked.

"I figured that while you're away I might be able to do something about getting Jason to pay what he owes you, so I looked up your Danville property." I took a sip of wine to wet my dry throat.

"Let's not get into that," John said. "It's my business and I'll take care of it."

"I found out something very interesting. Jason purchased the property, all right, almost twelve years ago, but according to the records, he didn't purchase it from you."

"Damn family! What have they done now to cheat me out of my property? When I get back from Cairo I'll have to get it straightened out."

"I don't see how. . . ."

"There's lots of ways to change legal documents. You don't know the half of it."

"Then I'll call Jason and ask him about it."

"Let it be, damn it! Don't meddle in my business. You are definitely not to call Jason. I'll get an attorney to meet with Jason and me." John poured more wine into his empty glass and took a huge swig. He almost drained it.

"Speaking of attorneys, we have an appointment tomorrow with Tom Landers to do our wills. We need to write drafts tonight." With the impending trip, I had felt it was prudent to update our wills, and John agreed. The attorney came highly recommended by George. I reached over for the manila folder, yellow legal pads, and pens that I had laid on the rattan étagère. "Maybe Tom will meet with Jason and me," John mused.

"Good idea. Now, let's get down to work. I'm naming you my executor, John. I want my Antioch property sold immediately after my death and the proceeds divided per my list."

"That's unwise. You should leave the timing of the property disposition to the executor. The real estate market is extremely soft right now. In fact, it would be best if you left the Antioch house entirely to me because it would be easier for me to handle if I had full control."

I bristled. "No! Antioch is my solely owned property and I want it disposed of exactly the way I said. You won't have any worries. You'll be getting my share of the Concord house, and you're the beneficiary on all my insurance policies, including the two-hundred-thousand-dollar life insurance policy at Excelsior. If I die on company business, you get double my salary to boot. That's another eighty thousand." I was adamant, and angry. Why was he being so greedy?

"I was just thinking about how to maximize your wealth," John said. "You're making a stupid decision."

"I don't care. It's my stupid decision and I will not budge. Let's move on." John let the issue drop, and I started to cool down. It was his turn. "I want to leave some of my fifteen-million-dollar estate to your nephew, and set up a scholarship at Juilliard School of Music in your dad's name."

"That's nice, if the money ever appears."

John continued writing, filling out a detailed list of more than five pages with his printed words. "Okay, that's done," he said, shuffling his pages and putting them in the manila folder. "We're ready for Tom tomorrow. Hopefully we can get a Friday follow-up appointment to sign them."

"That's rushing it," I said. "I have enough stress already. I leave for Hot Springs early Saturday morning and fly back from Indianapolis the following Wednesday. We'll get an appointment to sign the wills on one of the three days before we leave for Egypt."

"It's important to get the wills finalized as soon as possible,"

John said. "Anything can happen to either one of us, at any time." John would not give up. He bombarded me with reason after reason until he beat me down. After all, I did get to say how I wanted my Antioch property handled. "Okay, okay. I can't handle any more arguments tonight. We'll try to sign Friday."

My little voice was working but not hard enough. Although I had resisted John on some of the issues, what didn't register with me at the time were his suspicious demands. Why would John want complete control over my will, and why did it have to be completed before my business trip? I also didn't catch the clues with his reasoning about the real estate market, his deed of trust not being in his name, and his being adamant that I wasn't to bother his cousin for the monies due. I was too focused. *Debt free* was on the horizon. I still believed in the fairy tale of living *happily ever after*, even if it had become a bit fractured.

Perhaps if I had been more diligent, I would have taken these puzzle pieces and built enough of the picture to see them adding up to my imminent demise, instead of blindly moving forward, although the conclusion would have been so far out in left field that I would have considered myself crazy for thinking it. Hindsight is always clearer than the present.

NINETEEN

The Fog

It was dark by the time I arrived at the Holiday Inn North in Indianapolis, and the parking lot was packed. I circled, looking for an open spot. This did not help my mood. Weather had delayed my flights, and I was physically exhausted from a long day of dragging bags and uncomfortable airport seats. More important, I was mentally exhausted. The visit with my grandfather had been pleasant, but clouded with feelings of remorse.

Right before I left home, John and I sparred about Jason's unpaid obligation and the unfinished details of the Cairo trip. I was livid and downright nasty as I walked out the door. The next day John had called me in Hot Springs. He lovingly apologized and said I was right, and that he had set up an appointment with the lawyer for himself and Jason. "I miss you," he cooed. "The doggies lying at my feet miss you. The kitties napping on the bed miss you. We all love you."

His words softened my attitude and melted my heart. During every waking hour afterward, I wrestled with my feelings. Now I felt like a heel. How could I have doubted John? Why was I so hard on him? He tried his best for me, even if he wasn't always successful.

I found a parking space at the end of the lot and braced myself for the cold. I trudged into the foyer and up to the clerk at the registration desk. "We have the room you requested," he said, "secluded, at the back of the hotel. You won't be bothered by any noise."

"Excuse me?" I said. "I didn't—"

"It's right here, under your reservations."

I was in no mood to contradict him, nor did I want to be at the back of the hotel. "I want to be near the front," I said. The room was changed as I directed. I settled into it and freshened up, then headed to the hotel's restaurant. Maybe a nice dinner would cheer me up. Comfort food was what I needed.

The San Remo reeked elegance from its wrought-iron gates to the marble floor of the entrance, from its formally dressed staff to its ambient lighting, soft classical music, red linen tablecloths, and flickering candles. The waiting maitre d' flashed a warm, welcoming smile. "Table for one?" he said as he led me to the second small booth, not far from the entrance.

"Yes, unfortunately." I laughed. "If you happen to see a single good-looking guy, you can send him my way." I was joking. It never would have occurred to me to be unfaithful. It wasn't in me.

I perused the menu while I sipped my rum and Diet Coke. That, and the romantic atmosphere, helped me relax and unwind, and I found myself wishing John were with me. I wanted to caress him, whisper how much I loved him. I wanted to let him know how sorry I was I had been so unsettled lately. I was lost in such thoughts when I heard a commotion. I glanced up to see my husband bounding toward my table, holding one arm open for an embrace. The other arm was wrapped around his travel toiletry bag. "Surprise!" he sang out.

"Surprise" didn't cover it. I was flabbergasted. John was supposed to be in California with our animals. My remorse vanished, and a warm feeling engulfed me. My man was here in Indianapolis just as I wished. "John, what are you doing here?"

John slid his shaving kit onto the bench opposite me, bent over, and gave me a tender kiss. He removed his hat and coat and sat down opposite me. Our waiter took John's whiskey order.

"I'm on my way to Washington, D.C., to sign the contract with the admiral in charge of the peace project. The whole team is with me."

This was good news. Even if it was squeaking in less than a week before we were to leave for Egypt, we had a contract at last. John explained that the team had caught a military transport at Travis Air Force Base earlier that afternoon. When the plane made a stop at Indianapolis to pick up some equipment for the Gulf War, John requested that they leave him at the Indy airport so he could spend the night with me. The plane flew on to Wright-Patterson Air Force Base, but would return early in the morning to retrieve him before going on to Washington.

John's comings and goings were always complicated, and this explanation was no exception. Still, here he was, with me, and on his way to sign the contract. Life was good. The waiter interrupted and gave John his drink. I was full of questions. John was full of answers.

"Where's your luggage?"

"Don't need any. We fly in, sign the papers, and go home."

"What about the animals?"

"I took the dogs to Marie and Mark's. The cats are fine for one night on their own with some extra food and water."

"How'd you get from the airport to the hotel?"

"The hotel has a shuttle bus, so I hopped on it."

The waiter came and took our order: filet mignon for both of us, medium rare, and a good bottle of wine. "I have to be back at the airport at five a.m.," John continued. "The shuttle bus doesn't go that early. Can you take me?"

I hesitated. This did not fit into my plans, as I had a breakfast meeting with a business associate. John said I'd be back in plenty of time. He cajoled me, said the team and Jack Berger wanted to meet me. How could I refuse? My man needed me, and my only sacrifice would be losing a couple of hours of sleep. I agreed.

We finished dinner and took the elevator to the second floor. I stopped at the first room on the left and dug around in my purse for the room key. "I thought you'd prefer a nice quiet room at the back of the hotel where nobody would disturb you," John said.

"No, closer is better."

Inside, John went into the bathroom with his toiletry bag and closed the door. I tossed my purse on the dresser, sat down on the bed, and called the front desk. "What time does the shuttle bus leave for the airport in the morning?"

The clerk told me the hotel did not have a shuttle bus to the airport. I was stumped. John emerged from the bathroom and I handed him the receiver. "Here, John, talk to the desk. They say there is no shuttle bus."

John grabbed it and turned his back to me, blocking the phone. He braced himself on the nightstand and crumpled onto the edge of the bed. An animated conversation ensued. John was adamant that there was a shuttle bus, and after he hung up the phone he said the clerk was new. There was a shuttle bus, but it didn't leave until five a.m. I would still need to take him to the airport. I sighed. I had hoped I wouldn't have to go out that early in the morning.

"I'll take my shower now," John said. "That will save some time in the morning." I proceeded to get ready for the next day, organized my clothes and paperwork, and started to get ready for bed. John was still steaming up the bathroom when I opened the door.

"Mind if I come in and brush my teeth?"

"Not at all. Climb in the shower with me, if you like."

I laughed, set my cosmetic bag on the counter, and noticed that not only had John emptied his toiletry bag, but he had neatly arranged the contents on a hand towel, including two unusual items...latex surgical gloves and an amber pint bottle with no label. I reached for the bottle, unscrewed the cap, and took a cautious whiff. Ether! It was unmistakable. I quickly replaced the cap.

"What are you doing with ether?" I shouted above the din of the running water. John pulled the shower curtain back and poked his head out.

"Doc said to use it on the cut on the back of my neck so it will heal faster."

"Well, the bottle should be labeled. What are the gloves for?"

"To protect my hands when I use the ether. It's dangerous stuff, you know."

I shrugged. It sounded strange to me, but John did have a persistent open sore on the back of his neck. I quickly brushed my teeth and climbed into bed. It was eleven p.m. and I was exhausted.

John returned to the room and told me to set the alarm for three thirty. He'd get up first and shave and dress so I could sleep a little longer. I smiled, grateful for his consideration, and happy that I could snuggle up next to his warm body for the next four and a half hours.

The fog was low and thick when I drove to the airport. If it didn't lift I would probably be late for my breakfast meeting. The normal twenty-minute journey took forty minutes. John was concerned that he might miss his flight to Washington; he didn't know if they would wait.

The inside of the terminal was desolate. A lone janitor pushed a dust mop over the shiny granite floor. The only sign of commercial life was the coffee shop, which, thankfully, was open. "Stay here," John said. "I'll go check out the flight and boarding gate. I hope the fog hasn't screwed up the schedule."

He disappeared around the corner and was back in a couple of minutes. "Bad news," he reported. "All planes have been grounded because of fog. Why don't you order a cup of coffee, and I'll go see if I can get in touch with Berger."

I looked at my wristwatch. "I think I'll head back to the hotel, John. I have a morning meeting, and I don't want to feel rushed."

"Hang around just a little bit longer, please," he pouted. "Berger wants to meet you." All right. He seemed to be trying hard to please me. I watched him disappear down the near-empty corridor and checked my watch once more. It was five thirty. I would have to leave no later than six to make it back in time for my meeting.

I ordered a decaf coffee, black. The minute hand on the wall clock seemed to move incessantly slowly. Ten minutes. Fifteen minutes. Where was John? I began to panic. I finished my coffee and ordered another. Twenty minutes. Thirty minutes. Panic turned to anger; my stomach was tied in knots. Last night was merely a peaceful interlude, I thought. Forty minutes later John nonchalantly strolled up. He might have had all the time in the world, but I didn't. "Finally!" I exclaimed. I stood up and grabbed my purse.

"Sorry I was gone so long. It was difficult to get in touch with the group at Wright-Patterson. Berger says they're socked in over there, too, and the plane won't be able to pick me up until at least eight a.m."

"Sorry, I can't wait. I'm leaving."

"I'll go back with you to keep you company. I don't want anything to happen to you in this fog."

As I pulled up to the hotel, John announced he would come in, have a quick cup of coffee, and meet my business associate. "I'll have time," he said, over my protests. "The seven a.m. shuttle bus is sitting there right now. See? I'll hop on it and go back to the airport."

I was numb. My feelings had been stretched from one extreme to the other in less than twelve hours. I didn't know if I could take much more. In my state of mind, I never noticed that several additional crazymaking puzzle pieces had fallen into place.

Three days later, back home, I submerged myself in last-minute details and made several stops after work. The pressure was relentless as I tied up loose ends before we left for Egypt on Sunday. When

I walked into the house, I dropped into the first chair I came to, in the dining room.

"Hey, Babs," John called. "Come up to the office. I have some papers for you."

"Bring them down," I hollered back. "I don't think I can make it up the stairs right now. I'm beat."

John joined me in the dining room and handed me a power of attorney and a W-2 form that appeared to be from the University of California. "You'll need these to file the income taxes in April," he said.

"Thanks." I laid them on the table. Right now I wasn't worried about taxes. "John, I stopped by the vet's office to get heartworm pills for the dogs, and the receptionist said the strangest thing—that you were in a couple of weeks ago to pick up ether for the cat's ears."

"That's ridiculous."

"That's what I told her. The university vet didn't order any ether for Peaches."

"Guess she mixed me up with someone else."

John had said his medical doctor had prescribed the ether I saw in the hotel room in Indiana. I had no reason to connect it with the receptionist's story. There were other, more critical, loose ends to tie up. "Did the tickets and passports show up today?"

"No. Jack said he would bring them to the airport."

"Isn't that cutting it pretty thin?"

"I'm at the mercy of our government's bureaucracy. We have to be patient."

The circumstances left me unsettled. When I lamented that I had not seen the signed contract, John scolded me and reminded me that none on the team had received theirs. They would get them in Egypt.

I got up and dragged myself into the kitchen to make a pot of hot tea. John followed. "I talked with Tom today," he said. "He's worked out an agreement with Jason. You'll need to keep in touch with him while I'm gone."

My parents and I posed for my uncle in 1950. As an only child for ten years and the eldest of five children, I was considered to be the "responsible" child and became a third parent to my four younger siblings. *Photo by Paul Leo*

I celebrated my thirty-fifth birthday with friends at a posh Danville restaurant. Eleven months later, I met John Perry and clandestinely slipped this photo into his briefcase before he left for a business trip in Mexico. When he called me from Mexico City to say he had found the photo, he told me that he would never remove it—and he never did. I found it in his briefcase after he tried to murder me. *Photo by George Rammell*

After the 1982 wedding in Tijuana, John and I stopped at a small jewelry store to pick out a sapphire wedding ring. Later we celebrated at the elegant La Escondido restaurant on the other side of town, where John made a production of slipping the ring on my finger as he said, "With this ring, I thee wed." *Photo by John R. Clay*

In April 1983, we advanced into the world of collectible art, even though we couldn't afford it. *Freddy, Kitty, and Jack* was an $85,000 painting, one of two original Red Skelton works of art that John arranged to lease. We never actually took physical possession of the paintings. *Photo by F. C. Coffey*

In October 1984, we attended the San Francisco Fleet Week ceremonies. We sat in the reserved military stands for the Blue Angels show, and later toured one of the ships open to the public. When we came aboard, we were saluted as an admiral and his party and received a special tour of the ship—into areas normally off-limits to civilians.
Photo by Barbara Bentley

Gifts from friends for birthdays or Christmas usually had a naval theme. The twinkle in John's eyes showed that he was pleased.
Photo by Barbara Bentley

John said his father was Admiral Perry, who started the Seabees in World War II. On one business trip, we took time to find his father's grave at Annapolis. John was visibly shaken. After the murder attempt, I found out that John was indeed Admiral Perry's son. *Photo by Barbara Bentley*

John wore his Congressional Medal of Honor to a wedding in Napa Valley. This time, he donned a white shirt and pants, and added the admiral's bars on his shoulders. He was getting bolder in his impersonation. *Photo courtesy of Barbara Bentley*

In 1989, John wore his Congressional Medal of Honor to the Inauguration and Inaugural Ball for George H. W. Bush. We were crammed into the Kennedy Center like sardines, but John's medal got people's attention and they parted so that we could pass.

Photo courtesy of Barbara Bentley

John claimed he had secured a job with the University of California at Davis, teaching a psychology class so he could complete his doctorate. He showed me this letter to prove he was working. I was suspicious because there was no signature. Several months later, I found out that he had forged the letter.

Photo courtesy of Barbara Bentley

UNIVERSITY OF CALIFORNIA, BERKELEY

BERKELEY · DAVIS · IRVINE · LOS ANGELES · RIVERSIDE · SAN DIEGO · SAN FRANCISCO   SANTA BARBARA · SANTA CRUZ

DEPARTMENT OF Psychology   BERKELEY, CALIFORNIA 94720

John F. Perry, PHD

Dear Dr. Perry;
          It is with a sense of additional
capability and responsibility that we welcome you to
to our staff.
          You will serve in the capacity of
reserve associate professor for this semester
beginning October 22 at the Davis campus. Your
date of appointment is October 15 and it will continue through the Spring semester.
          The present schedule is:

Davis: 10 AM to 2 PM Mon., Wed., and Fri.
Berkeley: 1 PM to 4 PM Tues. and Thurs.

Two six hour symposiums per month to be scheduled:

          Remuneration at $24,000 per year and
$1,000 per symposium. Maximum 6 symposiums. Tenure
will not be included but all other University benefits
will.

          We welcome you,

          Chairman

          Asst. Vice Chancellor

I had planned a spring trip to Hot Springs, Arkansas, with my sister to visit our grandfather. At the last minute, John invited himself along. On Easter Sunday, John insisted that he drive me to the post office—very unusual, since I always drove. John ran off the road and wrecked the car, with most of the damage on the passenger side, where I had been sitting. I now realize that was a deliberate attempt to harm me.

Photo by Barbara Bentley

On February 15, 1991, John Perry tried to murder me. The bruises on my face provided mute testimony of the battle I waged to save my life.

Photo by Thomas Gregory Smith

During April of 1995, I invited myself to attend the annual Victim's Rights Day at the California State Capitol in Sacramento. I collected more than one hundred signatures and also caught the attention of an *Oakland Tribune* reporter. *Photo by Rex Johnston*

May 1995. I posed with the supporters of AB16 (including Assemblyman Richard Rainey, third from right) for a celebratory photo after the bill passed out of the Assembly Judiciary Committee without a negative vote. My lobbying efforts had paid off, for the moment. But that was only the first hurdle of many to come. *Photo by Bonnie Hilliard*

September 1997. Rex and I married in the same church where my parents were married during World War II. Our reception was held in a friend's restaurant, and the wedding cake was their gift to us. *Photo by Debbie Joseph*

This is the photo from Rex and my first Christmas card. Our merged animal family included Taffy the Terrier, Gaby the Golden Retriever, and Peaches the Escaping Cat. *Photo by Bruce Speights*

I pressed John for more details, but got none. I told myself I had to be satisfied that Jason would finally be honoring his commitment. In six months, with Jason's payment and the government salary, we would be almost completely debt free, and that prospect made me ecstatic, but not any less tired. The tea was ready, and I poured two cups.

"Bring your tea and come upstairs," John said. "I want you to show me how to use the computer."

"What? We've had it over two years and you haven't shown an interest before."

"It won't take long for you to show me the basics," he pleaded.

"Why bother? You're leaving for six months. I'll show you when you come back."

"I may need to use a computer in Egypt."

I continued to protest. I was too tired and we still had too much to do before we left on Sunday. John was relentless. Reluctantly, I agreed to start teaching him, but only for an hour. I didn't have any more spare time than that. After twenty minutes, I realized John was not a quick study. Even with the shortcut index cards I wrote out for him, he floundered. It was going to take more than this evening to show him the ropes. I was agitated at having been put upon at the last minute. He apologized and let his lessons drop.

"Come into the guest bedroom," John said. "I've been working on the billings for Westinghouse. I figure they owe us about eighty thousand dollars, and I'll have to take them to court to get it." I trudged down the hall after him. I got a shock when I saw the bed; it was covered with piles and piles of papers. He walked over, picked one up, and handed it to me, explaining that each pile was a separate billing and would become a separate small claims court case.

"I want you to move on these while I'm gone," he said.

"You're crazy. I don't know anything about them. Put them in a file box and proceed when you get back." I turned and left the room, unable to take it anymore. I was at my wit's end. It was too much to handle at this late date, and I couldn't fathom why he was insisting on things that made no sense, like learning the computer and going to small claims court. I went downstairs and dialed my mother to let her know how the visit with Grandpa Jonas had gone.

My spirits needed a lift, and talking to someone about the Egyptian antiquities I was going to see excited me. My mother seemed surprised that the trip was still on. "I thought John's health precluded him from going," she said. "That's what he told me when he stopped by here a couple of days ago."

"You must be mistaken, Mom. We're starting to pack tonight. Hold on, I'll get John on the line."

I used the intercom and asked John to pick up the phone. I listened as he told her she must not have understood him correctly. Despite her protests, John insisted the trip was definitely a go. Lift-off would be on Sunday morning.

The following Tuesday we should have been in Egypt, but we weren't. We were still at the San Francisco Airport Hilton Hotel in a room we couldn't afford, with six bags of luggage. Our discussion was heated.

"This is the third day, John. Where the hell is Berger?" I screamed. "I'm about to go mad. This is the most God-awful saga. I can't believe this is happening."

"I'll call Berger," John yelled back, his face fiery red. "I'm just as frustrated as you are."

The adventure started on Saturday evening, when we checked into the Hilton so we could use the complimentary shuttle to the terminal for our early flight and leave the car at the hotel until I got back. It was John's suggestion.

The first part of our plan worked out. The next part didn't. On Sunday, we waited in the American Airlines terminal for Berger to appear with the tickets and passports. He never came, and we had missed our flight. We hung around for more than six hours, and still no Berger. I was confused, angry, and troubled.

Finally, John left me with the luggage and walked across the lobby to a pay phone to call Berger. When he returned he told me that Berger had apologized profusely. The documents were delayed in arriving. The plan had been changed; we were to fly out on Monday. John talked me into spending another night at the Hilton.

The Monday plan hadn't worked either. Again, no appearance by Berger, and we missed our flight. I was appalled. This time John returned from his phone call and said there was something political going on. He had to go into the city to sort it out. I almost cried. We dragged our bags back onto the shuttle, and at the hotel had the bellhops put them in our car.

At the federal building in San Francisco, John told me to stay with the car in the nearby parking lot, because of the luggage. When he emerged he said everything had been fixed, but because of some last-minute paperwork, Berger would not be able to deliver the tickets and passports until the next morning at the airport.

To appease me, we played tourist at the Japanese Tea Garden in Golden Gate Park. The serenity and quiet of the gardens relaxed me. John surprised me by asking how to use the new Sony movie camera. He wasn't into taking pictures. Afterward, John talked me into staying at the Airport Hilton again.

When we returned from the airport and were allowed back in our room, I let John have it. He told me to shut up and reached for the phone. He turned his back to me and shielded the phone. I heard him dial, then carry on a rapid conversation. He slammed the receiver down and turned back toward me. "That bastard, Berger, is trying to nix me from the team. He wants to replace me with one of his cronies. He's stalling until it will be too late for me to go."

I collapsed onto the bed, distraught, and my eyes swollen with tears. *Not now, Barbara,* I thought. *Pull yourself together. Think. What can we do?* Then it came to me. "Why don't you call Admiral Lee in Washington? He's in charge. Tell him what's going on."

"Good idea," John said. Soon he was engrossed in an animated conversation. I sat on the other bed. All I could see was John's back;

the phone was hidden from my view. John thanked the admiral and hung up.

"You were right," he beamed. "Admiral Lee wants us to come to Washington, and he'll take care of the whole thing. Berger's ass is in big trouble. The admiral's going to get us the tickets for Cairo, and he'll pull rank to get us our passports."

"Must be part of the good-old-boy network," I said, elated that my plan had worked.

"But there's one thing," John said.

I felt my heart flutter and drop to the bottom of my rib cage. "What?"

"Don't be sad. It's not much. We have to buy our own tickets to Washington for tomorrow. The admiral will reimburse us."

"Can't. Our Citibank card is near the limit."

"That's okay. I got a new card in the mail before we left. It has a ten-thousand-dollar limit." John pulled the American Airlines schedule from his briefcase and flipped through it. "There's a plane today at two-oh-five this afternoon. I'll call and get us on it."

I went to the bathroom. When I returned, John seemed sad. "We can't get out until tomorrow, but I have the flight booked and paid for."

"Well, we can't afford another night here," I insisted.

We were drowning financially just to get out of town. What a helluva vacation this was turning out to be! We had two choices... return home and disturb the housesitter and cats, or go to Marie and Mark Passini's and visit with the dogs for the night. We chose the latter. We were lucky when Marie graciously agreed.

The next morning, when we were ready to leave for the airport, I couldn't find our car keys. Four frantic adults searched the house. I didn't think I had put them in John's briefcase, but when I saw it lying on the kitchen breakfast bar, I figured it was worth a peek. Time was definitely not on our side. I clicked the latches, opened the case, and found, not the keys, but the same amber bottle of ether I had discovered in Indiana, still unmarked. I was furious.

"John, I told you not to bring a lethal substance on the airplane. You don't need this in Egypt. A good cortisone cream will help you more."

"But the doc said..."

"I don't care what the doctor said. You don't need it."

"I won't be able to get more in Egypt."

I glared at him. "You don't need it," I said through clenched teeth.

I removed the amber bottle and set it on the kitchen counter. "Marie, if you don't mind, I'll leave this here and pick it up when I come to get the dogs."

"No problem," she said.

We continued looking for the keys. I decided to check my purse once more, and to my chagrin I found them nestled in the bottom. John and I pulled away from the curb, our six bags of luggage secure in the trunk. Marie and Mark stood in the driveway, the golden retrievers at their side, and waved. When they went back into the house, Marie decided to move the bottle of ether from the counter to the guest bathroom. She couldn't find it. The bottle had disappeared. In the final flurry to find the car keys, John had secretly slipped the bottle back into his briefcase.

TWENTY

The Attack

Two days later I walked into the coffee shop of the Key Bridge Marriott in Arlington, Virginia, and joined John at his table. He had already ordered. The waitress gave me a menu, and I quickly chose the waffles and sausage. She left, and I glared at John. "If we don't meet with the admiral this morning," I said, "I'm getting on the next plane home. I don't care what time it leaves. I don't care what you do. I've had it."

"We'll meet with him. I promise. He said to be at his office promptly at nine, so we can't dawdle."

"Meet with him, huh? Like yesterday, on Valentine's Day?"

"Look, it wasn't..."

"Don't bother. I'm sick of the excuses."

We had chased around from Fort Meade to the Goddard Space Center to the Annapolis officers' club, in the rain, and never caught up with Admiral Lee. The day was chaotic, confusion reigned, and I had tired of the harried itinerary. With each failed meeting John had apologized profusely. It was his fault. None of it appeased me, and we ended back in the bar at the top of the Marriott, where I cried my heart out.

"I'm frustrated, John," I said in a low voice, "not only over the events of the past week, but also from the disorientation of the past two days. I'm in total anguish."

The waitress approached and I stopped talking. She dropped off John's ham and eggs, then came back and filled our coffee cups, regular for John, decaf for me. My heart didn't need any extra stimulation this morning.

"Did you hear the TV news this morning?" John asked, stuffing a bite of yolk-soaked ham in his mouth. "The Gulf War may have ended and that might affect my assignment. Maybe that's why the admiral ignored me...the project is canceled."

"You said your mission had nothing to do with the Gulf War. Are you backpedaling?"

"Trying to figure out what's happened, that's all. We'll see the admiral in an hour and be on our way to Egypt this afternoon." He took a big swig of his coffee and wiped his mouth with his napkin.

"At this point I don't give a damn. I'm tired of running all over with six suitcases. I've used up a week of vacation for what? A wild-goose chase across the country! What the hell is going on?"

I took a sip of my coffee, stared out the window, and listened to the rhythm of the raindrops hitting the solarium glass. When the waitress delivered my breakfast, I came out of my trance and cut into my waffle. I needed something to squelch my uneasiness. John looked at his wristwatch. "I'm glad you talked me into wearing my old Timex," he said. "It would have been foolish to take my Rolex."

"Compliments aren't going to appease me. Only meeting the admiral and leaving for Cairo will do that."

John finished his breakfast, stood up, and said he would get the parking ticket validated at the front desk and meet me back at the room. I nodded. "Remember, John, if we don't meet with Admiral

Lee, I'm going home. I'm not wasting any more vacation on this nonsense."

Five minutes later I pushed my plate away, paid the bill, and negotiated the labyrinth of hallways and sets of double doors to get to our room. I remembered what the night clerk had said when we checked in...he had arranged a quiet room for us on the ground floor back near the parking garage. Our room was definitely out of the way, all right. When the garage appeared, I turned to the left, pushed on one of two solid doors, and entered a small foyer with access to four rooms. I crossed over to our door and saw it was ajar. I pushed it open and stepped inside.

My nose wrinkled and I coughed. The pungent fumes of ether assailed me. I followed the smell to the bathroom, where John stood near the toilet with a befuddled look on his face. I released the door. It shut, but didn't latch. "What the hell are you doing?" I shouted.

"I'm putting the ether on my abrasion, like the doc said."

"Come out of there or you're going to get sick."

Even as acrid fumes hung in the air, my mind ignored the fact that we had left the bottle of ether on Marie's counter in California. I was angry and confused and focused on the meeting with the admiral.

I continued on into the bedroom, grabbed my gray raincoat from the bed, and was on the last button when John dragged himself into the room. "What now?" I said grimly. "You're not going to feel good so we can't go the meeting?"

John bent and moaned, then shuffled closer to me. "Help me," he pleaded. I shrugged, stepped over to the blaring television, and turned it off. "Help you? Like hell!" Angry words spewed out of my mouth. "The last time I helped you I went down twelve stairs. I'm not going to let you make me fall again. You're acting sick just as you did when we were supposed to go to your seminar. Is this going to be today's excuse for not meeting the admiral?"

"Help me."

"This falls right in line with all the lame excuses this week and your secretive behavior, whispering into phones. I've had it, John. If we don't meet with the admiral, I'm flying home today no matter what."

John turned and limped around the divider to the dressing area and sink. I followed. He was now back in the bathroom and standing once more by the toilet. I stormed in after him.

"If you don't come out of here right now, you'll pass out on the tile floor."

"Help me."

"Go ahead, you son of a bitch. Fall. I'm not going to stop you, and I'm not going to call for help." I turned to leave. Fingers dug into my left shoulder as John spun me around. "Help me," John croaked.

His right arm flung around my shoulders and pushed me into his chest. My eyes widened. An ether-soaked washrag propelled toward my nose and mouth. I was scared. Adrenaline surged through my body, and my survival instinct kicked into full gear as I jerked my head back and forth. My thoughts raced. *Make a moving target. Ether can kill. Think fast. Don't open mouth. Don't let rag stay on face. Don't breathe or you won't leave this room alive.*

I wiggled and twisted, struggling to get out of his grip, but I couldn't. *Think, Barbara, think. Handicap bar on bathtub wall. Grab it!* I held on to the bar with both hands and created enough leverage to partially extricate myself from his bear hug. My left shoe came off. Fingers tightened around my left wrist. I thrashed about as the rag neared my face once more.

Must get out. Get to door. Desperate, I grabbed at the doorjamb with my free hand and pulled myself into the dressing area, right along with John. *Keep mouth shut. Move head back and forth, up and down. Don't stop. Oh my God, I'm going to die in a hotel room in Virginia.* My right ankle twisted, and that shoe came off. My free hand poked at his eyes but couldn't quite make contact.

It was a silent attack. I didn't scream. I didn't dare open my mouth and inhale the fumes; the ether was too powerful. John didn't say anything, either. He just kept wrestling with me and beating my face as he tried to cover my mouth and nose.

Suddenly, John snorted and his eyes widened. The washrag dropped. He grabbed the open ether bottle on the sink counter and doused my face with the liquid ether. I struggled harder. I had to survive! *Move head faster and faster. Twist around. Move up. Move down. Keep face out of liquid.* One earring fell to the floor and crunched under John's foot. A disconnected thought flashed through my mind...*this isn't real, it's like the movies.*

The battle continued. I inched closer and closer to the partially open door, visualizing the headline MURDER AT THE MARRIOTT. I kicked survival up another notch. I was getting closer. Another burst of energy. *Just a little more. Stretch.* I had the doorknob. *Pull. Pull.* It opened and I ran into the small foyer, but not before John had my arm once again. "Help! Help!" I screamed, but there was no one to hear me. The solid double doors were closed. John yanked me back into the room and kicked the door shut.

"Bitch!" he uttered.

Bastard, I thought, as I tried to kick his crotch. He pushed me and I stumbled backward, falling on my back in the dressing area. My energy was sapped. My adrenaline slowed. I was getting weaker and weaker, no match for the six-footer he was.

John knelt down and straddled my chest. He grabbed my left hand and pinned it down with his right knee. I tried to go for his balls, but my right arm was too short. I tried to knee them from behind, but only hit his soft butt. His left hand grabbed my flailing right arm and pinned it to the ground.

I had nowhere to go. No more leverage or energy with which to struggle. John groped around behind him. He retrieved the amber bottle, lifted it above my face, and poured the remaining ether. At least I could still move my head. I shook it, wildly. My remaining earring flew across the rug. John had trouble hitting his darting target, but I could feel the cool liquid make contact more than once. I told myself not to breathe.

"Bitch! Hold still," he seethed.

Then he stopped. He was panting. I looked into the mouth of the inverted bottle held above my face. He shook it several times, trying to release the last drop. John threw it to one side, scooted up, and sat on my chest, with all his weight on my hands, which were still pinned on either side of my head. He started wheezing, and his face flushed to an abnormal color.

He glared at me with wild devil eyes, vacant eyes, scary eyes, like nothing I had ever seen in my life. His eyes blazed like a wild beast, set to kill his prey. And I was that prey.

I stared back at him and subconsciously reached into the depths of my being for the right approach to let me survive. Without skipping a beat or consciously recognizing it, I slipped into my caretaking mode, which I had practiced for almost ten years. Smooth it over. Try to understand. Get him to change. I smiled weakly and kept constant eye contact with him. Then, from my heart—from my inner self—I uttered the words that saved my life.

"John, if there's a problem we can talk about it."

He cocked his head to one side. His muscles relaxed on my hands and chest, but he didn't move. I softly continued. "I think we both need a rest, don't you? Why don't you help me up?"

I firmly believe that if I had reacted any other way I would have died that day, in that hotel room. If I had not acquiesced, and instead had continued to struggle in my weakened condition, I know it would have triggered John into finishing the job in the heat of the moment. My words broke the momentum of his murderous attack.

For a moment, he did nothing. Then he loosened his grip, and his eyes lost the beastly stare. He didn't speak, just sighed and struggled to get off me and stand up. Once steady on his feet, he reached down and helped me off the floor. I leaned against the divider, frozen, as my mind reeled with what had just transpired, and I remained speechless while John picked up my earrings, straightened my shoes, and retrieved my gloves and the car keys that had been knocked off the counter during the attack. He stood between me and the door. Even if I had wanted to run screaming for help, I could not have escaped.

"Let's lie down," he said.

He grabbed my right hand and led me to the disheveled bed where we had spent the night, cuddled together. I looked at the pillows. Alarms sounded. Would they be his next attempt at snuffing me out? An eerie calm pervaded the room.

"I don't think I can lie down right now, John. I might get sick. I feel nauseated." That sounded logical, and it was the truth. "But I'll sit next to you while you rest."

John bought it, and why wouldn't he? I had accepted so many of his bad behaviors before. I followed his orders and sat down obediently on the edge of the bed, shoeless and in my torn raincoat. It still didn't even occur to me to try to escape. Something was broken and I needed to understand what, so I could fix it. John crawled to the middle of the bed and stretched out, then reached over and grabbed my right wrist. His grip was tight, and he didn't let go as he stared at the ceiling.

"Why did you do this, John?" I cooed, with care and kindness, with bewilderment and wonder.

"Right before we left, the doc called and said I had terminal cancer."

"But why did you try to kill me?"

"I didn't want to kill you. I just wanted to put you to sleep so I could jump off the Key Bridge and kill myself."

"We have good medical coverage," I said. "We can get you the best doctors."

"I don't want to live." John's eyes welled up with tears, and he coughed hoarsely. "I'm as crazy as your brother and should be locked up in an institution."

"We can get you mental help, too, if that's what you need."

A tear ran down his cheek. "You said this trip was one of the biggest disappointments in your life."

I paused. "No, John. Today was the biggest."

We both fell silent, lost in our own thoughts. I was completely thrown off balance, and confused. I didn't know if the cancer story was valid or if he was crazy. What if he tried to murder me again? My head throbbed. My mouth was dry. I asked if I could get a glass of water.

John released my wrist and rolled over to get off the bed. My pace was controlled, slow and easy. John followed directly behind me. I robotically passed the door and made no move to open it. At the moment it didn't seem to offer me an escape. I moved to the sink.

The ether aroma lingered in the air, and for a moment I thought I might throw up, but I didn't. I refused to lose control. I reached for a clean glass and shuddered. The empty amber bottle sat innocuously at the back of the counter, as did my wrecked earrings. Full glass in hand, I quickly glided back into the bedroom, passing my shoes that had been neatly arranged in the closet, and made my way to the desk chair. I took a sip of water, then another.

John followed but stopped at the end of the bed. His breathing was now less labored, and the redness in his face had receded. Perhaps he, too, still felt in control, so much so that he now removed his trousers, white dress shirt, and tie before he dragged himself back to the middle of the bed.

"Come sit beside me. I'm so tired."

I returned to my spot beside him and perched on the edge. Thankfully, this time he did not grab my bruised wrist. "Close your eyes," I whispered. "When you wake up, we can go to Bethesda Naval Hospital and get you checked out."

"You always take such good care of me," he said.

I gently laid his right arm in my left hand and lightly stroked it. His eyelids closed, his breathing deepened, and he appeared to be sleeping. Now I had to make the most important decision of my life.

I was in a dilemma. Beset with bold new facts and fears, I replayed the events of the morning and of the last several days. Is someone in the project out to get John? Is there actually a project, or an admiral? Does he have cancer? Did he go berserk because of the cancer news? Does he need mental help? Do I stay with him and take him to the hospital when he wakes up? Or do I try to escape and call the police?

Suddenly I understood how battered women feel, although I still didn't realize I was one of them. My beloved, my most trusted person, had just tried to kill me. Murder? Did he really mean to do it? He seemed so contrite. Was it my fault? Did I push him to the brink? What could I have done differently? My mind swirled with questions. My skin itched. My throat burned. I continued gently rubbing my fingers up and down John's arm.

Deep-sleep snores emanated from the bed. John was out, or so I thought. *If I'm going to do anything, this is my chance.* I reached into my inner self and found the strength I consciously lacked. The voice inside said, *RUN. If you don't, you won't leave this room alive. RUN for your life. Do it now. RUN! RUN! RUN!* For once I listened and decided to escape, but first I had to execute a safe plan.

I leisurely stopped rubbing John's arm. He didn't move. I softly laid his arm on the bed, slipped my left hand free, and sat very still with my hands folded in my lap. I hardly breathed. John snorted, stirred slightly, and resumed his snoring. Cautiously, in slow motion, I stood up, acting like I was going to take off my coat. John didn't move. I tiptoed to the end of the bed and stopped, still pretending I was unbuttoning my coat. His eyelids remained closed, and his chest heaved with deep breaths.

My heart pounded. After a few seconds that seemed more like two hours, I slipped past the divider, grabbed the door handle, and slowly, quietly, carefully turned it. The latch clicked. I froze and listened. John continued to snore. I pulled the door open just enough for me to squeeze through and then braced it as I let it come to rest, without slamming it. *Time is of the essence,* I thought. *Go! Go! Go!*

I pushed open the solid doors and bolted through, turned right, and ran in my torn stockings through the two sets of double glass doors, down the long hall past the meeting rooms. Crazy thoughts sped through my mind. What would I say? Murder? No, John had just gone berserk. He needed help. I needed help. We needed to get to a hospital. Denial obliterated reality.

I turned left and sprinted past the elevators, then right, past the house phones. People stopped and stared as I wove around them—a shoeless woman in a torn coat with disheveled hair, reeking of ether. I didn't care. At the main desk I caught my breath and blurted out the truth. "Call the police! My husband just tried to murder me with ether."

A manicured manager appeared, and she led me immediately into her office. "We called the police. They're on their way. Our security police are going to your room now. Is there anything you need?"

"Coffee, please."

I was alone, safe from John in a stranger's office, but not safe from my own thoughts. Denial slammed me. I had no weapons to vanquish it. I was weak, physically and mentally. I floated in a vacuum. I could see what was happening but unable to make sense of it.

Why did I ask for the police? I'm afraid of the police. What am I going to tell my family and friends when this gets out? No, I can't have the police. Why did I say murder? *John needs mental and medical help, and then everything will be okay. Then we can go to the admiral and John can join the project.* I had at last opened my secret bag of fears and the demons flew out, swirling around me, devouring me.

The door opened. A black female police officer approached me. "I need to take your statement, ma'am."

I answered her questions as best I could. When she asked where the ether bottle was, I told her it was on the sink counter the last time I had seen it. She continued, and all the while I implored her to ignore the police call. I didn't need her. She could leave. I just needed to get John to Bethesda. She shook her head, as if she understood, then smiled and left the room. I was alone again, and my apprehension increased tenfold.

What I didn't realize at the time was that my denial was a textbook reaction to domestic violence. I emerged from the attack confused and unable to face the truth that would set me free, I minimized the abuse, made excuses for John's behavior, and reverted to my caretaking role. His needs once more became the focus of my attention, and right now I believed he had medical and psychological needs. Ironically I wasn't too far off on the latter.

Five minutes later a slim, red-haired police officer entered the room. Her name tag read CATHERINE COBB.

"Where's John? Is he okay?"

"We caught him getting into a rental car with his briefcase. He told us he had a plane to catch. When hotel security woke him up earlier, he got dressed and nonchalantly checked out of the hotel. So far he's cooperated and has returned peacefully to the room. Can you tell me what happened, Mrs. Perry?"

I ranted on about what had happened. Cobb took notes. I begged that we be allowed to go to Bethesda and drop the police report.

"Can't do that, ma'am. Holly and I have both interrogated John, separately, and we feel there is something strange going on. We can't pinpoint it. We're going to take you and your husband to the Drewry Center to straighten this out."

"Drewry Center?"

"The county mental facility. The paddy wagon's on its way." My mouth fell open. Now I was being taken in like a common criminal.

"Don't worry," Cobb said. "The paddy wagon's for your husband. You'll go in our police car. Is there anything you want to take with you? A purse or something?"

"Yes, my purse, and my shoes, and…my camera. I don't want it to get stolen."

* * *

I stood at the door of the Drewry Center, clutching my purse in one hand and my camera bag in the other as raindrops pelted my unprotected face. *What now?* I thought, as Officer Cobb opened the door.

"Let's go inside, Mrs. Perry. We're going to get wet if we stay out here."

I didn't want to go inside. I wanted to take John to Bethesda Naval Hospital. Officer Cobb gently took my arm and led me into the foyer. "I have Mrs. Perry with me," she told the receptionist sitting behind a protective glass window.

"Up the stairs. Turn right and follow the hall all the way to the end for Ms. Lovato's office. I'll let her know you're on your way."

"Where's John?" I asked.

"In an upstairs room," Cobb responded.

"When can I take him to Bethesda?"

"I don't know. Come this way, Mrs. Perry. Ms. Lovato is waiting for you."

She led me up the stairs. We started down the hall; I glanced left and right, into each open room, hoping to see John. The hall branched to the right. I continued to look through open doorways. In the third room on the left, I saw him. He sat with his back to the doorway, his hands cuffed behind him. My breathing quickened. My eyes teared. My body tensed and stood riveted in place. The officer nudged me on.

At the end of the hall we stopped in front of an open door with LANA LUCAS LOVATO engraved on a brass plaque. A middle-aged woman with short brunette hair and Ben Franklin glasses sat inside at a green metal desk, browsing through a thick book. Officer Cobb knocked.

"Mrs. Perry is here," she said.

"Please, come in and have a seat," Lana said to me, waving her hand at the straight-backed chair in front of the desk.

I slumped into it and set my purse and camera bag on the floor, next to my feet. The officer patted me on the shoulder, smiled, and closed the door behind her as she left the room. Lana extended her hand and introduced herself.

"I'm a mental health emergency therapist, working with the Prevention and Intervention Unit."

"I don't need a mental therapist. I need to get my husband to Bethesda Naval Hospital," I said in a monotone.

Lana said she understood that was foremost on my mind, but there were several professionals who had to make an assessment of what happened in the hotel room, and it would take some time.

"My husband freaked out. That's all. He's been under a lot of stress lately."

Lana got up and poured us both a cup of coffee. When she sat down, the interview started. What happened in the room? What was the marriage like? Had my husband ever been physically abusive before? What was my background? I was bombarded with questions that invaded my privacy, and from a complete stranger. I was relieved when the telephone rang and Lana took the call.

"That was the poison control center," she said, hanging up. "They've advised that we wash your face to remove any residue of the ether. They also said any ether you inhaled would be gone. It dissipates from the blood within half an hour."

She led me to a small bathroom across the hall and switched on the light. "I'll wait for you in my office," she said as she closed the door.

I approached the sink and gasped as I looked into the mirror hanging above it. It was the first time I had seen myself since the attack. I stared at my reflection: sad brown eyes stared back. My hand gently touched my battered face. Was this person with scrapes, bruises, and welts all over her face really me? Tears escaped as I turned on the faucet. The water cooled the sting in my cheeks but could not douse the fire in my mind. I reached for the soft toilet tissue; the rough hand towels would have been too abrasive on my savaged skin.

Back in Lana's office I faced more insulting questions, many similar to what I had already answered for the officers. *How many times do I have to tell my story?* I thought. Lana carefully recorded my comments on a yellow piece of paper attached to a manila folder. Half an hour later she closed it.

"That's all for now. I'm going to interview your husband. Make yourself comfortable and don't wander away from the room, except to use the toilet."

"When can I take John to Bethesda?"

"I'll let you know if I find anything out."

She closed the door. I felt abandoned, afraid, and helpless. I wanted to get John to Bethesda Naval Hospital, but how could I when I was stuck in this office? I was still in denial.

For the next several hours, I existed in solitude, interrupted only by the occasional visit from Lana. When I said I was hungry, she gave me an apple. I would have preferred a sandwich, but they didn't have a cafeteria. She kept fresh coffee in the pot, and I drained it. Each time I asked about John, her answer was always the same: the matter was in the hands of the police.

I was exhausted from the attack, the questions, the monotony. Like a caged animal, I alternated between pacing and sitting. There were no bars on the window, but I was just as trapped. I settled into my chair, placed my elbows on my lap, lowered my head into my hands, and closed my eyes. I felt I was suffocating. When I heard the office door open and someone enter, I did not look up.

"Mrs. Perry, I have someone I want you to meet," Lana said. "This is Homicide Detective Greg Smith."

I opened my eyes and stared at a pair of brown wingtip shoes. My head followed to the tan slacks, tweed sport coat, a friendly smile, intense blue eyes, and sandy blond hair. My first thought, *He's gorgeous,* seemed wildly inappropriate. My second thought was, *Why did I have the first thought?* What I didn't recognize at the time was that God had sent me an angel.

"Call me Greg," he said, extending his hand. Then the detective's title shook me back to reality.

"Homicide detective?" I said. "Why homicide? My husband didn't try to kill me."

My denial ratcheted up several notches. My conscious self refused to believe it as my subconscious self struggled over and over to make me see the light.

"John has been interviewed by a team of specialists," Detective Smith said. "They all agreed there was something more than a domestic dispute taking place, so they called me. After talking with him, I support their conclusion."

"John didn't try to murder me. He's under heavy medication. I need to get him to the hospital."

"I've handled a lot of murder cases, Mrs. Perry."

"He *didn't* try to murder me! When are you people going to understand that?"

They just wouldn't listen. I needed to get John to the hospital, to get him medical attention, and everything would be okay. John would get the help he needed and we'd go home. I felt trapped in the clinic with therapists and police who wouldn't let me take care of John. I was as much a prisoner as he was.

"I've answered a lot of homicide calls," Smith continued. "Each time I see a victim, I ask myself what I could have done to help them. That's why I think I can help now."

"But I'm not dead!"

"I know, but I believe you could have been. John brutally attacked you."

"John never hit me before. He's under medication. He overdosed. He needs to get to the hospital."

"This is serious. I believe if we let you go with him tonight, we'll find your body in the morning."

"No! John loves me. He rubs my feet. He cooks for me. He buys me nice things."

"Mrs. Perry, please listen. I also believe if we let you go back to California with John after a three-day psychiatric hold, someone is going to find your dead body out there."

Dear God, I prayed, *please help me. Why is he saying these horrible things? Help me get out of here so I can get John to a hospital.* But the detective did not let up and kept insisting that, based on John's actions, he wanted to arrest him for attempted murder. I just about lost my mind.

"Attempted murder?" I whispered. "He has no reason to kill me."

Detective Smith explained that people kill for a lot of reasons. He asked more questions, looking for a plausible one in my case. We ruled out jealousy right away. When he asked about problems, I searched my soul and had to admit that we had been under financial strains, which was why the job offer for Egypt had been so critical.

"Would John benefit from your death?" Smith asked.

I hesitated, searching my life for answers, and thought especially hard about the past year. Yes, there was some life insurance from my work. John was the executor of my will and primary beneficiary. We had just redone the wills earlier in the month, but I didn't think there was enough money there for him to want to kill me.

"Has John ever hurt you, say, in the last year?"

"What do you mean?"

"Did you have any accidents or strange happenings?"

I replayed events from the previous year in my mind. It seemed so long ago. After the attack this morning, a lot of things seemed like a long time ago. Slowly, I found some of the crazymaking puzzle pieces that might shed light on the situation, if I would only believe their message. I explained the car accident in Hot Springs, the sleeping pills, and the telephone pole. Recalling the accident confused me. Could it have been a murder attempt? Why would he have wanted to murder me then? No, it was just an unfortunate accident, nothing more.

Detective Smith prompted me again. He was relentless. I tried to think of something else out of the ordinary.

"Well, there was this incident with the gun," I said, and went on to explain the Florida trip, John's heart attack, and the foil-wrapped gun in his briefcase. It didn't seem like a murder attempt, just carelessness on John's part—although it was strange that the banker didn't know John, and the attorney gave me an ominous warning.

"Was there anything else where you were hurt?" Smith asked.

The fall down the stairs came to mind almost immediately. I explained the circumstances, and that I had yet to prove that John was teaching at the University of California. Enlightening as some of these events could have been, my focus was still on getting John to Bethesda Naval Hospital.

"I'm sorry," Smith said. "I don't think that's possible at this time, but you can help John right now. I agree with you that he is sick."

Detective Smith said John could get psychiatric assistance in prison; a staff psychologist would evaluate him before trial, and the evaluation would be used to determine whether John should serve his time in the state's criminal mental facility. I perked up. All I had ever wanted to do was get John medical attention. This might work.

"How can I help?"

"Let me arrest John for attempted murder."

"What will I have to do after that?"

"Help us in our investigation. I suspect that a lot of evidence is back in California. And you'll have to testify against him at the trial."

I mulled it over. On the one hand, Detective Smith had brought up some interesting theories about the past year. I had been plagued with suspicions and troubled by missing family and mysterious loans. Maybe this was the way to help me shed light on them and help John at the same time. On the other hand, an arrest...and a trial? I wrestled with reality and faced the new chapter of my life that was about to unfold. The prospect frightened me. Reluctantly, I lowered my denial defense and agreed to let Homicide Detective Smith arrest John.

"Good decision," Smith said. "Now all we have to do is get some photographs of your face for evidence at the trial."

He went to the door and asked Officer Cobb to retrieve her Polaroid camera from the trunk of her patrol car. While we waited, I placed a bargaining chip on the table. "I'll let you arrest John on one condition," I said. "I want to see him before you take him away."

Detective Smith grimaced and shook his head. "It's not a good idea. You may change your mind if you see him this soon after the crime. Statistics prove that battered women are prone to recant and not follow through with prosecution of their perpetrator."

"I promise I won't change my mind. I don't break promises."

My inner resolve began to shine through as I started down a new path.

The door opened and Officer Cobb came in. "Brrrrr, it's cold out there," she said with a shiver. "I think it's going to snow tonight."

She handed the camera to Detective Smith, who tried to take several pictures of me, but the near-freezing temperature in the trunk of the patrol car had affected the film. The photos turned milky. All would have been lost, except for me. I pulled out my 35-mm Minolta and showed him how to use it. *Snap. Snap.* I removed the exposed film cartridge and handed it to Detective Smith. "The county will reimburse you," he said. I wasn't worried about that. It was simply another one of my life events. Providence intervened.

I gathered my belongings and followed Detective Smith to the room where John was being held. His hands were still cuffed behind his back and he had slumped over in the chair; his tousled toupee made him look unkempt, like a vagrant. *How did our relationship get to this?* I asked myself. I swallowed hard, took a deep breath, and walked around to where he could see me.

"Tell them I never touched you before," John pleaded.

"I did, but something serious has happened."

"I didn't mean to hurt you. I'll be okay now."

"I told you once that if you ever laid a hand on me, that was it. Remember?"

"I won't do it again. I promise."

"You need help, John. I want you to know I'm letting them arrest you because this is one way you can get it."

Detective Smith walked over and stood between us. He grabbed something from the desk next to John. "Time to go," he said, escorting me out to the hall. "I'll keep in touch with you." He handed me the folder with the airline tickets. "We found them in John's inside coat pocket. I think you'll need these to get home."

Lana was waiting, ready to take me back to the Marriott. She expressed concern for my being alone that evening. I told her I had called my friends the Baxters in McLean, and they were coming to take me to dinner.

"You will break down sometime. It's inevitable," she said as we pulled under the hotel portico. I grabbed the car door handle. "All the staff wants you to know how proud we are of you," she added.

"What do you mean?"

"You saved your life today. Most women would not have been able to extricate themselves like you did. You are truly an amazing and strong woman."

I didn't feel very strong when I walked into the lobby of the hotel. I felt disoriented. How could I face the room where I almost died? Fortunately, I didn't have to. "We took the liberty of moving your bags while you were away," the manager said. "We've put you in another wing, on the fifth floor."

Safely inside my room, I leaned against the door, exhausted and alone in deafening silence. But I knew I could not linger. My friends were due any moment. I dragged myself into the bathroom, splashed water on my face, and ran my fingers through my hair. *This will have to do*, I thought. *My friends will have to take me as I am.* The phone rang. *Dear God, please let me make it through this evening without disintegrating.*

At dinner I pushed my food around on my plate and ate very little. My friends said they understood. Thankfully they didn't grill me on the day's events as I continually dabbed the corners of my eyes and held on to some modicum of composure.

Later, when I returned to my hotel room, it was a different story. My purse and coat slipped to the floor. My feet shuffled to the bed and I lay down, fully clothed. But I couldn't relax. Through blurry eyes I stared at the six pieces of luggage lined up against the wall. My dreams of a happy marriage were packed in that luggage, as well as my hopes for being debt free. Now they both were gone, destroyed by my husband's ultimate betrayal.

My head pounded. My body ached. I longed for a hot bath to refresh my body and cleanse my soul. But in the bathroom, no matter which way I pulled or pushed the faucet, the water remained cold. I crumbled to the tile floor and broke into hysterical sobs, crying out loud to the empty room, "Why me?" There was no answer.

I stumbled to the bed and the telephone on the nightstand. While I waited for hotel maintenance to respond to my call, I replayed the unthinkable events of the day, my unpredictable emotional state, and my unhealthy plan to stay in town for three more days. Survival mode kicked in. I decided that for my sanity I had to go home as soon as possible, back to my familiar surroundings, to my family and to my dogs. The knock on the door startled me out of my reverie.

Maintenance politely explained how to use the faucet and left. But the hot bath would have to wait. A more urgent need pressed me. I retrieved the airline tickets from my purse and worked through choked sobs with a considerate agent who arranged a seat for me to fly home the next afternoon. Later, the hot bath failed to revive me, and sleep didn't bring much-needed rest. I had my first nightmare of John trying to murder me.

The next day I exited the elevator on the fifth floor of the Arlington County jail and went to a confined room about eight feet by eight feet, painted a hideous shade of green. Two women stood at a counter with forms and pencils on it, their backs toward me. The sign above the counter directed, TO VISIT A PRISONER....I shuddered. I had never been in a jail.

I moved toward the counter and gagged. One of the women smelled as if she had not bathed in weeks. The other woman's clothes were tattered and filthy; the two young children huddled at her feet wiped their hands across their runny noses.

I felt like turning back, but couldn't. I had to talk to John before I went home, to make sure he was okay and to bring him his medication, underwear, and $25 for his bank. He may have tried to murder me, but he was still my admiral and I couldn't totally abandon him. I worried about his health; he took so many pills. I worried that he wouldn't be able to survive the dynamics of jail. I wasn't sure *I* could, even for this short visit. The incessant din of the prisoners jawing and posturing behind the walls was deafening.

I pulled myself together. My plane was leaving in a couple of hours and I had to be on it. I realized that last night, when I broke down in my room and sobbed uncontrollably because the bathwater didn't get hot quickly enough. It was now or never.

I held my breath, grabbed one of the forms and a pencil, and went back to the wall nearest the elevator. A guard behind the barred window with the small pass-through processed my request and pushed a dated pass back at me. "Sixth floor," he said gruffly. "Present it to the guard."

The two women were still working on their original paperwork when I pushed the up button. The elevator doors opened on the sixth floor into an even smaller room painted with the same horrid green. Four orange plastic chairs, scarred by years of abuse, sat along one wall. At the far end, two women sat hunched into partitions similar to telephone areas. I presented my pass to the guard behind the glass and sat down. Soon it was my turn.

I settled into a beat-up chair and surveyed my surroundings. A small shelf lay underneath the thick glass on both sides, and gray phone receivers hung on the wall, just like in the movies. I wished this was a movie. Sadly, it was not.

I watched as John, wearing a navy blue jumpsuit, was led to the chair on the other side of the thick glass. He looked old and worn, downright pathetic without his toupee. He sat down, picked up his receiver, and started talking. I just sat there. I couldn't hear what he was saying. He motioned me to pick up my receiver. "You look tired," he said.

"I had a meltdown last night. Now I can't stop crying."

"Tell them I never beat you," John begged. "Tell them, and I can go home with you."

"I can't, John. You need help."

"I'll get help. I'll go to Kaiser as soon as we get home."

"No, you need help now."

"I won't get it here."

"The homicide detective said you would."

"Yeah, well, don't believe everything you're told," he snapped. Then he held his head downcast, with a shamed-puppy look. It was a posture I had seen many times before, and one that usually broke my heart. This time it didn't work.

"I've taken steps to prevent bail," I said. John raised his head and glared at me as I continued. "I canceled the credit cards and moved money into inaccessible accounts."

"What about a lawyer?" John whined.

I couldn't believe his nerve. He had just tried to murder me, and now he wanted me to get him a lawyer. I laughed. "We don't have the money, John. We're so far in debt I doubt I'll ever get out."

"What should I do?" he whimpered.

"Get a public defender."

John stood up, yelled "Bitch!" into his receiver, and slammed it back on the hook. He turned and motioned for the guard.

In the recent past I would have begged John to stay. I would have said we could work it out. I was a different person now. I made no sign to keep him from leaving. I had grown in the past day and was on the road to gaining my strength. John was losing control over me. I replaced my receiver on the wall, got up, and left.

* * *

That afternoon, as I sat in the airplane waiting for it to taxi down the runway, I was a sniffling, emotional mess. I was mourning the death of my dream, knowing that my life would never be the same again. Before I boarded, the concerned gate agent asked if I would be okay to travel. I convinced her I was, and that my friends, the Passinis, would be at the gate in San Francisco.

As the plane accelerated and the wheels left the ground, I looked below, scouting for familiar landmarks. There they were: the Smithsonian, the Washington Monument, the Reflecting Pool, the Lincoln Memorial. Brief thoughts of happy times forced a quick smile as the plane banked to the left over the Potomac River and headed west. When I saw the Key Bridge Marriott, tears flooded my face. It was my third major breakdown of the day.

I felt I was trapped in the middle of an impressionistic painting. All I could see were globs of different-colored paint dabbed here and there, surrounding me. None of it made any sense at all. A professional would be needed to help me step back until I could decipher the subject and understand the painting.

The Capitol area retreated below me, and I swore I would be a different person when I returned for the trial. The painting would be in focus. I had been raised to disregard mental health professionals, which would have meant sharing and exposing the family's private business to a stranger. As the plane headed over the Virginia countryside, I made the courageous decision to get mental help. Nothing in my life had offered me the emotional resources I would need to deal with and recover from such a brutal attack. I had to reclaim my sanity. I had to reinforce this decision that became the emotional turning point in my life.

PART THREE

Persistence

TWENTY-ONE

The Investigator

The plane landed in San Francisco. My fourth emotional meltdown of the day occurred when I fell into the Passinis' waiting arms. Their shocked faces reflected a woman spiritually broken and physically damaged with bruises, scrapes, broken fingernails, and chemical burns.

"I'm not the same person who left four days ago," I sobbed.

Unknown challenges lay ahead. The first was to get home safely. The Passinis insisted I spend the first night with them. The next morning, a Sunday, I headed home. First I stopped at my section manager's home. "Take as much time as you need," he said, "and mark it as personal time, not vacation." I appreciated his concern.

At my second stop I picked up my mother to stay with me for a couple of weeks. I needed someone with me to feel safe. John was incarcerated, but there were too many unknowns. Did he have an accomplice? If so, was it a woman or a man? Was I still in danger? When we walked into the guest room to get Mom settled, I blew a fuse. The Westinghouse billings covered the bed and dresser. "I told John I couldn't handle these."

"I can sleep in the twin bed downstairs," Mom offered.

"The file boxes are right here. It won't take that long to put them back where they belong. Give me a minute." I learned later that there was information I needed in those piles. I was too traumatized to look for it now.

Over breakfast the next morning I started a list, jotting down some chores for today, some for tomorrow. The locksmith rekeyed the house and I ticked off that chore. I double-checked my financial accounts and confirmed that my damage-control tactics in Virginia had been successful. John did not have access to funds for bail. I braced myself for the next task: the investigation of John's office.

Mom followed me into the paneled room at the top of the stairs. Stacks of papers covered the large wooden desk, the two chairs, the filing cabinets in the closet, the redwood bookshelves along the west wall, and most of the brown pile carpet. "How could he work in such a mess?" I groaned. It was anathema to my organized self and made me angry, especially because he was supposed to have been gone for six months. I knew I'd have to be carefully analytical to provide the homicide detective the evidence he'd need for motive. I embraced the challenge, sensing that this activity would also be crucial to my recovery.

"Where should I begin?" my mom said.

"Let me clear the chairs, so we can sit down and figure it out." I sat in the swivel high-back leather chair; Mom sat in the boxy office chair next to the desk. I spun around, surveying the chaos.

"I don't even know what we're looking for," I groaned, "but I do know we have to examine every single piece of paper."

I retrieved several new cardboard file boxes and folded them into shape. "We'll categorize the piles as we go through them," I said, "put them into labeled manila folders, and store them in these boxes."

It didn't take long for my mother to become bored. "I don't think I can be of any help," she said. She patted my hand, wished me luck, and went off to get us some coffee. I had made it through several more piles of innocuous notes when she returned with the full mugs.

"Got one box filled already," I said. "Now it's time for John's briefcase." I clicked it open. "Look!" I screeched. "It's the earrings I wore during the attack, and latex surgical gloves, just like the ones I saw in Indiana." I handed them to her and shuddered. "If the police hadn't stopped John at the rental car, there would have been no evidence to support the crime."

I searched further in the case and found a map of Indiana, notes about the Chicago Holiday Inn, and two rental car express cards for Chicago. When did he go to Chicago? I started a list, by dates and documents, then laid the items back inside. My lips trembled when I saw my tattered photograph, the one John had said he would never remove from his briefcase. I closed the briefcase, set it in the hall, and came back for a long sip of coffee.

"Your dad always said he felt there was something strange about John," Mom said.

"Why didn't he ever tell me?"

"He wanted you to be happy, and it seemed you were."

"I was, except for the financial part."

My stomach grumbled hungrily. I was shocked when I looked at the clock above the desk. I hadn't realized how much time we had spent going through the papers.

After lunch, Mom lay down to take a nap. Slowly, systematically, I made my way through the piles of paper on the top of the office desk, then progressed to the file drawers. In an innocuous, unlabeled folder I discovered a crazymaking puzzle piece . . . the contract for the second mortgage on my Antioch house, the one John took out while my father lay dying. Chills swept over me. My signature was forged. My name was not in John's distinctive scrawl. Someone else had signed it. Who? John must have had an accomplice. I made a note to visit the loan office the next day, and resolved to check my rearview mirror often.

Discovery propelled me forward. I shuffled through the rest of the desk file drawers but came up empty-handed. I attacked several piles from the bookshelves. The first one revealed nothing. The second pile provided another piece of the puzzle. I found the signature card John said he had taken to Kirsten when he picked up the funds, the card that required two signatures for advances on the last Concord second mortgage. He never turned it in.

I dug further into the pile. My heart sank when I saw, stapled together, the missing HFC loan statements I had never laid eyes on. John had been withdrawing against the equity loan for the past five months. I grabbed the calculator. His withdrawals totaled more than $17,000. Most of them were in the same increments as the deposits to our checking account for his supposed teaching salary. I retrieved the checkbook. I could not account for $5,000. I had stepped into financial quicksand, and no one was there to throw me a lifeline. I made a note to visit Kirsten and find out what had happened.

"Barbara, I'm up," Mom called from downstairs. Her voice startled me. "Julie is going to pick me up. We have some errands to run." My youngest sister, Julie, had moved back in with my mother. "Don't forget the new key. The doors will be locked."

I turned to one of the desk drawers and dug through layers of pads and papers. Near the bottom I found the unsigned department of psychology contract that John had shown me as proof of his employment, followed by a stack of University of California stationery. White-Out obscured the department name on the first sheet. Subsequent copies showed that the stationery was from the department of history. No wonder I had struck out when I called the university looking for proof of John's employment.

How could I have been so stupid, so naïve? I dug a little further and found an opened package of name tags with the UC Davis name and seal. The final proof of John's complicity about his teaching career lay at the bottom of the drawer; stapled together was a complete W-2 form, filled out in triplicate. John had given me a forged original. I made a note to call my CPA; the taxes would need to be redone.

I heard the key turn in the lock of the front door. I got up, turned the light off, and met Mom in the downstairs hall.

"I'm exhausted," I said. "Let's fix dinner and a cocktail. Have I got stuff to tell you! You're not going to believe what I found today."

Tuesday morning I tackled the telephone calls on my list. I arranged for counseling with Carolyn Pedrotti in Concord for Wednesday afternoon. I contacted Tom Landers to change my will. He could see me Wednesday morning. I called the phone numbers of Admiral Lee and Jack Berger. They were phantoms of John's imagination.

"Come on, Mom, let's take a ride," I said. "We have a couple of financial institutions to visit."

In Walnut Creek we marched into the mortgage company that had funded the Antioch second. "So you're the real Mrs. Perry," a man blurted out as he walked over to me, hand extended. He introduced himself as the loan officer. "We always felt there was something unusual about that loan." My body tensed at his words. I didn't shake his hand, and I couldn't contain my sarcasm.

"Great. That fits right in with how my life is running these days. Lots of things are out of the ordinary."

The loan officer told me John had arranged for the loan over the phone, but the head of lending insisted it be completed in person. John demanded that the loan officer come to the house, and when he did he met a woman named Barbara Perry. He described a woman who evidently looked something like me. I couldn't think who that could be. I jotted down *security* and underlined it several times.

"At the house John did all the talking," the loan officer said. "When I asked John to let you talk, he said he would speak for both of you. I asked for your driver's license and John produced an expired one. I accepted it, but I still had my doubts."

"Why did you process the loan, then?" I said, trying to remain calm when what I wanted to do was yell how stupid and unprofessional he had been.

"I talked it over with my boss. He said to get third-party identification. I met John and the woman at the Miwok Valley Bank, on Clayton Road, and the loan manager there identified you."

"The papers were notarized. How could that happen?"

"I did it, even though the photo on the driver's license was a stretch of the imagination."

"I want copies of all the documents," I demanded, "including your comments on the cover of the folder." I made a note to follow up with the bank, the police, and small claims court.

I dropped into the Walnut Creek police station. The desk sergeant called a detective to the front, and he told me that my loss of $15,000 was not enough to trigger a fraud investigation. Screwed again.

The visit to Kirsten at HFC in Concord held better promise. "John came in for another withdrawal in January," she said. "I told him it was the last one without your approval. I remembered how adamant you were when you wanted two signatures. He never turned in the new card we discussed right before the loan funded."

"Too bad you didn't follow through earlier. Now I'm left with another seventeen thousand dollars of debt." Another puzzle piece dropped into my hands. John had been cut off at the same time I told him I was investigating his teaching story.

The Clayton Road branch of Miwok Valley Bank was on the way home. The bank manager was skittish about his actions, and it was obvious John had conned him, too. My pity turned to disgust when he felt no remorse for his part in the fraud.

Back home I retrieved the mail and Mom made us some tea. We sat at the kitchen table; I sorted out the junk mail, saw the telephone bill, and opened it. Under long distance, there was a charge to Hot Springs.

"Mom, this is when John called me at Grandpa Jonas's." I gasped. "But the bill says it was placed from Chicago." I scribbled this on my expanding list of enigmas.

Later that evening as Mom watched television, I went into John's office and grabbed a pile of papers from the computer desk. Nothing new there. I filed them and snatched another pile. It contained an airline ticket stub in John's name for a flight to Chicago on February 2, and an Avis receipt for a Cadillac on the same day. On a piece of scratch paper were two phone numbers—one for our neighbor, a pharmacist, and one for a kennel in Walnut Creek. I picked up the phone. By the time I finished my calls, I came to a sickening conclusion. "Dear God! He planned to kill me in Indianapolis!"

"Don't take the name of the Lord in vain," Mom admonished. She had appeared at the door of the office on her way to bed.

"Can you believe it?" I told her. "As soon as I left for the airport to fly to Hot Springs, John took the dogs to the kennel, flew to Chicago, and spent two nights at the Holiday Inn. On Monday he drove to Indianapolis and the Holiday Inn North. He was waiting and watching as I checked in." I felt sick. He was the one who had requested the remote room in the back. I visualized the ether bottle and surgical gloves on the bathroom counter.

"Mom, he was going to smother me in my room, carry my body to my rental car, and have a car wreck, and it would have looked like I died in the wreck. The ether would have been out of my bloodstream by then." I fell silent. "He would have collected extra insurance because I died on a business trip."

"Why do you suppose he backed off?" Mom whispered.

"I guess my room location, and the fog."

"Where did he get the ether?"

A light went on. "From the vet, when he couldn't get it from our neighbor." I made a note to call our veterinarian in the morning.

Mom trotted off to bed, but I continued to unwind the shroud of deceit John had wrapped around me. I waded through more piles of papers and was rewarded. By midnight I figured out that John had altered his birth certificate to appear two years younger and used our Two Star stamp, the one we received when we incorporated the business years before, to make it look official. Most disturbing to me were the clues attached to the attempted murder in Virginia, the clues that revealed premeditation and plans to allow John to reap even more loot. He took out maximum insurance on the rental car at National Airport. He made sure the hotel room was secluded and close to the parking garage. The bastard was going to stage a car accident that would make it appear I died in it.

I stumbled off to bed but couldn't sleep. My mind raced as I continued to fit the pieces together. John's suspicious actions right before the trip came into focus. He failed to get the Antioch house willed to him, but he would inherit from my death. When I stubbornly refused the HFC life insurance, he continued with his plan to surreptitiously add to the loan. John wanted instructions on the computer and movie camera because I wasn't going to be around to use them. He left his Rolex watch at home and the Westinghouse papers on the bed so he could appear the grieving widower.

The ugly truth stared me in the face. John really had tried to murder me. I couldn't hide behind my denial any longer. I felt stupid. I had consistently ignored or denied every sign of fraud, deceit, and attempted murder. I was disgusted with myself and with him. What a devious mind he had. My denial disintegrated to dust, and I cried myself to sleep.

I rose early on Wednesday and called Homicide Detective Greg Smith to report what I had found. "Wish we could hire you." He laughed in his strong, deep voice. "You're good." His laughter dissolved into caution. "I have some bad news. John's bail is being reduced from twenty-five thousand dollars to ten thousand because he got booked into family court, and he only needs to post ten percent."

"What? He can get out with only a thousand dollars bail money now?"

"Because you are John's wife, the call went in as a domestic dispute, and that falls under family court."

"You mean if I had been a prostitute and he had done the same thing, he would have been booked directly into criminal court?"

"Yes."

"That says a lot about Virginia law, doesn't it? A wife is nothing but chattel. I'm a double victim."

"Sorry. Maybe what you've turned up will be enough to retain the higher bail. By the way, we still haven't been able to confirm or deny his rear admiral status."

"What about his fingerprints?"

"We haven't heard back from the FBI yet."

"It's been five days. I thought the police got faster results."

"Real life doesn't work like a TV show," he said compassionately.

I hung up. If I didn't have enough to worry about, now there was a chance John could get out of jail. I had taken care of stopping him from my end, but what about his accomplice? Could she be getting the money for him? I scribbled down *Confirm John is an admiral.*

The phone call was the beginning of a close working relationship between the detective and me, the investigator. Greg made me feel like someone cared that I was operating in uncharted waters. To divert me, he sent me cartoons with the words changed to fit my case, lending a bit of humor to a sad situation.

I called the local vet and confirmed that John had duped them out of the ether, not once, but twice, which gave him a lethal amount. John used our cat's ear problem for the ruse. For the first bottle, John convinced the local vet that it was recommended for the cat by the UC Davis Veterinary School. For the second one, he said he spilled the first bottle and needed a replacement.

My resolve kicked up a notch. It was errand time. My first stop was the law office of Tom Landers, where he handed me a bill for

$1,200. He apologized, and said the increase was based on the complexity of John's estate.

"What estate? I don't know if there is one. Does this include his meeting with you and Jason?"

"Jason? I don't recall having a meeting with John and anyone else."

"Do you mind if I call Jason?" Tom pushed the telephone my way. Jason was friendly, but didn't know what I was talking about. "I bought my house over twelve years ago," Jason said, "but not from John. In fact, I've only known him for about eleven years."

"What? I thought he was your dad's cousin."

"No, I met John first and introduced him to my parents. They hit it off and became friends." I thanked Jason and hung up the phone.

"John lied to me," I said grimly. "Now I know why there was never any payment. John didn't own the house."

My world tumbled in on me for the umpteenth time that week. With each discovery the ice beneath my feet got thinner and thinner. Now it had just given way. I made a decision. I would have to get a divorce for my sanity's sake, no matter what anyone thought of me. It was the very thing I had dreaded for the last nine years. "I want to start divorce proceedings immediately," I said.

Tom didn't practice family law, but he called someone who did. "They've had a cancellation. You can go right over."

My mother and I walked into Ross Grissom's office. A short, well-dressed man with a warm smile stood and walked over to greet us. We settled in, and the multiple volumes of California Family Code behind Ross faced me while I explained my situation.

"Strangest case I've ever heard of," Ross said, shaking his head. I could feel my internal pressure rise. Why couldn't this be a simple divorce, like my first?

"I can represent you," Ross continued. "What I need to start is a twenty-five-hundred-dollar retainer fee."

I gulped. My hands twisted around the wet tissue in my lap. Somehow, it always came back to money, no matter which way

I turned. "I don't have that much right now. Is there some other way?"

He needed the retainer to bill against. I'd hit a brick wall and didn't know where to turn. "I'll loan you the money," my mother said. "You can sign a promissory note later."

Mom wrote a check, and Ross hit me with the next bit of distasteful news. "We have to get John a divorce attorney in Contra Costa County."

"I won't have any part of it," I announced. "He's on his own. Besides, he's in jail in Virginia and has a public defender named Kent Whistler."

Ross explained that the Virginia lawyer practiced criminal law and probably hadn't passed the California bar, but he could be used to pass information along to John. Grudgingly, I retrieved my telephone book from my purse and gave him Kent Whistler's phone number. Too bad Greg Smith had given me the number, I thought. Ross called and arranged to fax a list of attorneys who sat on the family law board of Contra Costa County. I silently wondered if I was going to have to pay for the phone call.

More menacing, and unknown to me at the time, was that this phone call was the first step in a battle that would last for years as I struggled to be legally free of John Perry. Ross recommended stalling the divorce settlement until the Concord house sold. "It will make it easier to divide," he said.

"But I want to file for a divorce *now*. And I want a restraining order. He might make bail."

Perhaps Ross didn't understand the seriousness of my case. My panic accelerated when he said I had to keep paying the car and medical insurance on John. "What! He's in jail. He can't use them."

"It's the law. We're a community property state. In fact, John will get half your retirement fund and, based on what you've told me, he's entitled to alimony."

"Excuse me. He just tried to murder me and now I'm going to have to *pay* him?"

"Well, he's in jail and not working. It's the way the formula works. It's the law."

My hands worked the wet tissue into shreds. It was unbelievable. All I wanted to do was file and get a simple divorce, but it seemed nothing having to do with John was ever going to be simple. I felt my throat constrict and tears welling in my eyes once more.

"It's not fair," I whispered. "I'm a victim once more, this time of the divorce law of California."

Later that afternoon I sat alone in the reception area of the family therapist's office feeling like a fish out of water. The walls closed in on me. I knew I needed help. Carolyn emerged, a tall, professionally dressed woman with a brightly colored scarf draped around the shoulders of her navy blue dress. She introduced herself and called me into her office. "Please, have a seat."

"Do you want me to lie on the couch?"

"Only if you want to," she said, smiling. "Most people choose to sit in the wingback chair opposite me."

"I'd prefer that," I said, settling in right next to the box of tissues on the end table.

Carolyn gently probed into my family background and my relationship with John. It's a good thing the tissues were handy. I went through almost the whole box. Toward the end of the hour she looked at me intently.

"You have a decision to make," she said. "We can work on the grief you're feeling over the death of John, as the person you thought you knew, or we can work on why you allowed yourself to stay in a situation that almost cost you your life."

I chose the latter. I didn't want to make the same mistake ever again.

"Good choice," Carolyn said. "It sounds like John is a socio-psychopath. He has no conscience. Whatever he wants, he feels he has the right to take. He manipulated your feminine traits of caretaking and compassion, he assessed your loneliness at the time he met you, and his lies and deceit attacked your limits and boundaries. He snared you, and you became his victim."

She explained that my self-esteem had been shattered, and that there were many tools to piece it back together. She asked if I had ever heard the term *codependent*. I shook my head no. She scribbled something down on the back of one of her business cards and handed it to me, explaining that it was the one tool she felt would help me best.

"Here, I want you to read Melody Beattie's book *Codependent No More* before our next session. You can find it in any bookstore. Be proud of yourself; your positive action saved your life and you did not allow yourself to be frozen by your fear. You fought back intelligently and extricated yourself from a very dangerous situation."

My heart pounded as I left. I had survived and was on the road to recovery, although I didn't know if it would be a bumpy trail or a smooth path. Eventually I would find it was both.

In the bookstore, I stood and flipped to a page somewhere in the middle and read:

> We may even convince ourselves that we can't live without someone and will wither and die if that person is not in our lives. If that person is...deeply troubled, we may tolerate abuse and insanity to keep him...in our lives to protect our source of emotional security.

That was me! Melody Beattie, the author, had just described my actions, feelings, and emotions. I was frightened and excited at the same time as I clutched the book tightly and walked to the checkout stand.

Thursday morning I woke and counted six days after terror had invaded my life and turned me in a new direction. It seemed like an eternity.

After breakfast I went into John's office. Yesterday's appointments had slowed my progress. I still had a lot of papers to review, categorize, and file. The detective's comments about proving John's military rank were foremost in my mind.

What can you do to confirm an admiral? Of course, why hadn't I thought of it sooner? I'd get in touch with the rear admiral who was a consultant for John's company, the one who had formerly commanded Treasure Island. I had always wondered why he and his wife had stopped being our friends. When I mentioned it to John, he scoffed at the rift, saying it wasn't important. I found the rear admiral's number and dialed.

"Hi, this is Barbara Perry, John's wife." There was an uncomfortable silence before he acknowledged me. I explained what had happened and asked him if he could help me prove that John was a retired rear admiral from the U.S. Navy.

"Don't you know about the FBI?" he said.

"FBI? No. What about the FBI?"

"John is being investigated by the FBI for impersonating an admiral."

I just about dropped the phone. For all my suspicions of John, I had become fairly comfortable with his rank. I had lived the proof. We had been piped aboard ships. He had worn the Medal of Honor. We had been guests with other admirals on a commanding admiral's ship, and the Blue Angels had given us a photograph signed to Rear Admiral Perry. We had been allowed entry onto any base that we visited.

"I called the FBI and reported him in the fall of eighty-nine," the rear admiral said in clipped tones. "If you want any more information, call the Concord FBI office. And please don't contact me again."

I hung up the phone and dug into my memory. About the time the FBI showed up at our door, John stopped working. Could those events have been connected? I called the FBI office and spoke to the agent the rear admiral had contacted. I explained who I was and what I was looking for. He was respectful and confirmed what I had been afraid to admit to myself. John was the object of an ongoing investigation. "He has a history of this kind of behavior. Did you know he spent three years in federal prison for impersonating an Air Force officer?"

"No." I gasped. It was a good thing I was sitting down.

We continued the conversation. The agent gave me as much information as he was allowed to divulge. "I have the case of medals that we confiscated at your house," he said. "Since John's involved in a more serious charge, I think we'll stop the investigation. Can I drop them off to you?"

"Sure, just let me know when you want to come by. I'll let Homicide Detective Greg Smith know about your investigation. You'll probably get a call from him, as well."

"Oh, one more thing," the agent said. "The Medal of Honor wasn't in the case. Do you know where it might be?"

I didn't have any idea. I hung up the phone. *So that's what happened to the medals,* I raged. All those lies, all those times I was stressed out by John's indifference. "I hate you!" I shouted to the empty room. I immediately called Greg Smith and reported my findings.

"Great," he said. "With this information I think the PA can get the bail raised back to twenty-five thousand dollars. You're amazing. You've really helped this case along." Then he added that he had talked with the FBI agent. "Have you ever heard of John's aliases?" he asked.

"Aliases?"

"The FBI said he's gone by Calliet Delvin, Guy D. Delvin, Daniel F. Malley, Robert Lee Stuart, and Thomas John Mudge. Ring a bell?"

"I've never heard those names before," I said. "But I'll keep a lookout as I go through his office paperwork."

When I hung up the phone, I felt proud of myself. In spite of my grief, I had been able to function, to move forward, and in doing so I found enough evidence to allow the case to go to trial. But my job as investigator was far from over, and my recovery had just begun.

TWENTY-TWO

The Trial

Five weeks later, in Arlington, Virginia, I fidgeted with my foam coffee cup in the office of Alexandra Kouracos, the prosecuting attorney assigned to my case. She had been convinced John was a criminal from the start. Today, she had to convince the family court judge of the same, in order to move the trial to criminal court.

Alexandra whizzed into her office, a pile of folders in her hand. With her distinctive features and brunette hair, she closely resembled the portrait, hung prominently on one wall, of a judge in his court robes.

"My father," she said, smiling. She exuded strength and confidence. "Let's review your testimony while we wait for Greg Smith."

"I've worked hard to be ready for today," I said.

"You'll do great. I have to tell you this is the strangest case I have handled."

"Thanks. First my divorce attorney tells me that, and now you. I feel like a freak."

When Greg arrived we gathered our things and meandered

through a maze of hallways and elevator rides. Outside the court-room Alexandra asked me to take a seat on the bench while she took care of a last-minute detail. Greg also disappeared.

I was nervous. Today would be the first test of my newfound freedom. I had to be strong. John's intimidations during the pro-ceedings could not sway me. He no longer had power over me, and I had to let him see my determination. I wondered how it would play out. I twitched each time the prisoner elevator or holding cell opened and someone in a blue jumpsuit emerged.

It had taken a lot of time and hard work for me to regain my power. I made a major breakthrough when I discovered how to tap into my inner strength using techniques associated with healing the inner child. I was amazed at what happened next. This new self-realization propelled me through recovery, as Carolyn referenced my writings and drawings for our discussions. By the fifth session I was amazed at my emotional growth.

"I feel I'm progressing too fast," I confessed to her.

"Don't you know why? You had to regain your strength before the preliminary hearing. You persevered. You found that recovery takes more work than just sitting in my office for fifty minutes a week."

Today, seated on this hard bench in the corridor, I was in agony. Alexandra and Greg had not returned. Nervous anticipation ate at me as the minutes ticked away. Needing reassurance, I reached inside my purse and pulled out the horoscope from the morning's *Washington Post*, and found solace in the words: *You'll no longer fear the dark. Focus on inside information…Family member "explains" bizarre plan. Maintain balance, perspective. Say, "NO!"*

That's what I'm going to do today, I thought. *Say no to John. I will not crumble.* The holding cell door creaked and I glanced up. John shuffled out in handcuffs and shackles, wearing blue prison garb. An armed guard escorted him toward the courtroom. My breathing turned shallow and I turned away. I couldn't look him in the eyes. Not yet.

I needed to refocus and think of all the things I had recently uncovered. The paintings John said he owned were not his. He'd "borrowed" them from another woman and never returned them. Then he talked the same woman into a $5,000 loan. That was the $5,000 he said came from his grandmother. *Think of the pain he caused you, when you felt like a criminal as the divorce judge issued a restraining order against the both of you. Think how you told John from the start that honesty was the most important thing to you. Think of the nightmares that haunt you, your loss of sleep. He doesn't deserve your sympathy or support.*

Alexandra appeared and said, "This is it," and opened the courtroom door for me. Greg rushed up and joined us. The room looked like a church with blond pews, a middle aisle, and a wall of windows on one side. The "altar" was the judge's bench. Would I be the sacrificial lamb today?

John and his public defender, Kent Whistler, sat at the table on the right, with one man in the first bench behind them. Alexandra guided me to the left, and I sat with Greg and the rest of the prosecution witnesses. Just like a wedding, I thought, with the groom's family on one side, the bride's family on the other. The parody was that it was not a gathering for a celebration of beginnings, but rather one for the tragedy of endings.

The judge called the proceeding to order, asked the witnesses to stand, and had us sworn in, after which we were asked to leave. This was not like the Perry Mason trials.

Greg explained, "This way witnesses don't compromise their testimony based on what another witness has to say." His deep, caring voice grounded me.

We mingled outside the door. I sat once more on the bench and silently prayed, *Dear God, please give me the strength to persevere.*

The bailiff opened the door and called my name. I couldn't move. I took a deep breath and willed my feet to take me to the witness stand. I sat down, and immediately John locked his steely blue eyes onto mine and glared. In times past I would have averted my eyes and crumbled. Not today. I stared back at the old, pathetic figure in dark blue.

I silently projected my thoughts to John. *You no longer have any power over me. You no longer have any power over me.* Did he understand I had changed? I repeated my mantra. John squirmed in his seat and looked away. I won. I won! It didn't matter that no one else in the room was aware of my victory. I knew. I was ready to testify.

Alexandra asked questions about our marriage, our financial affairs, and how we got to room 173 at the Marriott. "I'd like you to take a look at these photographs, Mrs. Perry. Is this you after the attack?"

Kent Whistler rose from his seat. "I object, your honor. Only thirty-five-millimeter photographs are allowed as evidence."

Alexandra questioned me further, and I explained that the photos had been taken with my thirty-five-millimeter camera.

"I object. The witness took her own photograph. She could have doctored her face to look beat up."

The judge looked at Kent, shook his head, then turned to me and asked who took the photograph. I told him Homicide Detective Greg Smith. "Objection overruled," the judge bellowed. "The witness has given testimony to all conditions being met and the pictures will be entered in evidence."

I thanked God that He had intervened after the attack, and that the officer's Polaroid had failed to work. Otherwise we wouldn't have had photographs to enter as evidence.

Kent had his turn at me. He tried to distort the facts, to get me to change my story. He pounded away, but I did not weaken, even when John gave me another of his cold, hard stares.

I was released and allowed to remain in the courtroom to hear several police officers testify. The prosecution rested. Kent Whistler called only one witness, an expert to testify that John was addicted to ether. Alexandra blew his weak testimony out of the water. The defense rested.

The judge shuffled through the papers on his desk. It seemed like an eternity before he spoke. "Based on the evidence presented, I remand John Perry to criminal court to stand trial for attempted first-degree murder. His bail is to remain at twenty-five thousand dollars."

He banged his gavel, and it was over. I watched John slump out of the courtroom. My victory felt bittersweet. I knew John was mentally ill, and I prayed he would get the help he needed. I still didn't understand there is no changing a socio-psychopath.

Three weeks passed. I sat at my desk at work and waited for a phone call from Greg. We touched base often, sharing evidence that either of us had dug up. It was a strong working relationship built on mutual respect and trust. The previous night I had faxed him new information. I pounced on the phone when it rang.

"Guess what I discovered last night?" I told him excitedly. "I found the woman who impersonated me on the real estate loan."

I explained that when I took the garbage out I saw my next-door neighbor and struck up a conversation. We chatted briefly when, out of the blue, she asked, "How did your loan application go?" She told me John had asked her to sign for me; he said I was on a business trip and it was most important that the papers get processed. She was hesitant, but he told her not to worry, he'd do all the talking. Later, when the loan officer wanted a third-party identification, John had her stand by the bank door and smile and wave when he pointed her out to the loan officer and bank manager. Then they went to the car and signed the papers. The loan officer said he would notarize it when he got back to his office.

"Good work," Greg said. "She'll make a great witness."

"I don't know. She's pretty embarrassed about the whole thing. Said she didn't take any money, she was just doing us a favor. She's afraid she'll be prosecuted."

"I'll talk to her. She has nothing to fear from this end."

We reviewed the documents I faxed to him. There was the letter from the UC Davis vet denying he had prescribed ether. There was a letter from the travel agent confirming the dates John purchased tickets and his subsequent suspicious behavior. There was a letter from the Concord vet explaining how John had lied to get the bottle of ether from her.

"We need to have the Concord vet testify," Greg said. "Now that you have two witnesses, I'll fly out to California and take their statements."

As I hung up the phone, I wondered once more about the notary process. I always thought it was meant to keep fraud from happening. I no longer had faith in that procedure.

Between work, therapy, investigations, and haggling with John about the divorce, the next month passed quickly. Dealing with John was the most difficult. He sat in his jail cell and scribbled a list of everything we owned, from the Mercedes down to and including dish towels and washrags, and wrote his estimated value of them.

John controlled the divorce proceedings. He was clever, and it amazed me how much power he could exert from his jail cell. His latest tactic was to return my correspondence unopened. I felt as helpless and emotionally drained as I had when we were together. He continued to set up roadblocks.

In desperation, I arranged for the sergeant at the jail to intervene. That got results. John finally agreed to talk with me. The phone rang. I accepted the collect charges. After a bit of small talk, I jumped into the matters at hand. I needed John's consent to lower the prices of the Concord house and the 450SL. In typical fashion he led me along, acting as if he were all for it, then reneged. Even my rationalization about being able to pay his attorney with the funds backfired.

"I don't care about lawyers," he proclaimed.

Boy, was that a true statement! I had witnessed John toying with the attorneys I knew, so it didn't surprise me when I discovered he had stiffed another one in San Diego in 1975. That's when I learned John was previously arrested for car theft and credit card fraud around the same time. He had also severely beaten a woman, almost to death. My fear level increased at that news.

I finally understood that John was not a nice man. I also knew I had to be careful how I handled him. He was still a financial threat, and possibly a physical one. Next I proffered using the same divorce attorney, to save money, but he would have none of it.

I moved on to the next item on my list, the monthly annuity checks that had stopped coming. I had been using them to pay off the joint bills, and their disappearance created a strain.

"I heard the savings-and-loan has gone into receivership," John said. "I thought this might affect the payments."

"Hopefully you're wrong. I'll check it out."

"Don't bother. Leave it alone," he said, his voice rising. "Just leave it alone!"

I dropped the subject. I had nothing more on my list, and my pleas had fallen on deaf ears. My stomach started to twist. My head started to pound. I hung up the phone and sobbed uncontrollably for the next five minutes. My hopes of coming to some sort of an agreement had crashed and burned. Foreclosure loomed. I would probably lose my Concord home.

The trial began in the middle of June 1991. It would be short, and held without the glaring eye and feeding frenzy of the media. I was spared that agony because the original police call had been logged as a domestic dispute, boring stuff.

During the previous four months I had lived in fear, not knowing whether John had an accomplice, not knowing whether there was a hidden insurance policy on my life, with John as beneficiary. I also lived with the determination to find evidence of John's conspiracy and to work on my own psychological problems. I had been on one hell of a ride.

As I sat in the Arlington County Courthouse, room 601, with the other witnesses, waiting for the judge, I breathed calmly and appeared to be in control, but inside I was an emotional wreck. I was a key participant in an attempted-murder trial, not knowing whether I would be able to remain strong during the questioning. I had no idea how long the trial would take or whether John would be convicted. If he wasn't, what would happen? I was so deep in thought, the bailiff's voice startled me when he spoke.

"All rise."

The gallery rose, then sat when directed by Judge Madison. He proceeded with court-speak, and not all of it made sense to me. Madison asked the defendant and his attorney to stand. "How do you plead?"

"Not guilty," John responded, in a low monotone, his bald head bent forward, his shoulders stooped. He wore his own gray jacket and navy blue slacks.

Ten minutes later a panel of twenty-three jurors was sworn in, seated, and questioned en masse. Boring stuff, unless you're the defendant and those people would be judging you. Eleven jurors were excused and the panel accepted.

The trial proceeded. Witnesses were sworn in and secluded in two adjoining rooms furnished with minimal, stark gray metal furniture. The decor matched my mood. At the preliminary hearing I had come by myself, but this time two others from Concord were there...my neighbor and the vet who gave John the ether. I was grateful for their cooperation, but they provided no comfort. The first two witnesses were called. They did not return. The door opened once more.

"Barbara Perry," the bailiff said. I stood and moved toward the door.

"You'll do just fine," Greg said as he flashed a warm, friendly smile. I nodded and forced myself to smile back.

Alexandra questioned me thoroughly to set out the pertinent facts. Kent Whistler made many objections, and they bickered back and forth. There were sidebars at the bench. More than once, I grabbed the pitcher of water and poured myself a glass to ease my parched throat. More than once, John glared at me, but I didn't buckle under his attempt to control me. I glared back. By the time, two hours later, when Alexandra finished and the judge called for a lunch break, I was as limp as a wet dishrag.

After lunch, Kent took his turn at me. For another hour he manipulated facts to make me look like a gold digger. I deflected his jabs. He insinuated that I had overspent us into financial ruin. I deflected his insults. Then Alexandra asked for redirect, and Kent for recross. On and on it went. They hammered at the facts and picked at minute points. When they finally finished, I wasn't released. The bailiff escorted me back to the witness room.

One by one the remaining witnesses departed. By the end of the day only Homicide Detective Greg Smith and I sat in the dingy room. The door opened and Alexandra walked in.

"All the witnesses have testified," she said. "Court is adjourned. We'll reconvene in the morning for closing arguments." She came over and gave me a big hug. "You did great."

The next day I sat in the gallery with Greg Smith and Ashley Vandemeer, a perky blonde who had testified on my behalf as the Navy expert. She confirmed that John was not a retired rear admiral. We chatted until the judge called for order. The jury filed in. Kent Whistler gave his closing arguments, and my body tensed. He portrayed John as an aging man whose younger wife had deceived him, and who, in despair, had become addicted to ether. What a crock! Had the man no morals?

Now it was Alexandra's turn. A bundle of energy, she whirled around the room, pointing to a timeline displayed on a stand to make it clear that I was the victim, not the perpetrator. She built a strong case, point by point, and made sure the jury followed her reasoning. Then it was over. The judge instructed the jury, and at 10:10 in the morning they filed out. I was numb. It all seemed to have happened so fast, yet in my mind it had played out in slow motion.

Ashley stayed with me and we returned to Greg's office to wait. At lunchtime there was no word from the court. After lunch, more silence. We chatted and drank coffee as the afternoon dragged on. At four o'clock, the call came. The jury had a verdict.

I sat between Ashley and Greg; each offered me a hand to hold. The foreman stood. I held my breath.

"We, the jury, find the defendant guilty of attempted first-degree murder as charged in the indictment and fix punishment at five years imprisonment."

They had been lenient. They could have given John the maximum sentence of ten years. I didn't know if I was happy or sad. I squeezed the hands I held. The guilty plea echoed through my mind. *Five years...guilty...* Tears puddled in my eyes. *Attempted first-degree murder.* It's what I wanted to hear, yet at the same time it frightened me. It was fantasy and reality all mixed together. At that moment I couldn't make sense of my emotions.

"Ashley, can you take Barbara out for a drink until about five thirty?" Greg asked. "She shouldn't be alone right now."

Ashley and I walked to a nearby café and sat with our cups of coffee, killing time until the detective could take me to dinner. "You know," Ashley said, "this is the strangest case I've ever heard of."

I considered her words. "You're not the only one who's said that."

At work, two weeks after I returned home, I sat at my desk waiting for an important phone call from the annuity fund administrator. It would be the culmination of two months of investigative work about the missing checks. There was no way I could concentrate on work. My mind swirled dizzily from recent events, including the death of my cat Patches, who had died while I was at the trial. I was in mourning, not only for the loss of my beloved pet but also for the loss of what I thought had been a normal life.

The verdict catapulted me into another new experience I would have to find my way through. I interfaced with the probation officer and pleaded to get John the psychological help he needed. I also worked on my victim impact statement. It had to be compelling so that John would get the full five years. The judge had power to over-rule the jury's recommendation and reduce the sentence. I wished he could increase it to the maximum ten years.

When the annuity checks stopped coming to the house and John seemed indifferent, I got busy investigating. I followed a trail that led from company to company until I ended up with a fund admin-istrator in the Midwest. Today I anxiously awaited her call. When the phone rang, I grabbed it at once.

"I found a letter from John," she said. "He writes that you and he are moving, and you want the funds transferred to Miwok Val-ley Bank in San Ramon. I just faxed you a copy." San Ramon was a town twenty miles from Concord, near where John had lived for a short time before I met him. He had kept his account at the bank after we married and we used it for our business.

I laid the phone down, rushed into the next room, and grabbed the letter as the fax machine spit it out. The words danced before my eyes. Would the deceit never end?

"He forged my name!" I cried in anguish into the phone. "He's in jail for trying to murder me and he forges my name to illegally divert our community property."

I looked closer. The bank account listed was one I had closed right after the murder attempt. The fund administrator agreed to redirect the checks back to me. I immediately called the Miwok Valley branch in San Ramon and was connected to a bank officer. She checked the account.

"It's still active, Mrs. Perry. We have a notation in the account that Mr. Perry called and instructed that it stay open because his Social Security checks are automatically deposited into it."

"He can't do that."

"He opened another account. Money deposited into your joint account gets immediately moved into an account with only Mr. Perry's name on it."

"You accept his word and never even check with me? You're as crooked as he is," I seethed. "This is the second time you have helped my husband defraud me."

I slammed down the receiver and wrote in my day planner. *SF Annuity—confirmed John's forgery. WHEN WILL IT END?*

A month after John was convicted, the divorce stalled. The delay had me frantic and angry, especially when I met with my attorney, who informed me that John's incarceration complicated matters. Intent as I was on jump-starting the divorce, all I got was legal doublespeak from Ross Grissom, and $200 more added to my ever-increasing bill. I tried to explain to the attorney how John's latest delay tactic infuriated me and rendered me helpless when my correspondence to him was marked REFUSED AND RETURNED. How could I keep the divorce on track if John wouldn't communicate with me?

Defiant and anxious to get rid of the stigma of John's name, I demanded a new last name—Bentley—a fresh name to reflect the new me. John had always told me he would buy me a Bentley, and now I'd have it. I was ever the optimist; the name hyphenated well, should I choose to marry again.

I glared at Ross. "Please," I pleaded. "Help me get divorced as soon as possible. I'm married to a madman, and as hard as I try to resist, he's slowly driving me crazy."

I didn't realize at the time that my new name would sit on a shelf and gather dust for the next year and a half.

Several weeks later during a business trip to Indianapolis, I sat in my hotel room and pondered the events of the last nine years of my life. *Why has this happened to me?* I thought. *What good can come out of such tragic events?* I reviewed my therapy work on the yellow sheet of paper in front of me and it became clear. I needed to write a book. Yes, I'd write a book that exposed John's devious toxic behavior so that others would not fall into the same trap. With that bold decision I made a mental note—I would have to learn how to write.

I didn't realize the story was far from over.

TWENTY-THREE

The Crusade

It was two months after John was convicted, and my world continued to collapse around me. I was in danger of losing my home. John wouldn't agree to lower the selling price, and he had diverted funds I needed to meet our high mortgage payments. It seemed hopeless, and I was running out of time. Why was John doing this? How could he continue to torment me, even from prison?

I tried to negotiate with the lenders, make them see that it would be a win-win situation if I could pay only the interest until the house sold. The second mortgage lender agreed right away; the first lender said he'd have to get back to me.

The call came after lunch. The loan officer apologized, then slammed me with the news: they were going to foreclose. I went numb. The dreaded word echoed through my mind. Embarrassment engulfed me. Damn John for getting us into this position. How could I have been stupid enough to allow our debt to progress this far? I boiled with rage, but mostly I felt overwhelmed and defeated.

My lips quivered and my head fell onto my folded arms on the table. Sobs convulsed my aching body. My tormented mind conjured up questions that filled me with the paralyzing fear of shame. What would people think? I wallowed in self-pity. I cursed John. If it weren't for him I wouldn't be in this misery.

Let go and let God. I stopped crying and listened to my inner voice. I took a deep breath and absorbed the meaning of each syllable. It had become my mantra. *Let go of my troubles and let God handle it.* I raised my head, wiped my eyes, and folded my hands in prayer. Within moments, I sat taller and breathed deeper as trust released me from my fear, and I knew that I did not have to handle the foreclosure alone. Despair dissipated as strength and warmth radiated from deep inside me. I no longer shuddered at the thought of the word. "Foreclosure," I said aloud. "It's just a word. It no longer has any power over me." I met my fear head on, and won.

In early September, the homicide detective called to let me know he had found Janette Perry, Admiral Perry's widow, living in Georgetown. Greg said he didn't want to be further involved; I'd have to do any follow-up myself. I thanked him profusely. When we hung up I took a deep breath, punched the Washington, D.C., toll-free information number into the telephone, and scribbled Janette Perry's number on a piece of scrap paper.

I stared at the number for several minutes as I gathered my thoughts. What would I say to this woman, supposedly John's stepmother, who had remained a mystery to me for ten years? I picked up the phone and dialed. Janette answered with a cheery greeting, and then silence prevailed as she assimilated who I was and what John had done. She caught her breath and apologized, with a brief explanation that it didn't surprise her. It fit right into John's troubled history. I wanted more. I felt a compulsion to meet her, as if that would be my proof that John had told the truth about something. Janette agreed to meet with me.

At the end of September, I sat with Janette in her apartment, opposite a gallery-size oil painting of a naval officer. I couldn't help but gawk. John's resemblance to Admiral Perry was uncanny.

Janette confirmed that John was indeed the son of Admiral Perry. She debunked John's claim of four brothers, but revealed that he had had one brother, Pete, who'd died in infancy. She told me John's mother had passed away while they were living at the Great Lakes Naval Training Center, when John was only seven, and that she had married John's father when John was ten. Not too surprisingly, she could not confirm any relationship between John's mother and Rear Admiral Peary of North Pole fame.

I prodded her further about John's childhood. She said he was an ordinary child who got into the kinds of mischief one would expect for a boy. Then she mentioned an accident and how he had changed after that. I perched on the edge of my chair.

John had enlisted in the Navy against his father's wishes. He was barely legal age, but wanted to get into the action of World War II. On his first leave after basic training, he dove into a swimming pool and was knocked unconscious. He spent the next three months in the hospital. I explained how John's tales, in many respects, matched what she said.

"Maybe he felt he had something to prove to his father, who was career military. I always told my husband he was too demanding of his son."

I encouraged Janette to continue.

"Well, John changed. He was discharged from the service for medical reasons, as a seaman first class. That's when the trouble started...stealing cars and God knows what else. My John had his hands full trying to deal with him, and even had him committed to a mental institution in New Orleans when he was nineteen or twenty. It didn't help." I felt a pang of sadness that this decorated war hero had to put up with John's antisocial behavior.

"John had a story about living in the French Quarter in New Orleans," I said. "But not in a mental hospital."

"We believe John's misdeeds broke his father's heart and eventually killed him. We didn't want anything to do with John and didn't even tell our daughter that she has a half brother, because there was such an age difference anyway. After you called me, I broke the news to her."

The haze cleared. John always said he was the black sheep of the family and that was why he wasn't listed in his father's biography. I pushed Janette further about John's family. She confirmed that John's mother had a sister named Dorothy who had become a Catholic nun in Miami. Sister Dorothy would see John every couple of years. Once, in the early sixties, he showed up with a woman and four kids, but there was no way of knowing if they were his, and Dorothy had passed away years ago.

I related John's stories of his various wives, and that I had been able to track only one down—ironically, one that he had never told me about. She married John, who wore a Navy captain's uniform for the occasion, on the *Queen Mary*. A year later John was arrested by the FBI, and she had the marriage annulled. By that time he had maxed out her credit cards. It took her many years to climb out from under the debt. After sixteen years she was still reluctant to talk about it.

At the end of our meeting, Janette slipped into her bedroom and came back with a small gift bag for me. I pulled at the tissue paper and extracted a small jeweler's box. Inside was a delicate ring, made up of three separate bands of semiprecious stones.

"Janette, you shouldn't have," I protested. I bit my lip and tears welled in my eyes as I slipped it on my finger. It fit perfectly. I hugged her. "It's so beautiful. Thank you."

"You've been through a lot. It's the least I can do."

"You'd make a wonderful mother-in-law." I laughed. "Too bad I won't be your daughter-in-law much longer."

For the next three months, I worked with the jail system to get psychological help for John. By the end of the year, John was assigned to maximum security at the Powhatan Correctional Center, and he wasn't getting any mental help. The divorce was still stalled. John threw a monkey wrench into any proposed settlement, and foreclosure lay just around the corner. My last Christmas in the Concord house was definitely not merry, and the New Year did not look bright.

After the house was foreclosed in February 1992, I moved into the spare bedroom of a longtime friend. One month later my fragile world suffered another earthquake. Debbie, the friend who'd introduced me to John, called to tell me that he was up for parole and he needed a viable parole plan before he could be released. He wanted to live with her during his integration back into society. Parole! The word plunged me into a panic. He had been in jail for only thirteen months! I had not been notified. Fear engulfed me. I was about to play the victim part again. With our divorce still far in the future, if I were murdered now, wouldn't all our joint assets still go to him? Fortunately, Debbie had refused. He was stalled, for the moment. He would have to find another way out.

My survival was tied to my ability to act, not react, to John. I took immediate steps to protect myself. I contacted the prosecuting attorney, the homicide detective, the parole board, my attorney, and the three local police departments that had my restraining order. I received confirmation that John was up for parole, and that I had only the rest of the day to submit my victim impact statement. In the end, it didn't matter. A month later John was granted parole after only fourteen months in jail. Luckily, it would take him another eight months to come up with a reasonable parole plan. For the moment, he was still in jail.

Three weeks later I bounced into my mother's kitchen. "Hey, I've got something to show you," I reported cheerfully.

Julie looked up from stirring a pot of spaghetti sauce, and her son stopped rolling his Matchbox cars across the floor. My mom followed me to the table and we sat down. I grabbed a small box out of my purse.

"Remember the inaugural ball necklace and earrings? I've been waiting for the day I could afford to do something with them." I flipped the lid on the box and took out a shining diamond-studded ring. "This signifies my life—taking old and making new."

I handed the box to my mom and she ran her finger over the stones. Julie stopped stirring and looked over Mom's shoulder. Mom slipped the ring onto her right index finger and moved it around to catch its sparkle.

"Not to be outdone." Julie laughed, "I have something to show you." She grabbed a brown paper bag set by the back door. "I pried apart the two yellow plastic planters you gave me and this is what I found."

Mom laid several paper towels on the table. Julie opened the sack, extracted two decrepit boxes, and placed them on the towels. The boxes were moldy and stained from dirt and water. I picked one up and opened it. "Oh, my God." I gasped. "It's the Congressional Medal of Honor."

I carefully fingered the long-lost medal. Its ribbon was discolored and deformed and had a putrid odor. The next box contained the admiral's bars. "He's good," I said. "Imagine burying them so the FBI wouldn't find them! The FBI will get a kick out of this."

Four months later I had moved back to my Antioch house. It had been eighteen months since the murder attempt. John was still in jail after the two parole plans he submitted were rejected as being nonconducive to his rehabilitation, whatever that meant. The divorce was still not final. The property settlement was a shambles. I felt trapped by the attorneys' lack of action and once more confronted Ross Grissom in his office. "Ross," I said, "I want to be divorced *now*." He leaned back in his chair, thumped his pen on the desk, and drawled, "John keeps telling his attorney he's getting out any day. Trust me, it will be easier to wait until he's released."

It was the same old story, and I was tired of hearing it. "Delaying the divorce is costing me. Your bill is over six thousand dollars."

Ross leaned forward and looked me in the eye. "How would you like to be co-attorney on your case?" he asked. "Then you can deal directly with Alan Bradley, his attorney."

I walked out of the office, triumphant. From now on Bradley would have to deal with me. It would save time and money, and possibly bring sanity to my insane world.

John was released from prison four months later, in December 1992, after serving only twenty-two months in jail for trying to murder me. I got only two days' notice. My surprise and disgust turned to panic. John was now on the street, and might attempt again to kill me...or have someone else do it.

The Virginia victims advocate told me John was released under a reciprocal program to the state of Washington. A parole officer in Seattle would monitor him. I wouldn't find out until later that Hal Ledman, a former Two Star business associate who worked as a civilian contractor for the Navy, had vouched for John and gave him a place to stay, along with backing John's plan to start a plant import business. *Leave it to John to pick an area with a strong Navy presence so he could pick up where he left off,* I thought at the time.

I concentrated on the facts. John had continued to delay the divorce. If I died he could still try to get all the assets. John knew how to manipulate the system. I wanted additional protection, a new temporary restraining order, but when I called my attorney he said I was being melodramatic.

"By the way, Bradley called," he said. "John is willing to finalize the divorce and leave the property settlement until later, but he has one condition."

I braced myself. "What?"

"He wants you to relinquish the Perry name."

"You've got to be kidding." I laughed. "What an ass! John trying to control me through his name is a joke." At one time his request would have been devastating to me, when I was weak and basking in the history of his name. John's request showed that he still didn't understand how I had changed and what I had learned.

"Tell the bastard I decided I didn't want his name a long time ago. Let him know he's finally getting me my Bentley."

Then I turned serious. I offered to let John use the annuity until he died, on the condition that he back off my retirement and alimony. I believed my life was still in danger as long as there was a possibility of financial gain for him after my death. Yes, Ross had said I was being melodramatic, but he hadn't been the one with ether on his face, or glass in his hair, or bruises from a fall down the stairs.

When I hung up the phone, I took the next step to try to ensure my safety. I bought a cell phone. Later that evening, after I meditated, I wrote in my diary, *My mind is heavy. This has been the week from hell.*

TWENTY-FOUR

The Awakening

John roamed the streets at will, a chameleon who could outwit any parole officer, a snake who could easily slither away from Seattle unnoticed. I spent the weekend after signing the divorce papers in deep mourning and utter mental chaos.

Monday morning in my shower, my inner voice whispered, "*Call Melvin Belli.*" Melvin Belli, an internationally known flamboyant lawyer nicknamed the "King of Torts" for his work representing the rights of the individual, conducted business from his main office in San Francisco. His deep baritone voice set him apart, as did his work in sensational criminal justice or personal injury cases. In the San Francisco Bay Area, he was a legend, an aging legend.

"*Call Melvin Belli,*" the voice repeated. I dismissed the idea as fantasy and finished getting ready for work. No way was a world-famous lawyer going to listen to me.

Later that morning as I sat at my office desk, my persistent inner voice spoke once more. "*Call Melvin Belli.*" I gave in, got the phone number from San Francisco information, and dialed. Once the ringing started, I panicked. Who would I ask for? A deep male voice answered, "Law Office."

"Mr. Belli's secretary, please," I stammered. When she came on the line, she quickly assessed my situation and said, "Sounds like Mr. Belli should handle this. Can I have him call you around noon?"

"Yes. Yes, I'll be here."

The phone rang exactly at noon. On the other end of the line a booming baritone voice said, "This is Melvin Belli." Goose bumps rippled along my arms and I shook with nervous agitation. I need not have. Before the conversation ended, Mr. Belli had set up an appointment for me to see him in two days, even though he knew I didn't have a lot of money and there was no large estate. I hung up the phone and pranced around like a giddy schoolgirl.

My euphoria was short lived. Two days later, on the morning of my appointment, I got a call from Marie, in Cupertino. She told me John had brazenly shown up on her doorstep the day before. They not only asked him in, but had him spend the night. I couldn't believe it. He had used their former friendship to manipulate them, regaling them with his current exploits, and telling them he was in a government witness program. My dismay turned to terror when Marie told me John said he was going to cause me a lot of trouble. It made my trip today to see Melvin Belli even more critical.

That afternoon my mother and I sat in Belli's antique-filled reception area. When the receptionist called my name, Mom waved me on and I followed him into an office reminiscent of a bygone time. Mr. Belli rose to greet me. An old-fashioned gentleman, larger than life, he smiled broadly and extended his hand. Although now eighty-six, he was a striking figure with thick silver hair and deep wrinkles. Once we were seated, he prompted me for information and, as I spilled my story, I emptied my evidence from the briefcase. Bits and pieces of a once-happy life with the admiral lay on Melvin Belli's desk.

"He's even using his admiral rank again," I sobbed. "He showed up at the storage company in Martinez and said he was Admiral Perry. I promptly called the FBI."

"I'd like to beat this guy up and feed him to the sharks," Belli groaned. "Unfortunately, the law's the law. I'll have you talk to my assistant who handles the firm's family law." His assistant told me the law was not on my side.

I was looking for confirmation that the divorce law was insidious, while hoping there would be a way out of the financial injustice. I got the former, but not the latter. Disgruntled, I returned to the reception area and sank into the soft couch.

"What happened? Any luck?" Mom asked.

The ticking of the antique clock filled the room. I gathered my thoughts, analyzing what I had been told. "I thought Mr. Belli would have the answer, but there isn't any. He said the law is the law."

"What are you going to do now?"

I shrugged. I had no plan. As we rose to leave, innocently and out of ignorance, I spoke. "I guess I'll just have to change the law."

For the next three months I lived an endless nightmare, caught in a vise between the divorce lawyers, the judge, and John. I felt like a mime, moving my feet to get ahead while remaining in the same place, and it wasn't funny. No matter how hard I tried to keep the property settlement moving forward, John thwarted my efforts to reach a fair and even division, even denying the accounting in my copious detailed records.

We met twice, once in family court and once in Alan Bradley's office, without success. All I could see was my hard-earned money sprouting wings and flying into greedy hands. The lawyers were wrong to wait until John was out of jail. The negotiations were just as difficult, and the property settlement was at an impasse. I had not been able to appease John's appetite for my possessions, and I would not give in to his blackmail.

Was it any wonder I balked at the next settlement conference scheduled for the end of March in Judge Lawrence's chambers? I couldn't contain my disgust with John, the lawyers, the family law court, and the California divorce law. The frustration gnawed at me. It was a miracle I had not developed an ulcer by now. When I asked Ross to cancel the meeting, he offered a compromise. "You're co-counsel," he said. "Why don't you go to the hearing and represent yourself?"

"I never thought about defending myself in court."

"Why not? You've got all the facts. You know the case inside and out. You're intelligent. I'll fill you in on protocol and you'll do just fine."

Another door opened in my life. I stood at the threshold of this new experience, accepted the challenge, and stepped through to the other side.

In the judge's chambers, Bradley presented John's accounting. John figured I owed him $14,000. Ridiculous! Anger superseded nerves. I opened my briefcase, ready to pull out my ledger of detailed records and dispute each ludicrous demand. This was my day in court, and I needed to show my strength and intelligence so John would not get the best of me. "Your honor," I began. "I'm the victim in this case, not John Perry."

"I'm acquainted with the details," Judge Lawrence said wearily, shaking his head. "Very sad, and most unusual. This is the strangest case I've ever had in my courtroom."

Great, I thought. *Another one admits this is the strangest case they've come across.* That didn't help me as I struggled through the process, and more often it was a hindrance. Ignorance breeds delays. Without precedent to fall back on, we were forging our way through unknown territory.

"Your honor, I've negotiated with Alan Bradley and his client in good faith for over two years." I grabbed my green sheets in the briefcase and passed out copies to Bradley and Judge Lawrence. "I'd like to go through my detailed response from their last attempt to financially rape me."

The verbal and legal fisticuffs began. We argued over airline mileage, the annuity, the custody of the animals, monies expended by me to keep the household going, joint monies diverted by John into his personal account. In the end the judge glared at Bradley and growled, "Tell Mr. Perry he needs to accept Mrs. Perry's offer. She's being more than fair. I think that's enough for today." He rose and left the room.

Hooray! I had just won a victory in chambers, representing myself. We gathered our things, left the chamber, and paused in the courtroom. Bradley frowned and said he'd get back to me.

The next day Ross Grissom called me and ranted on for almost ten minutes about how I should get on with my life. I assumed that Bradley had whined about his client's stubbornness, and both attorneys were getting tired of the circus. "What's the matter, can't Bradley control his client?" I asked.

"He is having trouble with John."

"Just remember, I'm the victim here. Why should I settle for being victimized again? What kind of legal system do we have? And whose side are you on anyway?"

I slammed the phone down, feeling out of control, disoriented, fearful, and stressed. Constant nightmares about John, murder, and fraud disrupted my sleep. I realized it had been almost a year since my last session with my therapist, when I had sought her advice for a summer romance. It had been a wonderful summer in the California Delta, what my soul needed as I sunned myself on the deck of his houseboat or cooled off flitting about on his Jet-Ski. But by the end of the summer I realized that the relationship was toxic. The man was emotionally unavailable. We separated as friends and when I checked in with Carolyn, she affirmed my decision. I immediately called and set up an appointment.

In mid-April 1993, I sat in Carolyn's office and bared my soul about the effect John's crazymaking behavior had on me. Her good counsel had directed me to sanity before the trial and after the brief summer fling. Once more I looked for her guidance. At the end of the hour I left with a new resolve that John would not get the better of me.

Thirteen days later, Carolyn called me into her office for my next visit. She sensed at once that I was not the weak, emotionally distraught person who had dragged into her office two weeks before. I radiated energy, and it permeated the room.

"Walking tall today, I see," she said as she sat down.

I settled into the now-familiar wing-back chair, laid my briefcase in my lap, and zipped it open. I was a woman in command. "I feel liberated," I said as I shared with her how the emotional energy pent up inside me had burst into vigorous activity over the past weekend. "I've decided that John will not ruin my life, and that it's time I get on with it. I'm now ready to go beyond myself."

I showed her my handwritten letters: one contacting an advocate for victims' rights and one to Hannelore Hahn, the founder of the International Women's Writing Guild. I shared my computer-generated letters: one to Governor Pete Wilson; one to my assemblyman, Robert Campbell; and one to my state senator, Daniel Boatwright. Each had the same content. I stated my case and gave a brief background on the murder attempt and John's criminal history. I ended with an appeal for help in stopping the legal extortion and requested that the law be changed. "They're all in the mail," I said.

I hugged my pile of papers. By acting on my passions, with patience, persistence, and a belief in my process, I had emerged a victor. It was my last visit to Carolyn's office.

Three months passed. I was no closer to a settlement with John, but still moving forward with my life. When offered an opportunity to disprove John's stories, I jumped at the chance. That's how I ended up in Sacramento, at the Doris Tate Award Ceremony. Harriet Salarno, the founder of Justice for Murder Victims in San Francisco, and a recipient of one of the awards, had invited me. Bells clanged when I found out the governor would hand the awards out. Fate had intervened, and I planned to take advantage. I would find a way to speak to Governor Pete Wilson to confirm or deny two of John's stories that involved Wilson when he was the mayor of San Diego.

That day, when the inspirational ceremony ended and most people straggled away to the reception, the governor lingered by the podium. It was now or never. I picked up my briefcase and walked to the front of the room. An aide intercepted my path. "May I help you, ma'am?"

I took a deep breath to calm myself, and explained my cause. The aide listened attentively, then escorted me to the governor, whose gracious smile put me at ease. After presenting a brief rundown about the admiral, the murder attempt, the trial, and the divorce abuse, I reached into my briefcase and brought out several photographs of John Perry. The governor retrieved his reading glasses from his breast pocket and studied the pictures intently.

"John always told a story about knowing you in San Diego when you were the mayor," I explained. "It was something about him working undercover in a sting to catch car thieves. He said you helped bail him out of jail."

"I'm sorry, it doesn't ring a bell."

"He also said he visited you in Washington, D.C., when you were senator, to get your help on a government contract."

"Sorry. I wish I could help you," the governor said, "but this man doesn't look familiar." I suddenly realized John had been in San Diego, all right, when he was in jail for car theft and cheated a lawyer out of his fee. He was not doing undercover work for the mayor.

I thanked Governor Wilson for his time and moved to the reception. Fate intervened once more. I met Delores Winje, one of the six award recipients, whose husband had shot her in the face. She had gone beyond herself to counsel prisoners convicted of spousal abuse, just like Doris Tate. I felt honored to be in the company of such a strong woman. When I told her how I was going to change the unfair divorce law, Delores grasped my hand with both of hers, and her dark eyes looked intently at me. "I'll help you any way I can," she said.

"Let's hope it will be soon," I responded, explaining that my quest to change the divorce law was at an impasse. Senator Boatwright told me the deadline for bills this year had passed, and to get in touch with him in December. He also suggested I get an attorney to help me write the bill. The governor's office replied that the governor had no authority to give advice on private legal matters; I needed to go through the legislative process. To top it off, I still hadn't heard from Assemblyman Campbell's office, though it had been more than two months.

"Here's my address and phone number," Delores said. "Get in touch with me anytime." I stashed the paper in my purse. It would be almost two years before I would contact her.

The next month, in August 1993, I attended my first International Women's Writing Guild Summer Conference in Saratoga Springs, New York. It was a magical experience. I was forty-seven years old and going off to a college dorm for the first time. My mind opened to writing and new friendships, but most important, I learned I had a powerful voice.

The guild founder asked me to give a speech. As I prepared my notes, I came to the part about my efforts to change the law, and I couldn't help but feel disgusted. Less than three weeks before, Senator Boatwright had backpedaled and said I should deal with my assemblyman, the same one who had ignored two more letters from me. I scribbled about passion, patience, and persistence and how I would need all three to follow through. That evening, when I promised my audience I would change the divorce law of California, four hundred women gave me a standing ovation. I learned I had a voice, and I didn't need to feel nervous about using it.

Over the next seven months, John Perry routinely haunted my dreams. He chased, conned, manipulated, or tried to murder me. Cold sweats, headaches, and rapid heartbeats haunted my nights and made me afraid to return to sleep. It was pure hell. I held tightly to my recovery skills in order to stay focused and sane.

My chronic nighttime terrors reflected John's daytime activities. We still had not concluded the property settlement. A year ago Judge Lawrence had told Alan Bradley that John should accept my fair offer, but John would not concede. He insisted I be removed from the annuity, even though I had agreed he could have it until he died; that he get the dogs; that he get property and assets I owned prior to meeting him; and that I release the corporate file boxes stored in Bradley's office.

I wrote letters whenever I found someone I thought could help me, and listed John Francis Perry's aliases: Calliet Delvin, Guy D. Delvin, Daniel F. Malley, Robert Lee Stuart, and Thomas John Mudge. John was certainly a colorful character.

My friend Marie Passini and I went to Miami and scoured the Hall of Records to see if we could find any previous marriages in Dade County. We didn't. I contacted the Miami, Coral Gables, and Hialeah police departments to trace one of John's stories that his second wife's father, Carl Shirrow, had been a former police chief. He wasn't.

Up to now, I had not relinquished the Two Star corporate file boxes, even though they were in the physical custody of John's divorce attorney, Alan Bradley. I wanted the corporation dissolved and a letter from John absolving me of any part of the business. Unexpectedly, John agreed. I went to Bradley's office to go through them one last time. It was March 1994.

"The boxes are in the conference room," the legal assistant

scowled when I walked into Bradley's office. She was a middle-aged paralegal, and she didn't like me. I can imagine what John must have told her about me.

I opened the first box and started to collect names and events, routine items. When I got to the middle of the fifth box I found a folder marked RESEARCH with pages copied from law books related to estates, death, and contracts. Premeditated murder came to mind. I made copies, stuffed them in my briefcase, and was on my way out when Bradley stopped me.

"You know, John feels terrible about what he did to you."

"Really? He's never apologized to me."

"His remorse is genuine. He's told me about the good times you had together and how much he loved you."

"Then why doesn't he settle?"

"I think he's coming around. He doesn't get angry now when we talk about you."

I thought of John's charming persona, how he could turn it off and on to seduce people into believing in him. "Be careful, Alan," I said. "I don't know what his game is, but he can't be up to any good." Outside, I breathed a sigh of relief as I walked away from one part of my life. The boxes were gone. If only John would disappear as well.

Three months later, in June 1994, I went into the work lunchroom to get my morning cup of coffee. The refrigerator door opened behind me, and I jumped. "Sorry," Elizabeth said, "Bad night?"

"Yes. And that's not the half of it," I complained. "It feels like my life is falling apart." The dam burst. "The last ten months have been a living hell. I can't get John to settle. He wants more and more. He's challenged the joint annuity and he drags his feet whenever it comes to answering my counterproposals. One time it took almost five months just to get an answer out of his attorney, and then it wasn't an acceptance, but another attack proposal. My attorney has backed away. I'm left alone to work it all out."

"You sure have your hands full," Elizabeth commiserated.

"That's not the worst. A couple of weeks ago, it came to me that John's actions might be related to getting himself off parole. It scares me. I still don't trust him."

"What did you do?"

I paused and hugged my coffee cup. "The next morning I confirmed my fears. John was getting off parole and, as usual, I had not been notified. So I wrote and faxed letters to the judge, John's attorney, and my attorney, and included a detailed step-by-step description of why I figured John was still out to murder me. The last time I felt threatened, I almost ended up dead. I learned my lesson. John isn't going to have the same advantage over me ever again. Not as long as I have a breath in my body!"

"Good for you," Elizabeth said. "Did it help?"

I leaned forward on the lunch table. "I thought so, but it just spurred John into action. He appeared in town four days ago, on Monday, as Admiral Perry no less, and claimed his stuff from storage. It's been eighteen months since he was released from prison. Why show up now to retrieve his stuff?"

"It is strange. The strangest thing I've ever heard," Elizabeth said.

I took a sip of my coffee, sat back in the chair, and grinned. "Yesterday I figured it must have something to do with my appointment with John's attorney to settle the case. Sure enough, Bradley called me and cancelled our appointment."

"Why?"

"John called him and said he was too upset to agree to any proposal. He said when he got his stuff back to Seattle he couldn't find any of his valuables, like his Rolex watch. That son of a bitch accused me of stealing all the good items and leaving him the dregs. What a liar!"

"Whew."

I continued my tale of woe, describing how I had fumed at Bradley and told him I made sure every box of John's was packed and labeled by friends, just to insure against this type of accusation. I had detailed lists for each box. I was ready to battle him in court. My friends would testify. I challenged the idea that John even *had* enough time to go through two hundred boxes in less than two days. My insides boiled just thinking about John's deceptive behavior.

"So what's up now?" Elizabeth asked.

"I don't know. I wish I knew what he was up to. I wish...I wish...Oh, my God!"

I jumped up and started to pace. "I just figured it out," I shrieked. "He's setting the stage to try to kill me! Once I'm dead he can go into court and claim he's due my estate because I didn't give him all of his joint property, and there will be no one to contest it. My mother's too old, and the rest of my family live out of state. He'll have his lawyer testify that several months ago John expressed remorse for what happened, and that he really missed the good times with me."

Elizabeth was speechless.

"I've got to go. I have letters to write and fax. I've got to stop John once and for all. Thanks for letting me vent. Without talking to you, I might not have figured it out." I grabbed Elizabeth, gave her a big hug, and whispered in her ear, "You helped save my life."

Back in my office, the phone line burned as I made calls to Judge Lawrence and Ross Grissom. Then I called Bradley. He tried to alleviate my fears and downplay John's actions, but I would have none of it. By this point, I knew John far too well. When Bradley suggested a final conference hearing on Saturday, at his office, I readily accepted, though I was apprehensive. Would this mess finally be over?

Saturday morning I woke up with a splitting headache and a pain in my gut. I had experienced another nightmare: John was chasing me with a knife and threatening to kill me. I took it as a warning and called Alan Bradley as soon as it was eight o'clock. "I can't meet you at your office," I said shakily. "I'm afraid John will try to kill me today."

"He's not here. He's in Seattle."

"You're on the third floor, right? My car will be in the parking lot for a couple of hours, unprotected. It would be easy for John to have someone tamper with it, maybe cut the brake line. Then I'll die in a car accident, like I was supposed to four years ago." Tears fell and I sobbed into the phone. "I'm not paranoid or delusional, and you're not the one who's suffered from John's psychopathic behavior."

"What do you suggest?" he asked.

"Let's meet somewhere neutral, and very public."

"How about the Pleasant Hill Park on Gregory Lane?"

I consented and we agreed to meet at our scheduled time. "Don't tell John," I added.

Two hours later I sat on a picnic bench with my two golden retrievers at my feet. It was a late-spring morning, warm and fresh. My cell phone rested on the table, next to my briefcase. The table was next to the parking lot where I'd left my car in full sight.

About five minutes later a sports car zipped through the parking lot and pulled in next to my car. A man in shorts and a golf shirt, carrying a briefcase, got out and walked my way.

"I didn't recognize you." I laughed. "You look different when you're not wearing a suit, almost human." He laughed, and it set the tone for an amicable working meeting. We both opened our briefcases and extracted papers.

"John agrees to everything except for three issues." *Here we go again*, I thought. "First, he wants to file separately on Concord's capital gains."

"Really?" I laughed. "That's what I've said for the last two years. Second?"

"John doesn't think the airline mileage voucher will work to transfer your share of the joint mileage."

"It will. He just has to sign it. You know what Judge Lawrence thinks about this item. What's the third wish for the genie?"

Bradley handed me a list. John wanted six of the twelve Waterford hocks, the Anthony Quinn vellum, the blue goose cookie jar, the modernistic statue acquired in Spain, and the bathroom scale. Would John's greed never end? I looked at the dogs at my feet and embraced the sun on my face. Peace settled over me.

"You've got a deal," I said, "provided I get three of the last six annuity checks that have remained uncashed, and that John pays to have Martinez Moving pick up these last few items and the Mercedes 450SL at my house."

Bradley looked relieved. "I didn't think you'd give them up." I shrugged my shoulders. "They're only things. My peace of mind is more important. I want John Perry out of my life."

As Bradley drove away, I remained at the table feeling smug. I was no longer John's potential victim; there was nothing he would gain financially from my death. I grabbed the morning paper and turned to my horoscope. It read, *You know all the right things to say and do today. Others welcome your leadership. A recent success could make you feel heady; do not act foolishly.*

TWENTY-FIVE

The Stakes

The melodrama of my meeting with Alan Bradley in Pleasant Hill Park strengthened my resolve to change the unfair no-fault divorce law of California. Although I was at peace with the agreement, the journey to get to a place where I could feel safe and let go had been long and arduous. It wasn't right. No attempted-murder victim should have to undergo this additional trauma.

I returned home after the meeting with Bradley and reread the rejection letter from Assemblyman Campbell. It irritated me. Why should it take a year to get my assemblyman to take a stand, one way or the other, on a request from his constituent? Campbell indicated that a change in the law would be a major departure from the state's longstanding history of no-fault divorce, and it wasn't his specialty. He was afraid to buck the system, but he provided me with a list of family law legislators.

I had forgotten about the list of names and now read it with the curiosity of a prospector looking for a lost gold mine on a torn map. I didn't recognize any names in the family law section and moved on to public safety. Bates…Gotch…Isenberg…Lee…Rainey. I stopped. Dick Rainey was the former sheriff of Contra Costa County. I had met him when he came to Excelsior to give a campaign speech. I immediately wrote him a letter. Three weeks later, in June 1994, I sat in front of him in his Walnut Creek district office, crying as I told him what had happened and why I wanted to change the law.

"Your story is a tragic case. The law is ludicrous and must be changed. I'll carry your legislation."

I inhaled deeply and moved a wadded tissue to my eyes to dab at the happy tears. "Thank you," I whispered.

"The next step," Dick said, "is to get the bill written. You'll need to help my legislative aide to do that."

From my first utterance in Belli's office, it had taken me nineteen months to get someone to agree to help me change the law. What I didn't realize as I walked out of Dick's office was that a new set of struggles was just beginning.

Now I had another ball to juggle in the many that made up my life—work, the law, my book, victims' rights, and fighting John in divorce court. I looked for opportunities to advance each one. During the International Women's Writing Guild's annual summer writers' conference, I connected with Nancy Weber, a nurse and psychic, who helped the police solve crimes. I asked Nancy to do a psychic reading on John. She said she had to hold something that person had touched, so I told her I would mail what I could find at home.

"Fine," she said. "We'll set up two half-hour phone conferences, one for his past and one for his future." I left at the end of the week looking forward to the readings.

A month later, my mother and I made our first trip to Sacramento to meet with Rainey's legislative aide, Eric Burlington. It wasn't that I needed the emotional support; I just liked taking my mother along to give her a change of scenery. I knew the trip would be successful. That morning my inspirational calendar told me, *Today, maintain your purpose in life, act on it, don't just wish for it to happen. Persevere in your attempts to achieve your goal.*

"What do you want to do with the bill?" Eric asked.

"I want to give financial protection to victims of spousal attempted murder in divorce court. I don't want the perpetrator to be able to get half the victim's retirement fund, to be able to collect alimony from the victim, or to have the victim pay the perpetrator's medical and car insurance until the divorce is final."

"Have you had any luck writing a draft?"

"No. My divorce attorney keeps putting me off. I can't get him to commit."

"That's okay. I'll have the legislative counsels work on a draft. Then I'll ask for your comments and revisions. In the meantime, you need to start looking for a sponsor for your bill."

Eric explained that the sponsor is the group that spearheads getting support for a bill and rounds up witnesses to testify before the committees. I scribbled notes as fast as I could while he talked. This was important stuff, and I didn't want to forget a word.

My mother and I gathered our things and got up to leave. As we walked toward the door, I turned around and looked Eric directly in the eye. "I am going to change the law," I said.

Two weeks later, on October 6, 1994, I stood in the American Airlines terminal at JFK International Airport in New York, waiting for the commuter flight to take me to Hartford, Connecticut. I was on my way to a writers' retreat and workshop. I strolled around concourse D, killing time. At gate 49, the door opened and a planeload of passengers spilled into the area.

With nothing better to do, I watched as they deplaned. A middle-aged woman in a black business suit emerged, then a bald man with a wrinkled coat, followed by a couple of thirtysomething men carrying briefcases. Next, an older man in a Burberry raincoat and Stetson...*oh my God! No, it couldn't be. What's he doing here? He's no longer on parole. Is he following me?* My heart pounded. My breathing escalated. The man wearing the raincoat and Stetson hat was John. He moved to one side, checked his itinerary, and looked at the direction sign above. Then he winced as he limped to the next gate and sat down.

Fearfully, I melted into the wall and crept along it until I got to my departure gate. I sidled up to the podium, as close to the gate agent as I could get, checking the concourse all the while. "The man who tried to murder me just got off the plane at gate 49," I panted. "He may be following me. He may try again to kill me."

The agent escorted me behind the partition, out of sight, and listened intently as I spilled my story between sobs. "Stay here. Let me check out the flights," he soothed. After five minutes that seemed more like five hours, the agent slipped around the corner with a passenger manifest in his hand and a security guard behind him. "I confirmed that a John Perry was on the flight from Geneva, Switzerland," the agent said. "He's booked on a connecting flight to Seattle that leaves in two hours."

A coincidence. It was a coincidence, albeit a highly emotional one! I stayed behind the podium with the security guard until time to board my flight. Even after all this time, seeing John made me panic and stirred up demons I thought I had laid to rest. My emotions spilled into my writing over the next ten days. When I shared the encounter that night with the writing group, I was told it was the strangest event to have happened on the way to one of the retreats. "Great! Now I get to add you to my 'this is the strangest case I've known' fan club." I laughed.

In late October, a week before her retirement, my friend Pam popped into my office and invited me to join her for lunch, with the added caveat that I could reconnect with our former workmate, Rex John-ston, who was meeting her at the Potato Barge. I accepted.

During lunch the three of us laughed as we recounted stories from our lab days. We brought each other up to date on what we had been up to for the last couple of years, including some about my encounter with a psychopath. On that one, we didn't laugh. Before we parted, Rex invited us to a dinner party at his house on the third Friday of November.

The following week Rex was gone on a Mexico vacation and I dealt with the devastating loss of my beloved golden retriever Gobi only four days after our re-acquaintance lunch. At fourteen-and-a-half, Gobi had lived a good life, but it was hard to let him go. I couldn't stop crying. I took two days off from work to grieve then concentrated on my job, getting rid of John, and changing the law. When Rex returned the first week of November, I invited him to the Justice for Murder Victims dinner dance in San Francisco, which was a week before his own dinner party. We enjoyed each other's company on both occasions. With success at hand, I extended an invitation to him to join my mom and me for Thanksgiving dinner at my house, and he gladly accepted with an offer to bring a smoked turkey. I insisted he also bring his small dog, Taffy. The dinner was delicious, Rex's laugh was infectious, and our pets integrated with ease. Rex told my mom the story of how his ex-wife had adopted Taffy at the Oakland SPCA a day before the dog was to be snuffed. It seemed that no one wanted a one-year-old scraggily blond mixed terrier with a horrendous overbite complicated by too many teeth. I picked Taffy up and gave her an extra long hug. Mom eagerly engaged in the conversation and, after Rex left, she commented that he looked and acted somewhat like my dad. Her observation shocked me. She was right. Rex, from Illinois, had some of the same Midwestern traits of my dad, who was born and raised in Kansas, and they were of similar build and coloring.

Rex and I started to date, slowly. With each date I noticed that our common interests and values meshed into a comfortable relationship. I had trusted my Higher Power. My trust was not misplaced, in either my Higher Power or in Rex.

Many mystical happenings have no obvious explanation but produce amazing results. My first psychic reading with Nancy Weber had been one such. She told me things about John's past that chilled me, including that he had murdered three women in the Miami area around 1960. Nancy also "saw" events that coincided with what John's stepmother had told me, things that Nancy would have no way of knowing. Eerie. Now I sat perched on the edge of my chair at work at the end of November, ready for the second reading. It was noon and Nancy was due to call any minute. We were going to deal with John's future.

I jumped when the phone rang. Nancy said she was holding John's photograph and his money clip once more, and that visions were popping into her head. "This time I see money being exchanged for shipments of something...crates with straw sticking out...and the something is being imported illegally."

I hadn't told her John was importing plants. What she said chilled me. "I see him with connections in Zurich...something about arms dealers and money laundering."

"Oh, Nancy, I ran into John in the airport when he was on his way home from Geneva, not too far away from Zurich."

"You're always in danger from him, Barbara. Especially if he thinks you are following him." I took heed of her ominous warning. I would watch my step, even more than I was already doing. When I didn't think it could get any worse, it did.

"John's connected with a woman," Nancy continued. "When he gets this way, he gets violent and possessive. But it's not jealousy; it has to do with possession of wealth, and it's starting to happen."

Her prognostications turned darker. "It's dangerous for her to be with him," Nancy said. "He's going to try to murder her. He's a sociopath with psychopathic serial tendencies. You've got to warn her and let her know her life is in danger, but you must do it anonymously."

When the consultation ended I sat like a zombie, mulling over all the details I had scribbled on my white lined paper. I had to share this amazing event with someone. I went to Elizabeth's office and told her what Nancy said. "What are you going to do?" she gulped.

"I don't know, but I trust in my Higher Power. He will give me the way."

For three months I worked diligently on the bill. Finding a sponsor was paramount to my success, so I wrote letters, made phone calls, and visited offices, to no avail. No one was interested in taking on my cause, including my divorce attorney. Oh, they all agreed the law needed to be changed, and they would support me. They just didn't have the staff to commit. More likely, they lacked my passion.

However, Eric Burlington worked with the Democratic and Republican legislative counsels to structure the bill, and I had the opportunity to review their results. The legal language was strange to me, and I was often confused, especially regarding a section on fiduciary duty. I didn't understand why the bill amended both family law and the civil code, when the bill was to address a divorce issue only.

One afternoon, Eric called me. "We have a number. It's Assembly Bill Sixteen."

"Sweet sixteen. Never been kissed." I laughed, then slipped back to serious. "Are we ready for next week?"

"Rainey has five bills he's carrying this year," Eric continued, "but he can only introduce one on the floor on opening day. He's chosen AB Sixteen."

"Mine? Assembly Bill Sixteen?"

I asked if I could come up; Eric advised saving my vacation time for the committee hearings. He was right. It would have been a waste to drive to Sacramento for the opening day; it was a fiasco.

The political climate was explosive. Democrats and Republicans were equally represented and the speaker, Willie Brown, who was supposed to step down, refused to relinquish his seat. There was a lot of yelling. Because no regular business could be conducted until the speaker issue was settled, no bills were introduced. A rumor began to spread that not much would get passed in this year's session if the assemblymen voted on party lines. My bill was in limbo.

I have learned to trust my Higher Power, and I find that I'm given what I need when I need it. In mid-December, Hal Ledman, the man who had helped John with his parole plan, called me in a panic. "John's criminal activities are continuing," he complained. "He's not who he says he is. I believe you now. I'm sorry I didn't talk to you first before letting him come live with me." Hal relayed that John was no longer living with him, that he had moved in with Trudy, a sixty-five-year-old woman who owned a twenty-acre ranch in Redmond, thirty miles east of Seattle. Hal was a long-time friend with Trudy and her brother.

I thought it strange he would call and cry on my shoulder. Then I remembered my conversation with Nancy and realized I was being given the moment I needed to warn the woman who was living with John. This man was her friend. "You must warn Trudy. John is going to try to murder her, but you can't say it came from me." He agreed to talk to Trudy's brother, and the two of them would approach her. "Her life depends on it," I warned.

In December, Rex and I cultivated relationships with friends and merged closer together. We attended George's sixtieth birth-day party. We took our first trip together to a romantic cabin on the Mendocino coast, accompanied by our dogs, Taffy and Gaby, who made us laugh as Taffy dodged the crashing waves and Gaby pounced into the foaming surf. We spent Christmas with my mom at Pam and George's home.

We renewed our friendship with Cathy and Carl Crenshaw, a couple from our Excelsior Chemical days, and attended a New Year's Eve dinner and party with them at Snooker Pete's restaurant. The party crowd counted down the seconds. Rex squeezed my hand. At midnight we clinked glasses, sipped champagne, and lingered over a tender kiss. *It feels good to trust someone's arms.* We toasted with Cathy and Carl. *It feels good to trust friendships.* I thought about the challenges that lay ahead: balancing a budding relationship with changing the law, writing a book, and legally eliminating John from my life. *It feels good to trust my Higher Power.* When the crowd broke into a raucous rendition of "Auld Lang Syne," I fought back tears of joy and struggled to join in the lyrics. *I'm too emotional, just like my mom.*

TWENTY-SIX

The Sponsor

At lunch on a Wednesday in February 1995, I sat at my desk nibbling a tuna sandwich while editing the latest procedure for the global quality team. The double ring of the telephone startled me; I wasn't expecting a call. I quickly swallowed and answered. A soft female voice introduced herself.

"I'm Anne Dunsmuir, a legislative aide from Assemblyman Rainey's office. Dick asked me to take over your bill from Eric Burlington."

I felt uncomfortable about the change. I wondered if Rainey thought my bill didn't have a chance, and worried that Anne might not be as competent as Eric.

"Will this change anything?" I asked.

"It shouldn't. I've reviewed the file and I'm excited to be working with you to get AB Sixteen through the system."

She asked for background information. I wanted her to hear the passion in my voice and understand how dedicated I was to changing the law. "One thing has troubled me, Anne. I haven't been able to find a sponsor, and I've been trying for almost six months. Can you help?"

"You *have* a sponsor, Barbara," Anne said.

"What?"

"Look in the mirror. *You* are the sponsor."

"But...I'm not an organization."

"Haven't you been writing letters? Haven't you been directing the outcome of the bill? Aren't you the driving force?"

"Yes, but..."

I suddenly realized that through my efforts during the last several months I had evolved into the sponsor of AB16, as an individual, not an organization. My shoulders sagged under the weight of this added responsibility.

"The sponsor of my own bill, huh?"

"That's right," Anne giggled. "Now you need to get some public support and think about who will testify with you. The heat is on. The bill was introduced into the assembly this morning and has been assigned to the Judiciary Committee."

"It's really happening," I said, choking with emotion. It had been more than two months since Willie Brown disrupted the new session by refusing to step down. My bill, along with everyone else's, had languished in the interim.

"The hearing has been scheduled for May seventeenth," Anne said. "Just about three months from now."

"What do I need to do?"

"Write letters to the committee members, asking for their support. I'll fax you a list of members. I'll be at Dick's office in Walnut Creek in a couple of weeks. Maybe you could come by and we could meet face to face."

"It's a date," I said, scribbling a note in my organizer. When our conversation ended, I hung up the phone and squealed out loud. I had to release my excitement somehow. Good thing no one walked by my office at that moment.

Five minutes later I pulled the list of names off the fax machine and settled back. There were fourteen members of the Assembly Judiciary Committee. That evening, while visiting Rex, I wrote my first round of letters to the committee members. Rex believed in me. He believed in my quest to change the law. I smiled as he plopped down beside me, grabbed the stuffed envelopes, licked them closed, and stamped them.

Two weeks later I sat with Anne in Rainey's regional office in Walnut Creek. I was confident as I outlined my recent activities that ranged from writing letters to getting a video produced. Then Anne dropped a bombshell.

"We're starting to get negative feedback. The way the bill is worded and the sections of law it is trying to amend, both civil and family codes, are causing concern. Because the bill has become controversial, it has been assigned two hearings. The first is scheduled on April nineteenth for the punitive damages; the second will be on May third or seventeenth for the family law portion."

The news upset me. These new hurdles seemed higher than the previous ones. I didn't know if I could negotiate them in order to win the race.

"I'm worried," I said. "What can I do to pull AB Sixteen back into a positive light?"

"We have to keep the judges neutral," Anne warned. "If they come out against it, AB Sixteen is dead. Marty Montano, who works for the California Judges Association, told me the judges are coming out against it."

I looked her square in the eye. "I'll do whatever it takes to win them over," I said.

When Marty Montano ignored my letter for more than three weeks, I called him. He told me the judges were against Assembly Bill 16 because they believed it would open up a whole new can of worms with the revision to the civil code. I explained my goal. Marty was sympathetic, but stood his ground.

"The judges are against changing a thirty-year-old law they fought hard to develop and implement in order to alleviate a lot of unnecessary courtroom antics."

"But we have changed some words."

Marty would not budge. I asked him what could be done to have the group at least remain neutral. I can be stubborn, too, especially when an important issue is on the table. Marty and I went back and forth, neither of us willing to move, when out of the blue a potential connection between us popped into my mind.

"By the way, did your dad work for Excelsior?" I asked.

"Yes."

"What a small world! I worked with your dad over twenty years ago. My first husband and I took your family's portrait at our house in Concord."

"Oh, my gosh," he exclaimed. "I was in that photo."

"All I can remember is that there were a lot of kids." I laughed. "And it was hard to get everyone to smile at the same time."

I had brazenly joined the "good-old-boy network," and it didn't let me down. Marty agreed to reevaluate AB16; he'd try to come up with wording that might appease the judges. I thanked him profusely, hung up the phone, and immediately dialed Anne to give her the good news.

Anne reciprocated with good news of her own. She told me Rainey had received a compliment about me from a representative of the California Federation of Republican Women.

"I remember talking to her," I said. "She teaches advocacy at the local college. She was very helpful, gave me lots of information on lobbying, and suggested whom to target on the committee. At her request, I sent her my appeal letter."

Once more in my journey, I had been given the right people at the right time to help me or teach me new skills. In less than a month I would use this new insight as I rattled around the halls of the capitol.

* * *

Two weeks later, in Sacramento, Rex and I set up my folding table, chair, signs, pens, and box of petitions near the sunny eastern entrance of the state capitol. Today was another new adventure for the sponsor of AB16, and a bold one. I had invited myself to participate in a victims' rights ceremony.

The crowd began to swell. It was close to lunchtime, and my table generated interest from victims' rights supporters, curious visitors, and the press. A man walked up to me, handed me his card, and said he was a reporter for the *Oakland Tribune*. "I'll watch for your testimony," he said.

Anne came down to check on my progress and prompt me for my speech. "Can you get it to me by Friday?" she asked.

"Sure." I knew it would be easy to capture my passion on paper.

"I'm still working with the legislative counsel on some amendments, to see if we can keep Isenberg from killing the bill. You need to be available for the next couple of days."

I frowned. "I'll be in training classes the next two days, and away from my desk, but I'll check in with you during morning and afternoon breaks, if that's okay."

"That'll work," Anne said. "What about your witnesses for next week?"

"All three are confirmed."

"You've done a great job as a sponsor, Barbara," she added.

It was time for participants to clear our tables and move to the big white tent set up on the lawn behind us. After the catered lunch, State Attorney General Dan Lundgren gave a moving speech about victims' rights. That ended the program. I gathered my courage, made my way to the podium, and introduced myself to Mr. Lundgren.

"I'm the sponsor of AB Sixteen," I said. "I'm in the process of changing the no-fault divorce law to help victims."

"I wish you well," he said, with a broad smile and a strong handshake. "Keep up your good work."

TWENTY-SEVEN

The Lobbyist

Six days before I was to testify before the Assembly Judiciary Committee, I sat trapped in a training class at work, counting the minutes to the morning break, and when the instructor released the class, I bolted down the hall, desperate to reach the phone bank before the others from my class got there. I had to know whether the bill I sponsored had survived the night.

When I reached the communication room there was, thank heaven, one available phone. I took that as a positive sign. I punched in the number for Assemblyman Rainey's office, set my notepad on the shelf, and held my pen poised for the notes I wanted to take.

The phone rang and rang. While I waited for someone to answer, I reviewed my notes from yesterday's phone conversations with Anne Dunsmuir, Rainey's legislative aide. I was sure the wait would be worth it. Anne would get on the phone, set my mind at ease, and assure me that my Assembly Bill 16 was not in trouble, after all. Wouldn't she?

Uneasy, I realized I expected no such thing. I expected trouble.

Still, I was glad Rainey had assigned Anne to work with me on the assembly bill I was sponsoring to change California's divorce laws. Anne was bright, effervescent, and an extremely helpful guide through the many mysteries of politics. At twenty-eight, she had proven to be a remarkably mature confidante as well. There was no doubt in my mind that if the bill was still in trouble, she would do all she could to help me turn things around, and she'd tell me the truth whether it was what I wanted to hear or not.

Yesterday she'd informed me that the chairman of the Assembly Judiciary Committee, Phil Isenberg, was not happy with the wording of AB16. She had met with the committee's counsels and with Isenberg's legislative aide and massaged it once more. When she faxed me their revision for my approval, she expressed the belief that the changes would satisfy Isenberg's concerns.

Nevertheless I worried, because before she hung up Anne asked me to phone her this morning, and there was a cautionary tone in her voice.

As I waited for her to come on the line I glanced at my notes. The words in front of me blurred as my eyes misted. AB16 and I had been a team for an arduous two years. Passion, patience, and persistence had brought us this far, abetted by my organizational skills, my attention to detail, and the copious records I'd amassed. Feeling optimistic again, I looked forward to next Wednesday, when AB16 and I could...no, *would*...finally have our hearing before the Assembly Judiciary Committee. All of us, my witnesses and I, were lined up and ready to testify. The bill had to make it out of committee. If not, that would be the end of it.

"Barbara?"

Finally!

"Sorry," Anne said breathlessly. "I was in Marty's office."

I wet my lips. "So? What's the word from Isenberg?"

There was an uncomfortable silence. My palms began to sweat; my heart beat faster.

"I'm sorry, Barbara," Anne said when she finally spoke.

No, I thought. *Don't say it. Please don't!* I held my breath.

When she did say it, I thought I might collapse. "Sorry, he still wants to kill the bill."

I couldn't speak.

"Barbara? Barbara? Are you still there?" Anne yelled into the telephone. "Did you hear what I said?"

My heart pounded. This was the all-important call I had awaited with such mixed feelings, and Anne had just confirmed my worst fears. "I'm here, Anne. I can't believe Isenberg still wants to kill my bill. We've worked so hard these last couple of days...the faxes...the editing...the phone calls. My God, what else does this man want?"

"His aide said he still doesn't like the wording."

"The wording? We've changed it a dozen times."

"You know Isenberg; he's a lawyer, so he scrutinizes all the legal implications."

Anne always explained legal matters in terms I could understand. I appreciated her for that. "Well, I'm no lawyer," I answered, "but I know what I want the bill to do. Quite honestly, the way it's written has always confused me. Why does it have to be tied to that section on fiduciary duty?"

"I don't know. Anyway, it's what the committee came up with."

When I decided to get the California divorce law changed, I asked my divorce attorney to help me draw up the bill. He turned me down. Too busy, he said. Or maybe he just didn't want to get involved. I approached other groups. They didn't want to get caught up in something that looked like a losing battle. It was always the same old story; there wasn't a snowball's chance in hell to change the law. Damn sacrosanct no-fault divorce! Ultimately I had to rely on the Republican legislative counsel and legislative committee to draft the bill. Perhaps I had misplaced my trust. The wording had become a major roadblock.

"We'll need a miracle," Anne said. "Without the chairman behind the bill, we can kiss it good-bye. He told his legislative aide to pull it from next Wednesday's agenda."

"He can't. I have witnesses all lined up to testify."

"He can do anything he wants."

Her words stung. I leaned against the wall. I had not come this far to let one man blow away what I knew must be done. Deep inside me, anger and frustration bubbled up and took control. Out of some deep survival instinct, I uttered words that astounded even me. "Guess I'll have to come up next Tuesday and lobby the committee assemblymen on my own."

Lobby? I knew nothing about lobbying, but I believed that if the committee members saw me and heard me, they would see my point of view. I was so naïve.

"That's fourteen offices, Barbara."

"Fourteen, huh?" I had to change my strategy fast. "Okay. I'll come up Monday and Tuesday."

"Good plan," Anne said.

I hung up, determined not to let AB16 languish and die in some fusty old committee.

The following Monday morning I arrived at the capitol ready for battle, spiffed up in a smart two-piece navy print dress with jacket and clutching my black briefcase. It was a businesslike look I hoped would impress committee members and get their attention, then their support.

I found Assemblyman Rainey's office, took a deep breath, and entered a small reception area. A pleasant-looking woman in her early forties stood, removed her reading glasses, and extended her right hand.

"Hi, I'm Daisy. You must be Barbara. Anne told us you were coming today." I shook her hand and quickly scanned the room. I saw no one else. I shivered even though the room was warmed by sunlight streaming in the large windows.

"Yes. I have an appointment with Anne at nine. Is she here yet?"

"I'm sorry, she won't be in. She called in sick just a few minutes ago."

Another roadblock. I squeezed my briefcase handle. *Breathe, Barbara, breathe.* It took all my concentration to keep smiling, even though I was close to tears.

"Don't worry," Daisy continued. "Anne said you could use her office. She's really sorry. But she says you'll do fine."

Daisy walked around her desk and pointed me to one of two small offices at the end of the reception area. "Make yourself at home. Coffee's in the kitchenette, back the other way. Let me know if you need anything."

"Thanks," I whispered, knowing Daisy would be unable to provide what I needed. I would have to find it on my own.

I trudged into the cluttered office, cleared a space on the desk, and laid my briefcase down. I glanced back into the reception area and focused on the light streaming through the windows. Because I needed every bit of self-encouragement I could muster, I took it as a positive sign that I would prevail. Without Anne, though, the day ahead looked bleak and ominous.

I unzipped my briefcase and took out the ammunition I had prepared for my assault: fourteen letters, one for each committee member, containing the picture of my swollen, bruised face, photographed after John's murderous attack. I planned to visit the offices by area, to conserve energy and time.

Daisy stuck her head in the door. "One more thing. Anne said it would be hard to see assembly members on such short notice, without an appointment, so first introduce yourself. Then ask to speak to the legislative aide handling AB Sixteen."

"Thanks."

I grabbed the first stack of letters, my notepad, and my pen and headed toward the door.

"Here goes the lobbyist," I giggled, "a very nervous lobbyist pushing off into uncharted waters."

"You'll have smooth sailing." Daisy smiled. "The wind is at your back."

Perhaps I was wrong. Daisy did have something to offer me—her kindness and encouragement.

Off I went, into the dark depths of the capitol. It didn't matter that I was the most inexperienced lobbyist roaming the halls. I was on an adventure, armed with passion, patience, and persistence, a trio that had helped me rise like a phoenix out of my tragedy. Together we were strong and effective. I entered the first office full of fire and met immediate resistance.

"Who's the sponsor of your bill?" the middle-aged receptionist asked.

"I am."

"No, I mean which group is sponsoring the bill?"

"I am. There is no group. It's just me, an ordinary citizen."

The receptionist furrowed her brow, pursed her lips, and shook her head. "It's a hectic Monday morning. Come back later, in the afternoon."

Undaunted, I recorded this on my notepad and prepared for my next assault. My lobbying juices started to flow. It would be a morning fraught with frustration, when negativity chilled the air and my spirits sagged. It would be a morning of exhilaration, when positive remarks warmed my soul and my spirits soared. Each office responded differently, and when I even lobbied in the hallway, as I caught one legislative aide dashing out to the travel office, I was proud of my ability to think on my feet and survive under pressure.

Right before lunch I dashed up to the sixth floor to deliver my most important letter of all, the one to Assembly Judiciary Committee Chairman Phil Isenberg. His office, with its intimidating set of double doors, stood alone and smacked of importance even before I entered. I took a deep breath and slipped inside. It was elegant, richly paneled in wood and handsomely decorated. I approached the smiling receptionist and repeated my now-familiar introduction.

"Have a seat," she said. "I've paged the legislative aide. He'll be just a few moments."

Around me, men and women hurried about. Busy, busy, busy. More than once my heart skipped a beat as a man approached, only to say good morning before he left the office through the double doors. It felt like hours had passed, but it was only minutes according to the antique clock on the wall behind the receptionist. Finally, a tall, lanky man with sandy brown hair approached, smiled, and extended his hand.

"Let's go into the library," he said. "It's quieter and more conducive to conversation."

I sidestepped a pile of law books and seated myself at a round wooden table covered with stacks of books and a few single volumes, laid open. *This is where it all happens,* I thought.

"Isenberg's sure to like the bill now that the revised language has been inserted," he said, sitting down opposite me. "Requiring a felony conviction for attempted murder in order for the law to apply tightens it up."

"Wait a minute. Anne told me last Friday that Isenberg still wants to kill the bill, even with the new language." I could still hear her words and feel my fear.

"She must be mistaken. He hasn't seen the new wording yet. I can't imagine why he would be against it now. I'm going to push him on it. It's a law that makes good sense."

I pressed my luck. "Would it be possible to have an appointment with Mr. Isenberg today so I can discuss AB Sixteen with him personally?" I pleaded. I realized this would be the only way to discover where he stood. Enough of this middleman stuff; I needed to talk to the main man.

"I wish I could accommodate you, but his schedule is very tight. He serves on five committees, and two of them meet today. He's at the first right now. After lunch he'll be in the second one until the end of the day."

That was not what I came to hear. *Do something, Barbara!* I mustered my persistence and my passion and found the answer. "What time does Mr. Isenberg leave for his afternoon session?"

"It starts at one thirty. He usually leaves about one fifteen."

"Could I meet him here at the office and walk with him to his meeting?"

"You sure are one determined lady. Let me check with his schedule."

He sauntered over to the receptionist's desk. After a short discussion, she made a call, then wrote something down while I kept my fingers crossed. "You're on," the aide said when he walked back into the library.

"See you at one fifteen," the receptionist said. I gathered my things and floated toward the massive double doors. I had just done the impossible...gotten a same-day appointment with the chairman of the Assembly Judiciary Committee.

At lunch in the nearby cafeteria I snatched a leftover newspaper and flipped it open to the horoscopes. I had become a horoscope junkie ever since John tried to murder me. It was amazing how many applied, like guiding beacons of light showing the way, or reflecting my past actions. Virgo. My finger traced down the page. What did Jeane Dixon have for me today? I gasped as I read, *Influential people like the way you think and work.* Why not? After all, Isenberg had agreed to meet me. *Your business acumen helps you meet an important deadline.* My testimony was only two days off. Maybe I'd be able to testify on Wednesday. *New fame and fortune will follow. Keep your own counsel about emotional or financial concerns.* Did this mean my bill would pass to help others?

My heart raced. It was a wonder how the words fit so closely to my day. I ripped out the horoscope and stuffed it into my briefcase, another addition for my expanding horoscope file.

After lunch I arrived five minutes early. I couldn't take a chance that I'd be late for my golden opportunity. Fifteen long minutes passed before a man wearing a navy jacket and tan pants came rushing out from the back, carrying a briefcase. I stood, sensing this was the big moment. I could scarcely breathe.

"I understand you won't take no for an answer," Isenberg said, smiling. "I admire determination." He extended his hand and apologized for being late.

He took my arm as we left the office and led me through an unmarked door to a narrow, crowded hallway. "Welcome to the assemblymen's labyrinth," he said. "It's a shortcut to the assembly wing. Careful. It gets a little tight as we all rush to our afternoon meetings."

What a thrill! Here I was, walking in a secure pathway designed for the restricted use of legislators alone. My high heels clicked on the shiny linoleum floor as I tried to keep up with Isenberg's long-striding gait.

"I appreciate what you're trying to do," he started, "but the language of AB Sixteen could create all sorts of legal ramifications. For example, the bill does not specify any difference between a felony conviction and a misdemeanor conviction. Also, there's the embedded fiduciary duty and family sections that muddy up the water."

"Frankly, I've always been confused about the fiduciary duty and family sections." I began, then proceeded to explain what had happened to me, the unjustness of the current divorce law, and what I was trying to accomplish with AB16. I bombarded him with words as we maneuvered our way down two short flights of stairs and around several bends in the tube. "All I want is to protect crime victims from being victimized again, financially and emotionally, by the divorce law," I pleaded. "I want to protect their retirement funds, and block alimony, insurance, and medical payments to the criminal."

"I understand. However…"

"Last Thursday we changed the language of the bill so it applies only for criminal convictions. Haven't you read it yet?"

He stopped walking and I bumped into him. Had I gone too far?

Should I apologize? Hell no! I was in this to win, working like a dog to get the wording right, and I wasn't going to back down now. I held my breath and noticed that we were now in the middle of a solarium, a large area drenched in light with potted ferns and seating areas. The journey was almost over. Maybe I was, too.

"My committee room is just ahead," Isenberg said. He held out his hand. Mine trembled as I took it.

"You know," I said, "I had to trust in the committee I've been working with on the language. They're the experts, not me. But we did limit it to a felony conviction."

Isenberg nodded and relaxed his grip. "All right, I'll take another look at the bill tonight. If what you say is true, I'll have no objection."

I thanked him and he disappeared into the committee room. My rubbery legs gave way. I melted onto the nearest bench, exhausted, but exhilarated and ecstatic. I jotted down his support in my notebook, checked my watch, and evaluated my list. There was no time to rest.

At the end of the afternoon, I trudged into Anne's office and collapsed into her chair. It had been quite a day for a new-fledged lobbyist. Pen in hand, I recorded *yea* or *nay* by each assemblyman's name, for those whose vote I could determine.

I had made it to all fourteen offices, and only six had rescheduled me for tomorrow. I did the math. I had achieved a fifty-seven percent success rate for visits, but the *nay*s on my list worried me. To get my bill out of committee I'd need more than fifty percent of the vote on Wednesday, even with the support of the chairman, which I now felt I had.

Daisy poked her head into the office. "Good news. Anne called. She's coming in tomorrow."

It was music to my ears. I needed all the moral and tactical support I could get. I retrieved my horoscope and reread it. I smiled. *Yup, Jeane Dixon, you were right on.*

*   *   *

The next morning Anne eagerly greeted my mother and me. She led me into her cubicle. I was jazzed to finish up the job I had started yesterday. "I've got good news and bad news," Anne said. "Which do you want first?"

"The good news, I guess."

"Okay, Isenberg no longer wants to kill the bill. Your little walk-and-talk impressed him."

"And the bad news?" I braced myself for what Anne would say.

"Isenberg wants to table the bill, put it on next year's calendar. He believes in what you're trying to do, but is still bothered by the civil code portion."

It was that wording about fiduciary stuff, still a roadblock after all our work. I'd have to learn a lot more about writing a bill, and I'd have a year to do it.

"Well, at least it's not dead. That's positive, I suppose." I couldn't quite contain my disappointment. "Does this mean our hearing tomorrow is canceled?"

"Yes, unfortunately it does."

I let out a deep sigh and hung my head as I fought to keep the tears from coming. I had battled through two long years of telephone calls, letters, and faxes, all pleading, prompting, cajoling. To come so close, only to face a delay of one more year was hard to accept. I had spent so much time getting witnesses lined up. Oh, no! "Anne, I've got to call all the witnesses and tell them not to come." I snatched the witness phone list from my briefcase. Within half an hour I reached them all, apologizing and thanking them profusely. Fortunately, no one had yet left for Sacramento. As I hung up the phone from the last call Anne bounced into the office, with a happy smile on her face.

"You're not going to believe this," she said. "Isenberg's legislative aide called me a couple of minutes ago. The counsels and attorneys and aides want to give it one more try...with you!"

"Me?"

"Yes. They believe in your cause so much they want to work

with you to see if the bill can be reworded and revived in time for the scheduled hearing tomorrow."

I jumped out of the chair, hugged Anne, and grinned at my mother. Things were happening too fast, throwing me off guard and taking my breath away. I couldn't stand still.

"The biggest surprise," Anne said, "is that Isenberg encouraged the meeting. What a great start for a first-time lobbyist! You brought around the powerhouse of the committee in five minutes."

An hour later I sat once more at the round table in Isenberg's office library, amid the stacked law books, half-filled coffee cups, and piles of pads and papers. I was nervous in the presence of lawmaking specialists, flanked by Anne and the Democratic and Republican legislative counsels and two aggressive female attorneys.

We rolled up our sleeves and got to work. Or, rather, the assembled experts did. Round and round they went, tweaking this word and that. Legal jargon flew. I rubbed my temples, still confused over the fiduciary part they were discussing. I couldn't take it anymore. The pressure built up until I had to release some steam.

"Why can't you write this bill in plain everyday English?" I sputtered. Mouths shut. Heads turned. Eyes widened. They looked at me. They looked at each other. "And why must you include civil code in the bill when this is strictly a family code matter? Why not just say that the convicted criminal loses certain financial rights in the divorce."

Silence.

I gulped. Stupid me, thinking I could rewrite a bill. Then one by one, they spoke and said I was right. Law books were consulted and found unhelpful. "Nothing we can pick up. We'll just write a new section," the Republican legislative counsel said. "Who wants to transcribe?" Anne volunteered. She leaned forward in her chair, pulled her yellow legal pad closer, and picked up her pen. All eyes turned to me.

"Okay, Barbara. Here's your chance," the attorney said.

I prayed I would find the right words to make this come out okay. I inhaled deeply and began. Within an hour we had a new bill written in plain English. My bill, composed the way I wanted it.

"I'll inform Isenberg that the bill is clean, and all of his objections have been addressed," the Republican legislative counsel said. "I can't see why this shouldn't be a go tomorrow. It's still on the schedule."

Back in Anne's office, I got my next lesson on the way the legislative system works. "We have a clean bill, but it's a new bill," Anne said. "The legislative council will reprint and make copies of the new version of AB Sixteen, and you'll need to pick those up and distribute them to committee members before the end of the day."

The timing would be tight, very tight. The legislative aides would have to review the new, very different AB16 and prepare their position for the committee members to be able to vote the next day. Then it hit me.

"Anne, the witnesses I just dismissed...we need them again."

We scurried back to her office. I began furiously dialing the phone while Anne filled my mom in on the latest development. My mom gave me a thumbs-up through the open doorway.

After lunch in the cafeteria, we returned to Rainey's office and sat down. Anne was on the phone with other business. Daisy came around the corner. "Barbara, I have some messages for you from some of your witnesses." She thrust them into my trembling hand. "All good," she said. "They can all make it."

I closed my eyes. *Thank you, God.* This surely was a positive sign, like the rays of sunshine yesterday morning.

Every quarter hour over the next two hours, I hurried up to the third-floor printing office but came back empty-handed. My concern mounted as the minutes slipped away. Finally, at 3:25 p.m., Anne reported, "Just got the call. You can pick up the revised copies on the table in the hall just outside the printing office."

Now began a mad dash to fourteen offices, to convince fourteen legislative aides in less than an hour. Thank goodness I was wearing comfortable shoes. Time whizzed by when I needed it to crawl. Somehow, within an hour I met with each legislative aide, gave my two-minute spiel, slapped the new bill into their hand, and extracted a promise they would review it before making a recommendation. Each time I jotted down what I thought that recommendation would be.

I got on the elevator to go down to the fourth floor and recognized the aide for Assemblyman Murray, already inside. "I've been thinking about your bill," she said.

"All good, I hope."

She shook her head. "I'm worried the criminal would get to retirement age and have nothing but Social Security to live on."

"Excuse me, shouldn't you be thinking about the victim? Heck with the criminal." Bile rose in my throat.

"I've made up my mind to recommend a *nay* vote."

I looked daggers at her. "I hope you're never a victim," I said through clenched teeth. The doors opened and I stormed off the elevator.

Back in Anne's office, I reviewed my notes with her. "Looks like nine confirmed. We only need eight to get out of committee, right?"

"Yes, but legislators are a tricky bunch to read," Anne said. "I'd feel better if I knew for a fact that Isenberg was happy about this new rewrite."

My mother walked over, put her hand on my shoulder, and gave it a squeeze. "I'm sure it will be just fine," she said.

Later that evening, at the Holiday Inn near Old Sacramento, I stood by the window of our sixth-floor room and glanced over at my mom, lying on her bed, already resting from our long day. I was glad we had decided to stay in the city, avoiding the two-hour drive home tonight and the two-hour drive back to Sacramento tomorrow. My mom had been my rock during the last couple of years, always there if I needed her, never telling me "I told you so" when things went south with John. For that, I was grateful. Now I wondered if I told her often enough how much that meant to me.

I turned back and stared out the window. The Sacramento River meandered like a lazy snake along the western edge of the city, and the *Spirit of Sacramento* floated by, churning up the water with its fake paddle wheel. Mesmerized, I was drawn into the reflection of the setting sun in the river's dark current. It was time for the new lobbyist to rest to gear up for the big day.

TWENTY-EIGHT

The Assembly

The next morning I stood by the window in my hotel room in my white linen dress and watched the sun dance on the Sacramento River. *It's a sign,* I thought, *a good sign about my testimony today before the Assembly Judiciary Committee, for AB16 and changing the law.* I had plunged into the lawmaking game more than two years ago, a game I never thought I would be playing. I wasn't political. I had never considered holding a public office or changing legislation. Yet, here I was, in the state capital, learning something new each day about the rules of engagement. I was naïve, but I was on a mission, and I had fought hard to get here.

I picked up my speech and read it slowly, out loud, placing emphasis on the right words to make sure the assembly members would understand the importance of what I was saying.

"You'll do fine," my mom said, bringing me a cup of coffee. "You've always gotten whatever you put your mind to."

"Thanks, Mom. I know I can do it. I learned that I had a voice at Skidmore."

I sipped my coffee and smiled as I remembered the International Women's Writing Guild's empowering conference two years before at Skidmore College in Saratoga Springs, New York. Five days into the conference Hannelore Hahn, the inspirational founder of the guild, had approached me in the hallway and asked me to give a speech that night at the evening gathering.

I have come to believe we are offered doors of opportunity during our lives. Sometimes it's frightening to go into the unknown, so we resist, bracing our arms against the doorjamb and refusing to go through. But there's a reason we have that door—personal growth. If we don't go through, we may never again have the opportunity, and that would be tragic. So, with trepidation, I accepted her offer and went to my next workshop. After lunch I wrote my speech.

That evening, as I sat near the stage while Hannelore introduced me, I realized I was not nervous. No butterflies in my tummy. No pounding headache. No sweaty palms. It was as if speaking before four hundred women were a daily routine for me. When Hannelore called my name, I climbed the stairs and strolled to the podium, notes in hand. By the time I finished sharing my thoughts, I had the audience laughing, crying, and cheering. That night I learned I had a strong voice, one that could be used to help others.

I was going to use that voice today, when I did battle with the Assembly Judiciary Committee. My quest was at hand. Was I the lamb, about to be slaughtered? I looked at my wristwatch.

"We'd better go," I said. "We're supposed to meet Delores in the lobby for breakfast."

Delores Winje, from San Luis Obispo, was an outspoken voice against domestic violence. Several years earlier, her husband had shot her through the jaw, permanently disfiguring her face. As she recovered, she found her voice and became an advocate for change. She visited prisons and explained to perpetrators what their crimes did to the victims and their families.

We met with Delores and her friend at the hotel's coffee shop, and twenty minutes later four women with a passionate desire to make a change stormed the north face of the state capitol. We made our way to Rainey's office. As I opened the door, I bumped into the back of a man standing inside.

"Looks like a full house," I said to my group. "Better stay out here while I find out what's happening." I squeezed in. Daisy, the receptionist, caught my eye. "What's up?" I asked. "Why are there so many people?"

"It's always crazy on days when legislation is being presented in committee," she said. "I'll ring Anne for you. Why not wait outside where you can breathe."

Back in the bare hallway, I rejoined the ladies and glanced around, hoping to see my other two witnesses. They weren't in the motley group milling about. I checked my watch. It was almost 8:30. I tapped my foot and wet my lips. *Relax, stay calm*, I silently reminded myself. *Harriet and Kevin won't let you down*. But I kept staring at the corner. Lately I could go from confidence to doubt without much effort. That wouldn't do today. I had to remain strong. Thinking about how strong Harriet and Kevin were going to be as witnesses helped.

Harriet's teenage daughter, Catina Rose, was murdered in 1979. Stunned, and then abused by the criminal justice system, Harriet and her husband, Mike, became victims' rights advocates to help survivors deal with their grief and the inadequacies of the justice system during and after a criminal trial. It was the group I had turned to when I decided to help others.

Kevin Washburn, a tall, imposing man, was the president of Citizens for Law and Order, a group originally formed in 1970 as a response to the liberal policies of State Supreme Court Justice Rose Bird. Although originally focused on judges, the group decided to provide support to victims' rights groups. I met Kevin through Harriet and felt his voice would be forceful in the fight for AB16.

"Traffic was a bear," Harriet huffed as she rounded the corner and headed straight to me. We shook hands. "And the parking! Don't ask."

"Where's Kevin?" I questioned, looking around.

"Here I am," Kevin panted. "I tried to catch up with you, Harriet, but it wasn't easy."

A moment later, Dick Rainey turned the corner at the end of the hall and wove his way through the crowd, shaking hands and smiling. He disappeared into his office. I breathed easier knowing all my witnesses and my assemblyman had arrived.

I heard Anne call my name. "Over here," I gestured.

Anne made her way through the noisy crowd filling the hallway. I introduced her to my witnesses, and she gave us a brief rundown of what would be happening. Anne disappeared back into the office to check on Rainey. When she reappeared, she was juggling stacks of papers in her arms.

"Let's go to room four forty-four," she beckoned.

"Where's Assemblyman Rainey?" I asked as the door closed behind her.

"He'll join us in the committee room as soon as he can," she advised, unruffled by the unexpected change in plans. She was calm; I was not. I was confused and apprehensive. It must have shown on my face.

"Don't worry. This happens all the time. He has another bill today, in another committee. He needs to sign that one in, too. It's first come, first served, and he wants to get both of his bills heard today."

"Hope he doesn't get delayed," I gulped. "My witnesses have come a long way to testify."

"Dick won't let you down," Anne smiled.

"What if the bill doesn't get heard today?" Delores asked.

Delores said what I had been thinking but afraid to verbalize. I couldn't let on that I was concerned. I had to be the strong leader, even if I didn't feel very strong right now. "It will be fine," I said. "Just remember—passion, patience, and persistence, everyone. That's our mantra."

Anne led the way down the hall to the elevator. When it arrived, we trotted inside after her like a herd of sheep. I breathed a silent prayer: *Please, dear God, be with us today.*

On the ground floor Anne ushered us toward the west hall. We scrambled up the marble steps and spilled out into the ornate rotunda, at the back of a three-figured sculpture. "It's Christopher Columbus," Anne said, as we whizzed by. "The queen is agreeing to finance his expedition."

How appropriate. Columbus ventured into uncharted waters. I was doing the same. He was told he couldn't sail around the world. I was told I couldn't change the no-fault divorce law of California. He was successful. My fate remained to be seen.

Anne kept up her pace, coming to a stop before another set of elevators labeled ASSEMBLY NORTH WING. We exited on the fourth floor and approached the dark mahogany door at the end of the hall. To its right I noticed carpeted stairs that climbed to a sunny solarium. It was where I had concluded my talk with Isenberg, the chair of the Assembly Judiciary Committee, only two days ago.

My heart skipped a beat and I felt myself flush at that success. Today I had a bigger mountain to climb. We rewrote AB16 yesterday, at the last minute. I didn't know if Isenberg liked the new wording, and it was critical that he did. Without his support, AB16 would not make it out of his committee, and would die.

We maneuvered through the crowd near the committee room door. I reached for the handle, but before I could grab it, the door flew open. A man rushed out and almost knocked Anne over. She shrugged it off with a smile. "It gets crazy around here on committee days," she said.

I glanced over my shoulder, looking for Rainey. He wasn't there. My paranoia began to grow, but I beat it back. *He must be inside,* I assured myself. He wasn't, as far as I could see when we entered the windowless room with its raised ceiling and recessed fluorescent lights. I scanned the gallery's theater-style seats, all hooked together and upholstered with shiny green velvet. There were plenty of bodies, but no Rainey. I looked behind the spindled banister that separated the room like a communion altar rail. There was plenty of activity at the dais, the raised U-shaped committee desk, with some members already sitting in their high-back leather swivel chairs. He was not there, either. My stomach tightened and I frowned.

"Don't worry," Anne said. "He'll be here." She marched to the short front row on the right of the room and showed us where to sit. The committee was scheduled to start at nine a.m. sharp. I checked my watch. It was 8:53. Still no Rainey. I pulled out my speech to read it over once more. Anne shuffled her stack of papers.

"Here, this is for you," Anne said, handing me a small newsprint pamphlet. "This is the Assembly Daily File. All the assembly committee meetings for this week are listed."

My heart pounded as I flipped through its one hundred pages until I found what I was looking for on page 73, under the header: *Wednesday, May 3, 1995 JUDICIARY*. There it was, the second measure listed: *AB16—Rainey—Exemplary damages*. My lower lip trembled and I fought back tears and passed the pamphlet back to my mother and my witnesses. I pinched myself. It was real. I was here. It was going to happen.

A woman stepped down from the dais, walked in front of the railing, and smiled at me. "Nice dress," she said as she passed me by. The compliment felt good. I had dressed for success and someone noticed.

Loud chatter filled the air. I looked at my watch and held my breath. In the crowded room there was standing room only. No Rainey. I slowly turned back to focus my attention on the dais. Piles of papers were being delivered to each seat, and technicians were adjusting their equipment for closed-circuit television.

"Anne, where are all the committee members? There are a lot of empty chairs."

"Some are still standing," she said. "Not all assembly members attend their committee meetings. Today our quorum is ten members. Don't worry. Sometimes the sergeant-at-arms has to make a call to their offices to pry them away."

I started counting...one...two...three...Isenberg entered from a door behind the dais and sat down in the middle seat. Several members scrambled for their chairs. Four...five...six...Papers were shuffled. Microphones tapped. Seven...eight...The side door opened and three more members slipped into their seats. Eleven. We had one to spare. Another hurdle cleared.

In spite of that, I couldn't help feeling disappointed. *Where were the remaining three?* I had visited the offices of each committee member more than once. They all knew how important this was to me and to other victims. *What could be keeping them away?* As I have done most of my life, I personalized my fears when people don't show up. *Maybe they didn't like me. Maybe...* I felt a hand on my shoulder and looked up.

"Sorry I'm late," Rainey said as he slipped past me to the other side of Anne, giving me a warm smile and a thumbs-up. "We're number two on the calendar."

Here we go, I thought, sucking in my breath.

"AB Nine-Twenty," Isenberg barked, and the gallery hushed. I looked in my daily file. The bill had something to do with corporations and shareholder derivative actions. It sounded Greek to me.

Four people positioned themselves at the tables behind the railing; two faced west, two faced south. "The proponents are the ones with their backs to us," Anne whispered. "That's where you and Dick will be sitting."

"What about the others?" I whispered.

"They're the opponents, the ones against the bill."

The opponents! Anne's words hit me like a sledgehammer. In all the excitement I had forgotten about the opponents, like the Judges Association, who thought my bill would open up a legal can of worms. I had worked with their representative to get them to understand, but I didn't know if they would send someone to testify.

My facial muscles tensed, my mouth went dry, and I felt lightheaded. The unknown was chipping away at my confidence. I turned and looked at the crowd in the packed gallery, wondering whether any of my enemies were out there. I faced forward, gripped my speech to my chest, and slumped in my seat.

The drone of those who were there to observe the procedures made me think they were not paying attention. At one point they drowned out the proceedings up front. Isenberg pounded his gavel and bellowed for silence. The shock brought me out of my stupor. The gallery quieted down and testimony continued.

As talk about the first bill became more contentious, my attempts to remain calm failed. I feared the same thing would happen to my bill. It would not be clean and swift, as I had imagined, but dirty and vengeful. I was not prepared for the reality of politics.

The opposition grew more boisterous, and so did the gallery. The battle of words went on for more than an hour. Would they ever take a vote?

I dabbed at the tears welling in my eyes. I began to feel like a victim once more, caught in an ever-tightening vise. Today I was a victim of time and an unfamiliar process, held at the mercy of eleven committee members. I couldn't seem to shake the role. I rested my throbbing head against my hands and closed my eyes, trying to fight the constriction in my throat. As the bickering in the front of the room grew louder I wanted to yell *STOP!* But I couldn't.

Chairman Isenberg pounded his gavel, and I emerged from my reverie with a rapidly beating heart. The gallery continued to buzz. The gavel smacked once more, and the sound level diminished, but it did not completely disappear.

"That's it. Enough of this disagreement," Isenberg barked. "Go back and work out the bugs before you set foot in this room again. There will be no vote today."

He slammed the gavel down once more, cutting off Assemblyman Cunneen as he tried to speak up for his bill. I was stunned and scared. Could this happen to my bill, after all these months? *Oh, God, please don't let this happen to my bill, please let there be no opposition.* The cluster of witnesses gathered their papers, stuffed their briefcases, and shuffled out of the room. There were still vacant seats on the dais, and I leaned across Anne to murmur my concern to Rainey. Anne patted my hand. "Don't worry," Dick said. "It's not unusual to have only a quorum, especially at the beginning of the session."

I settled back in my seat just as someone bellowed "AB Sixteen. Author: Assemblyman Rainey. Please come forward." Every muscle in my body went rigid. I swallowed hard. Dick rose and looked at me. "This is it," he said.

Dick motioned me to join him. Anne asked the rest of the witnesses to follow. Dick directed Delores and me to the witness table. Harriet and Kevin stood to one side, in back of us. I didn't understand why they couldn't join us; there were several empty seats at the table. Then I remembered that the empty seats were reserved for opponents. I waited breathlessly. No one came forward to fill them. Was I safe? Dick approached the podium. I laid my speech on the table and rested my folded hands on top of it.

"Good morning, Assemblyman Rainey."

I hardly dared to breathe as Dick reeled off a quick synopsis of AB16. I felt suspended between reality and fantasy; between hope and despair, caught up in the drama of legislative proceedings.

"I've read yesterday's rewrite," Isenberg said. "No need for the second committee meeting. Today is it."

I gasped and tried to decide whether that was good news or bad. *Good,* I concluded. *This way it doesn't get strung out, and I don't have to impose on my witnesses.* Dick jotted down a note, thanked the chairman, and continued.

"Mr. Chairman, I would like to introduce Barbara Bentley, the sponsor of AB Sixteen."

I choked back tears of excitement. Isenberg stared directly at me and smiled. "I've seen Barbara around the last two days," he said. "She's been doing a great job as a sponsor."

I was thrilled at his words and smiled back. This was it, the goal I'd fought for during the past two and a half years. I felt in charge; my palms weren't sweaty, my stomach was not queasy, and I didn't have a pounding headache. I had learned my Skidmore lesson well.

Ready to do battle, I picked up my speech, adjusted my reading glasses, and leaned toward the microphone on the desk.

"Mr. Chairman and members of the Judiciary Committee, my name is Barbara Bentley and I am the sponsor of Assembly Bill Sixteen. I come before you today representing all victims of spousal violence as they seek a divorce from their convicted partner."

My voice cracked and I began to quiver. Hearing my words pierce the legislative air triggered the pain pent up from years of abuse, emotional and physical. *Don't cry now, Barbara, not now.* But I couldn't stop the salty tears from rolling down my cheeks.

"In February nineteen ninety-one, my husband attempted… attempted to…to…murder me…by ether asphyxiation."

I choked on my words. An assemblywoman went over to a service table, poured a glass of water, grabbed some tissues, and brought them to me. The gallery sat in total silence while I composed myself.

Remember your three Ps, Barbara. Passion, patience, and persistence will get you through this as they did after the murder attempt, the investigation, the trial and recovery. Remember, it's been an uphill battle since you walked out of Belli's office, saying you were going to change the law. I silently repeated my three Ps and concentrated once more on the task at hand. I would prevail. My eyes focused on my written testimony. I blew my nose, took a cool drink of water, and continued.

"When I started divorce proceedings, I became the victim of the community property divorce laws of California. It mattered *not* that my husband had tried to murder me for financial gain. It mattered *not* that I lost twenty-five thousand dollars when he surreptitiously added to the home equity loan…"

I was on a roll now. With each word, with each sentence, my voice grew stronger. The committee members watched me, and I stared back into their eyes, one by one, as I emphasized my words. I used positive action to remedy my pain.

"The law said he was entitled to fifty percent of everything obtained during the marriage. The law said he was entitled to half my pension plan. The law said I would have to pay him alimony. A victim of spousal abuse is often a silent victim. It takes great courage for a victim to overcome her fear and testify in a criminal trial. Let us not continue to traumatize the victim in the divorce court. In the name of victims of spousal abuse, I respectfully ask for your *aye* vote. Thank you for your kind attention."

I sat back in my chair. It was done. My voice had been raised to right a wrong, but would it make a difference? Dick thanked me and introduced our next witness, Delores Winje. She leaned closer to her microphone, cleared her throat, and began to read. Within moments, her pain boiled to the surface. Her words began to falter, ramble, and drag.

Isenberg glanced at his watch more than once. When Delores finished, Dick thanked her. Isenberg intervened. "How many more witnesses do you have?"

"Two."

"We're running late. The committee would like the rest of the proponents to give only their names, what organization they represent, and their stand on the bill."

My heart sank. Harriet and Kevin had come all the way from the Bay Area, and now they would not be able to testify. Damn that first bill. They had no right to usurp time like they did. Harriet and Kevin moved forward to the podium, did as they were instructed, and returned to stand behind me.

"Are there any opponents?"

I turned and looked over my shoulder. The gallery had maintained a modicum of decorum since I testified. My eyes scanned the crowd. Gratefully, no one seemed to be moving forward. Anne smiled from the gallery and gave me a thumbs-up.

"This is the second and final call for opponents," the chairman said.

I barely breathed as once more I glanced over my shoulder. What about the Judges Association? Would someone race in at the last moment and sabotage the bill? I never did get a final answer from Marty. No one moved, not even to go out the door.

"Then let's vote," Isenberg said.

I swallowed hard and took a sip of water. My throat and lips were parched. I watched intently the actions and reactions of the committee members as they were polled. Some were already collecting their papers and filling their briefcases. Some tapped their pens. Some said *aye*. Some abstained. Not a single one said *nay*. I felt victorious.

"AB Sixteen passes out of committee with eleven *ayes*," Isenberg declared. He banged his gavel and called for the lunch recess.

Sweet success! I had made it past the first hurdle in this final race, with the endorsement of family, friends, my witnesses, and strangers. I paused and thanked God for their concern and support. The witnesses started down the ramp with Dick, and as I passed the assemblyman seated at the end, he leaned down.

"Congratulations on your courage."

"Thank you," I whispered.

Anne rushed up to me and gave me a bear hug. "I knew we had it in the bag when Isenberg acknowledged you at the beginning," she grinned. "He rarely does that, and only when he supports what's on the floor."

"I wish I had known that." I laughed. "It would have saved me a lot of worry."

The Rainey contingent now forged its way through the standing-room-only crowd at the back of the chamber. One observer patted me on the shoulder. "Powerful testimony." Outside the door another gentleman approached me. "Great job."

We made our way up the short flight of stairs and stood in the solarium. I pulled out my camera and accosted a stranger as she walked by. "Would you mind? I'd like to document my victory today."

The woman obligingly poised the camera. "Say *cheese*," she said.

"No, no. On three, say *victory*." I laughed.

The next morning, the article "Brutal Alimony Story" appeared in the *Oakland Tribune*, right next to a report on the O. J. Simpson trial. I had not sought publicity out of fear of John Perry's litigious soul, but seeing my victory in print gratified my soul.

Two weeks later I sat in my office, trying to concentrate on my job, but I couldn't. No way. AB16 was on the assembly floor today, and I was waiting for the phone to ring. Anne said she would call me as soon as there was a vote. I needn't have been so apprehensive. The recent signs seemed to bode well for passage. Even the judges' position had mellowed. The previous week Marty had called to tell me so. The double ring of an outside call interrupted my thoughts. I grabbed for the receiver. It was Anne.

"Are you sitting down?" she said.

"Yes, I'm at my desk."

"Congratulations, girl, the assembly passed AB Sixteen on to the senate," she giggled, "with a vote of seventy to zero. AB Sixteen came out as a bipartisan bill!"

"Oh, my God," I squealed. "Seventy to zero! I can't believe it. Not one negative vote, even with all the political bantering going on." Happy tears formed. A major battle had been won in the war to change the law.

I hung up the phone and sat silently, staring at the computer screen but not seeing anything on it. Then, in gratitude, I bowed my head and prayed. My hand swiped at the solitary tear that trickled down my right cheek and I continued to sit in silence, unsure of my feelings. I thought I should probably run up and down the hall, screaming with joy, but I didn't. Instead, I remained in the chair, voiceless.

I wanted to remember this moment and was puzzled that the excitement wasn't there. I should be bounding around the room with the good news. Perhaps the struggle had been too long, or too exhausting. Perhaps I knew this was just one more notch toward the goal, not the goal itself.

My thoughts now turned to the senate.

TWENTY-NINE

The Senate

Coming off my victory in the assembly, I was not prepared for the sinkholes that appeared in my road to the Senate Judiciary Committee. I soon discovered that there would be no superhighway through the senate to the governor's desk. Anne broke the news to me with a telephone call.

"Chairman Calderon is looking at AB Sixteen as a typical domestic issue, another women's thing." There was a definite pause, and Anne cleared her throat. "He's against the bill."

I gasped and clenched my fist. I knew enough from my recent experience with the Assembly that this was not a good thing. Without the chairman's backing, a bill would languish and never make it out of committee. We needed to show that the bill would also help men, and as the bill's sponsor, it was up to me to prove it. But how? I hung up the phone and prayed for guidance.

My prayers were answered two days later when Anne called.

"A male victim has appeared," she said excitedly. "Steve Peterson. He saw the latest AB Sixteen story in the *Oakland Tribune*."

Twenty years earlier, Steve Peterson's wife hired two people to kill him. He survived the attack, and his wife and the hit couple were sentenced to prison. In another fine example of the skewed legal system, his ex-wife was incarcerated for only three years. When Steve retired, his ex-wife retained an attorney to go after her share of Steve's retirement pension. She got twenty percent.

"He'll make a great witness," I exclaimed.

"Yes, but we may have a problem," Anne said. "He wants the law to help him, to be retroactive, which we can't do. I told him I would have you call him."

It took all of my negotiating skills to sway Steve into lobbying and testifying with me. I talked to him on the phone and met with him in person. Each time he spoke of the attack he broke into tears. When you've been a victim, the pain is never far from the surface, especially when you've just learned that you are going to have to pay the woman who tried to murder you $500 a month. Reluctantly, he agreed to my request. I had my male voice.

Four days later at work, I filled my coffee cup and slipped back into my desk chair just in time to catch the ringing phone. It was Anne, and she was alarmed. "We have a problem," she blurted. "We heard from the Judges Association, through a letter from Marty Montano. The judges...well, there's no easy way to say it. They've come out against the bill."

"What! Marty assured me the judges would remain neutral."

"On the plus side for you, it's too late to get their opinion into the senate analysis."

"Thank God for small favors." I sighed.

I hung up the phone and sat quietly at my desk to catch my breath and gather my thoughts. Why, at the last minute, did these things always seem to happen? I took a swig of coffee and dialed Marty's number.

"What went wrong?" I asked. "Anne says she got an unfavorable letter from you."

"I'm sorry," he mumbled. "I was forced to send it. The judges were adamant about not changing their law."

"*Their* law? I thought the law belonged to all of us, that it was to help the victim, not the criminal."

"I put a positive statement in the letter, but they edited it out."

"Bastards."

"There is a silver lining," Marty said. "I'm not going to add it to the schedule. So, if any judges show up, they won't be from me." He assured me he thought the bill would pass. "I haven't heard from Calderon's office, and if there were any doubts about the bill, I would have."

"Thanks, Marty; I need all the encouragement I can get."

On Monday morning, four days later, Steve and I stormed the capitol, stopping first to check in with Anne. "I learned from last time," I said wryly as I handed her our schedule. "I've made appointments." Our first stop was Chairman Calderon's office, where I asked for Morgana Swanson, his legislative counsel. She wasn't available, and we continued with our appointments.

"Is this one of your good signs?" Steve laughed.

"Of course, we're just saving the best for last. Don't forget that positive thinking is cumulative."

Each legislative aide we met with listened intently to our stories and agreed that the law should be changed. No doubt Steve's loss of composure and his tears helped. We handed them our letters and left. I recorded their responses and began to feel invincible. Our next stop was Senator Bill Lockyer's office.

Lockyer was president pro tem of the state senate, and his digs were impressive, nothing like the smaller offices we had been in. After we announced our appointment, a short, stocky woman, impeccably dressed and militarily erect, emerged. She introduced herself, stiffly shook our hands, and never smiled.

"I'm worried about the reverse effects on a battered woman," she said crisply. "If she's convicted of attempted murder, she won't get half of her husband's retirement."

I bit my lips and counted to three before I answered. I said attempted murder was wrong, and that the courts probably wouldn't prosecute her anyway, because of battered wife syndrome.

"But," she continued, "this would be an exception to the no-fault divorce law." She scribbled a note on my letter that sat on her desk. We were dismissed.

When we walked into the hallway, Steve asked, "What went on in there?"

"Some people can't think straight, and they misconstrue the facts."

"I would have been at a loss for words."

"That's why we're a team. We support each other. Come on, let's go back and check in with Anne."

We returned to Rainey's office, helped ourselves to some coffee, and waited for Anne to get off the phone. She smiled and motioned for us to come in and sit down. When she hung up, she was excited.

"A newspaper reporter called about ten minutes ago. It looks like he's updating his story for the *Tribune* and he'd like to interview Steve, if that's okay."

"I don't mind," Steve said. "I just hope I don't say something stupid."

"Talk from your heart," I said. "You'll do just fine."

Anne handed Steve the receiver as she dialed the reporter's local phone number. Steve hesitated. Then he spoke slowly, stammering through the reporter's questions, his discomfort raw and apparent. Steve handed me the phone. After I confirmed several facts for the reporter, he asked to be transferred to Dick. I handed the receiver to Anne.

"Sorry, he's just leaving for the afternoon assembly session, and he's running late." Anne scribbled on a notepad, agreeing with whatever the reporter was saying. Then she hung up the phone. "Here," she said, folding the notepaper. "You need to get this message to

Dick on the assembly floor. If the reporter doesn't get to talk to him, there won't be a story."

Steve and I delivered the message to the sergeant-at-arms and rushed back to Calderon's office. This time Morgana was available, and she met us in the foyer. "Calderon has no problem with the bill," she said. "It should make it out of committee just fine."

My heart raced and I felt like giving her a big hug, but I kept my composure. I floated back to Anne's office, with Steve at my side. "We've got it!" I exclaimed, giving Anne a high five. "Morgana says it's a go."

"I'm surprised," Anne said. "I just got a copy of Morgana's analysis and I'm not too pleased with it."

"But she seemed so sure."

"I'll trust your judgment. You've been right so far."

The next morning, Steve and his second wife, Poppy, rang my doorbell. "Come in. Come in." I said. "You're not going to believe what happened this morning." I ushered them inside, introduced them to my mother, and took their coffee orders. Mom said she would pour and bring the cups into the living room.

"Are you going to keep us in suspense?" Poppy laughed as she sat down.

"ABC Channel Seven News in San Francisco is going to interview us this morning," I blurted out. I was excited, but cautious. I knew publicity was what the bill needed, but I had been afraid to seek it because of John Perry's vindictive nature. "Apparently their news scout read an article in the *Oakland Tribune* this morning."

Poppy opened her purse and handed me a newspaper clipping. "This is what they must have seen," she said, handing it to me.

"Injustice Rife in Divorces," I read out loud. I grinned. "It's another fine tribute to the efforts that Steve and I are making to get the law changed."

Minutes later the reporter, Eric Thomas, and his cameraman,

Sean Overly, rang my doorbell. I jumped. *Don't be nervous*, I told myself as I opened the door and let them in. When I saw the TV news van in front, I snatched my camera from the side table and snapped a photo for my album. When we finished the interviews I expected the crew to leave, but they didn't.

"We're going to follow you up to the capitol and do a live report for the evening news."

Surprised? You bet! We gathered our stuff, piled into Steve's car, and wound our way through the Delta to the capitol, with the white van trailing close behind.

At one o'clock, the AB16 contingent met in Rainey's office. Delores and Kevin, who had once more generously offered to testify, showed up together. Eric and Sean had gone ahead to the committee room. Anne led the way. We marched across the floor like a small army ready to do battle.

"I'm very nervous," Steve said.

"Don't worry," I reassured him. "I'm nervous, too, but we're going to do just fine. We have justice on our side."

"This is it," Anne said as she opened the senate chamber door.

We filed into the back of the room. The spectator seats faced the horseshoe-shaped dais to the left. Empty high-back leather chairs waited for the senate committee members. Sean set up his camera in the far corner and made last-minute adjustments. Eric sat in the first row, with a nonobstructed view of the arena. He'd get to see the proceedings close up.

The room bustled with energy; most gallery seats were taken and we had to split up. Moments later there was a standing-room-only crowd. Once settled, Anne handed me the Senate Daily File. I flipped through it and found our session on page 47.

It was 1:30. Chairman Calderon sat, reviewing stacks of papers in front of him; the lights reflected from his partially bald head. Senator Wright seated herself a few moments later, put on her reading glasses, and buried her blond head in her stack of papers. I figured they were the bills that were to be heard.

"Where is everybody?" I asked, my old fears resurfacing. Were they out because my bill was controversial?

"This committee can be a challenge to round up," Dick explained. He assuaged my fears, for the moment, but by two o'clock only three senators sat in their swivel chairs, and Chairman Calderon was one of them. He looked at his watch and shook his head in disgust. He reached over and pressed a button on what appeared to be an intercom system.

"All committee members need to get to room twenty-forty. NOW," he bellowed. "I don't want to have the next two sessions overloaded with sixty to seventy bills each." He released the button and turned to his two colleagues.

"We'll operate as a subcommittee until a quorum appears. Let's consider SB Two Sixty-Six, about earthquake insurance."

They shuffled their papers and launched into a discussion, droning on for an hour, when all I wanted to do was get my testimony over with. I squirmed in my seat. I fingered my speech, lying in my lap. Occasionally I glanced over at Steve, who smiled and shrugged his shoulders.

By the time the discussion ended, eight senators were perched around the horseshoe. The legislative aide for the missing senator sent word that he was out of town. Calderon called the session to order.

"Assembly Bill Sixteen. Assemblyman Rainey."

I clutched my speech and nodded at Steve, Kevin, and Delores. We approached the front and were directed to sit at the mahogany table in the middle of the horseshoe. Steve sat next to me on one side; Kevin and Delores sat at the opposite end. In our seats we had to gaze upward at the senators as if they were superior beings. I didn't like the feeling. Dick settled in at the podium located behind me.

"We have some amendments to discuss," Calderon said. He

went through several items I didn't understand. Rainey then spoke, introducing me as the sponsor.

I leaned forward, closer to the microphone, picked up my speech, and adjusted my reading glasses. I quietly cleared my throat; the noise level in the gallery subsided. My speech was the same one I had used before the Assembly Judiciary Committee. It was an old friend, and I figured there was no sense fiddling with success. But something was different this time. I came charging out of the gate with a voice that projected strong and steady.

"It mattered not..." I was adamant, precise and I did not break into tears. "The law said..." Immersed in my quest, I forgot that the television camera was rolling and recording every nuance, every breath, and every emphasis on righting a wrong. Once more, my voice spoke out for victims.

Then it was Steve's turn. He was about to show the senators that this was not strictly a women's bill. He picked up his speech and started reading, his deep voice shaky and uncertain. "In nineteen seventy-six my wife hired two people to rob, kidnap, and kill me..." His voice broke; he sobbed. After almost twenty years, his tears reflected the injustice and cruelty he had endured at the hands of someone he loved. Steve had been strong for the interview in my backyard; now he bravely tried to overcome his emotions and continue, but he was unable.

Senator Lockyer spoke up. "We will discuss some points until Mr. Peterson can continue. I'd like to start out by saying I think this bill will have an adverse effect on battered women."

I had hoped that wouldn't come up. I might have truthfully said I was one of the battered women he was supposedly looking out for, but it never occurred to me I was part of that group. Fortunately for our side, no one else seemed concerned about this point.

Senator Mello spoke next. "I'm going to vote for the bill, but I'm concerned about what would happen if the attempted-murder conviction is later reversed."

"The crime is so heinous," Calderon said, "it probably doesn't matter."

"Is the committee ready to vote?" Lockyer asked.

"Excuse me, senators, but Mr. Peterson has not finished his testimony," Rainey interjected.

"My apologies, Mr. Peterson," Lockyer said. "Please, continue."

Steve picked up his speech and struggled to maintain his composure while reading his powerful words about injustice and victimization. I mentally cheered him on. He faltered through and made it to the end, thanking the senators and heaving a sigh as he laid his typed speech on the table.

"Are we ready for a vote?" Calderon asked. The senators nodded affirmatively.

"Excuse me, senators," Rainey interjected, "I have two more witnesses who have traveled great distances to be here today. Please give them the courtesy of their comments."

"Our apologies," Calderon mumbled.

Kevin leaned into his microphone and introduced himself as the president of Citizens for Law and Order and also a board member of Crime Victims United. "My organizations and I support AB Sixteen."

Delores Winje pushed her chair forward and spoke. "I am a victim of attempted murder. My husband further victimized me with the divorce laws of California. This law must be passed." Her few words were more powerful than a five-page speech. I appreciated her loyalty and candor. Calderon questioned Delores about the abuse, and her testimony ended.

"Do we have any opposition to come forward?" Calderon asked.

I curled my fingers into fists, and prayed that there would be none. I was afraid to look around for fear some nasty judge would appear and voice his old-school mentality. The room was momentarily silent.

"This is the second and final call for opposition testimony," Calderon said. No one spoke up or came forward. I let out a long sigh of relief. "Then let us vote," he said.

"Mello?"

"*Aye.*"

"Lockyer?" I crossed my fingers.

"*Aye.*"

"Wright?"

"*Aye.*"

It continued, one by one, until all eight senators had voted *aye.* It was amazing. Once more I achieved victory with not a single negative vote.

I looked at each senator and mouthed *Thank you,* my eyes shining. We gathered our belongings, threaded our way through the crowd to the hallway, and hugged each other. I couldn't stay still and squealed with happiness more than once. Eric Thomas offered his heartfelt congratulations.

"Don't forget to watch the six o'clock news tonight," he said. "We'll be broadcasting live to our anchors, Richard Brown and Terilyn Joe."

Later, after the Petersons dropped my mom and me back home in Antioch, I flipped on the news. It was half over, and our story didn't appear in the last half. I rewound the VCR tape and got something to drink for both of us. We settled on the couch and I hit the play button.

"Mom, we're a lead-in story," I exalted.

We sat glued to the screen as we watched Eric's report, interspersed with snips of the interviews and testimony. When Richard Brown asked about the law helping Steve and me, Eric, standing with the state capitol visible behind him, responded that I knew it wouldn't help me, but I wanted to be sure others did not have to suffer the way I had. When the camera cut back to Richard and Terilyn in the studio, they were shaking their heads.

I replayed the segment and timed it. The report was three minutes long. Usually, a TV news story runs for thirty seconds. Passion, patience, and persistence had made this a successful day.

* * *

Two days later Rex and I flew into Springfield, Illinois, as a stopover on one of my business trips to Canada. I had obtained a free companion ticket and pointed out to Rex that we could take advantage of the opportunity to visit with his parents on our way to Quebec and take in Henry Ford's Greenfield Village on our return. His acceptance pleased me. After my years of yearning and pleading to meet John's family, only to have my hopes dashed repeatedly, meeting Rex's parents became a major step in furthering our relationship, but not because I longed for a wedding band. I had determined in recovery that meeting family and friends was a way to help cement trust between two people.

I immediately liked Rex's parents, down-home folks with no pretensions. They were excited that Rex was home and surprised us with an afternoon mini–family reunion in their backyard. During the party, his Aunt Susie started introducing me as Rex's fiancée. I politely declined. "No, just a good friend," I would say, shaking hands. Many responded, "You must be doing something right. We've never seen Rex smile so much in his life." Rex would break out in a silly grin, put his arm around me, and, as if to change the subject, regale them with my efforts to change the divorce law of California. About halfway through, the Midwest skies dumped a hard rain, and we all scampered under the back porch. We continued eating and talking. The downpour couldn't dampen the festive familial mood.

Three weeks after we returned from our trip, on Thursday, July 20, 1995, I sat at my desk at work, waiting for a phone call from Anne. After several delays, AB16 had finally made it to the senate floor, and she would be calling me with the vote. During the month I had continued to work hard as the sponsor of AB16, writing letters, making phone calls, garnering support whenever and wherever I could. I was exhausted.

What pulled me down and tired me out lately was not the lobbying and politicking. It was John Perry. He continued to be a thorn in my side. We had signed a property settlement one year ago, but John had reneged on five issues and Bradley could not move his client.

It was the craziness surrounding John that spurred me on to change the law. My physical uneasiness and emotional breakdowns prompted me to work even harder. Perhaps helping others wasn't my only motive. Deep down it may have been revenge. Now I looked forward to Anne's call. I wanted one more notch in my belt.

I grabbed the phone on the first ring.

"I've just come back from the senate," Anne said. She let a pause hang in the air. "You've cleared the senate! AB Sixteen came through with a block of noncontested bills, with a vote of thirty-eight to zero."

I hung up the phone and realized I felt complacent, at peace, and not overly excited. I suppose it had been such a long, arduous fight that I felt this result was inevitable. Also, I didn't want to set myself up for disappointment if the assembly blocked the bill during the reconcurrence vote or if the governor decided to veto it. I grabbed the copy of AB16 from my corkboard and held it to my bosom. AB16 and I had been a regular twosome for more than two years. Now it was almost law.

The next day Anne left a phone message. "Congratulations! The assembly voted sixty-eight to zero to move AB Sixteen to the governor's desk. You're one signature away from changing the law."

The numbers echoed through my mind. Eleven to zero, seventy to zero, eight to zero, thirty-eight to zero, sixty-eight to zero. How had I made it this far without one negative vote? *With my Higher Power,* I reminded myself, along with my powerful three Ps...passion, patience, and persistence.

THIRTY

The Celebration

Extraordinary events take place in ordinary lives, and when they happen it can seem like good luck or a miracle. Since the murder attempt, I found that my good luck was the result of planning and hard work, and miracles the product of my deep belief in my Higher Power. I also experienced excitement that overflowed with each success along the way...a giggling scream, happy tears, a jump for joy, or a big hug. But when the major culminations of my efforts evolved and I learned the results via telephone, I was calm. There was no overriding euphoria, an unusual feeling for me. It was the same when I heard the news about the governor.

In August 1995, I was on vacation with Rex, staying at a bed-and-breakfast in St. George, Utah. At the time we left on our vacation, I had not heard about the fate of AB16. Though the chance was slim, there was always a possibility that the governor would refuse to sign it. Anne said to go and have a good time; she would leave me a message on my work voice mail.

I crawled out of bed and made my way to the phone. Might as well get the daily phone call out of the way, I thought. I sat down in the chair next to the antique desk and punched in the sequence of numbers to reach my voice mail. I scribbled down several messages and hung up the phone.

"Well?" Rex said.

I floated over to him. Tears welled in my eyes as I choked out the words.

"I changed the law of California. The governor signed the bill late yesterday afternoon."

On August 9, 1995, the *Oakland Tribune* ran a follow-up on my story titled "Woman's Crusade Becomes State Law." In late December, I received a call from a reporter for Antioch's *Ledger-Dispatch*. She had heard about my story and wanted to do a feature, because AB16 would become law on January 1. I agreed. We established a good rapport, and she respected my concerns about something showing up in print that might prompt John Perry to sue me. He was still a specter in my life.

On the morning of December 30, I got up early and drove to the newsstands at the newspaper office, collected the sack of quarters on the seat next to me, and approached the metal racks. When I got close enough to see the top of the stack of papers, I burst into big, chest-heaving tears. My color photograph, the one where I sat at my table in Sacramento gathering signatures to support AB16, dominated the front page. I plunked in my quarters, grabbed my copies, and hurried to the car. I snatched up the top paper and avidly read the article. It took me a while to calm down enough to drive home.

On December 31, I hosted a party at my home in Antioch. It was not a New Year's Eve party, but a birthday party, complete with cake and balloons. Just before midnight Rex poured the champagne and I lit the candles on the cake; guests donned their party hats and held their whistles. As the mirrored ball dropped in Times Square, the crowd in my dining room did not belt out "Auld Lang Syne." We raised our glasses of champagne.

"A toast," Rex said, "to the birth of a new law. Barbara's law. A law to help others."

We clinked our glasses together and drank to AB16, then sang "Happy Birthday" before I blew out the candles on the cake.

My success in the halls of the capitol was not mirrored in my dealings with John. Eight months after my bill was signed by the governor and nearly four years after the property settlement had ostensibly been agreed upon, it was still not finalized. In early April, Ross Grissom asked me to meet him in his office so he could review court procedures with me. I was about to battle John in the courtroom, over the airline mileage, representing myself. I glanced at the family law books on the wall shelf behind Ross. Goose bumps rippled up my arms.

"My law is in those books, isn't it?"

"Yes, it is. In all my years of practice, I've had many clients who sit across from me and say the law should be changed, but you are the only one who has done it. I'm very proud to know you, Barbara Bentley."

On April 11, 1996, I strode into Judge Lawrence's courtroom, with my head held high and my trusty black briefcase by my side. I wore my metaphorical attorney's hat, ready to stand up against John and collect my long-due airline miles. I had changed the law, and now I wanted to win against John in court.

A psychopath like John is motivated by greed. Like a wild animal,

John Perry had bitten into my flesh and would not let go as he flung me back and forth. He was determined to drain me emotionally so he could profit financially. I refused to let him and was tenacious, especially when it came to collecting the airline mileage he owed me. Now we would settle it in court.

Bradley greeted me as I made my way to the front. He sat at the defendant's table on the right. I settled in at the plaintiff's table on the left and extracted my papers from my briefcase.

"All rise," the bailiff bellowed. "Court is now in session, the Honorable Judge Lawrence presiding." The judge appeared in his black robes and made his way to the bench.

"Please be seated," he instructed. He scanned a page in front of him and peered over his glasses at Bradley.

"I thought I told you to settle this months ago, Mr. Bradley," he said testily. "What are we doing here today?"

"Your honor, Mr. Perry and Ms. Bentley can't seem to agree on the airline mileage."

Judge Lawrence scowled, looked at me, and said he would hear first from the plaintiff.

"Your honor, I know you are aware of the details of this case. I won't bore you and the court with rehashing them except to say that the defendant, Mr. Perry, attempted to murder me by ether asphyxiation in 1991 and was convicted of attempted first-degree murder. We signed a property settlement agreement in August 1994. I have tried to settle all matters pertaining to this divorce in a timely manner, but have been stonewalled by Mr. Perry. Because he has chosen to ignore his legal obligations, I have come before you today to seek remedy. I have a copy for you of the letter detailing the history of the airline mileage, and one for Mr. Bradley."

The bailiff came forward, took the copies, and handed one to Bradley and one to the judge. Lawrence scrutinized the document and made some notations on it.

"Thank you, Ms. Bentley. You've outlined the situation in great detail."

The judge looked back at Bradley. "Well, what do you have to say to this?"

"My client contends that..."

"Contends what? It was decided that he had to forfeit one-half of the miles."

The judge looked at my calculations once more, made another notation on it, and raised his eyes. "I find for the plaintiff, Ms. Bentley. The respondent shall forthwith transfer to the petitioner either choice one or choice two as contained in the letter dated April third, nineteen ninety-six."

Judge Lawrence added a caveat that made my victory even sweeter. "Should the transfer and payment not be concluded prior to May first, nineteen ninety-six, this judgment obligation shall commence to accrue interest at the legal rate of ten percent per annum, simple interest."

Interest? I hadn't thought about that. I'd won a double victory.

Judge Lawrence slammed his gavel. It was over. I gathered my papers, and Bradley came over to me. "Congratulations. I'll try to get John to cooperate."

Forgiveness frees the soul. Within months of the murder attempt, I had forgiven John for his treachery and criminal behavior, but I had also decided to stand up for my rights against him. I refused to be his willing victim again.

As I stood outside the courthouse and looked back at the stately columned building, I reviewed my journey of the last fifteen years. It had been one of adulation, victimization, discovery, recovery, and advocacy. I had donned the hats of a bill sponsor in the legislative process and a lawyer in the family law courts. I chose life unhampered by guilt and neediness, and embraced it. I had established a loving relationship with Rex based on trust and mutual respect and continued to nurture it. Out of the ashes of victimization by John and the divorce law of California, and of myself, I had become like a phoenix rising.

I took a deep breath, grinned, and turned to go home. With my additional tools, I knew I could face the future, no matter what came my way.

EPILOGUE A

The Prince and the Pauper

Although convicted and sentenced to five years for attempted murder, John Perry was up for parole after only thirteen months. It then took him eight months to come up with an acceptable parole release plan in an area with a naval presence, and in November 1992, the Virginia parole board released him into the Washington state parole system. A parole officer in Seattle would monitor him. But on the street again, John easily slipped into his old habits and directed his energy to establish a new life in Seattle while continuing to make my life a living hell. I was not just his victim. I was his enemy.

After the murder attempt I kept a close watch on John's activities. It was imperative to my safety. I hired a private detective and constantly consulted with John's current and previous friends and associates, who provided accounts of their conversations with John, their meetings, and their observations of his actions. Although I have not been able to verify all the information I received, their input, plus my personal experience with John's modus operandi, has led me to believe that the following closely represents John's movements after his release from jail.

It didn't take long for John to violate his parole stipulation that disallowed impersonations. He once more rebuilt his self-esteem and marketability by passing himself off as a retired navy rear admiral, retired navy captain, doctor of psychology, executive vice president of an investment company, Westinghouse executive, former undersecretary of commerce, and director of a hospital in Canada and an alternative-medicine facility in Seattle. John cast his net with the old stories he told me and embellished them with even more outlandish tales. He sprinkled his conversations with the names of well-known public figures he supposedly had met: Linus Pauling, Bill and Hillary Clinton, and Al Gore.

With his magnetic personality and intrepid style, John quickly caught his first female victim, a wealthy Florida heiress on an extended vacation in Seattle. He was priming her to be a major investor in his plant business. He swept her off her feet. Before long the romance hit a rough spot. She missed Florida and asked John to move there with her. He was unable to do so, as his parole plan tied him to the Seattle area. Try as he might, John could not persuade her to permanently relocate to Washington. The relationship ended.

John turned his attentions to Trudy Biltmore, a middle-aged friend of Hal Ledman, the man who helped John make parole. John turned on the charm. Within weeks Trudy and John were living together in Trudy's rundown ranch house on twenty acres in Redmond. Trying to elicit sympathy, John lamented that he didn't get what he should have out of our divorce. She invested $65,000 in John's plant scheme.

Within two years, John's relationship with Hal soured. John illegally used Hal's credit card, charged $2,300, and stole two boxes of his checks. By the following year, in September 1996, John's relationship with Trudy had deteriorated. It was a familiar story. There was little profit in the plant import company, and John's financial contribution to the living arrangements was sparse.

Monetary arguments between John and Trudy became commonplace; she wanted a return on her investment and help in running the house. John found ways to put her off. He insisted that because they loved each other, they should take out life insurance on one another and name each other sole beneficiaries in new wills. She agreed.

One evening they had a big argument over finances. John became violent. Trudy left her home and stayed away all night. The next morning she returned to an empty house. John was off on a three-day business trip, and Trudy felt guilty. Perhaps she had been too harsh on John; he was in ill health, after all, and he was trying to make money. When John returned, they made up for a couple of days, but the honeymoon didn't last.

A week later, Trudy and John got into another quarrel about money. This time John grabbed a loaded shotgun and stormed off to the master bedroom, saying he was going to kill himself because Trudy didn't appreciate him. He slammed the door behind him.

The little voice inside Trudy told her to run, and she did. If she had turned the handle on that bedroom door, it is my contention that she would have been blown away with a shotgun blast and John would have claimed it to be an accidental shooting. Trudy checked into a nearby motel. The next morning she found John, slumped on the kitchen floor in his bathrobe, with a can of soda in his hand. He was dead. John died on Friday the thirteenth.

Monday morning Ross Grissom called me at work with the news. I hung up the phone and sobbed. I could now mourn the person who, for me, had died five years earlier, on that Friday morning in the Key Bridge Marriott in Arlington, Virginia. John, tormented by all his demons, was now at rest. I prayed for his soul. Then I sprang into action to protect my interests.

I needed a death certificate to complete the legal transactions precipitated by his demise. My call to the mortuary triggered a two-month delay in getting John's body released from the county morgue. There was no family member to legally identify his body, and they needed identification to complete the temporary death certificate. I stepped up. I had to in order to complete legal papers.

In a bizarre set of circumstances I confirmed that the body was John Perry, by reviewing faxes of his corpse and providing details of his unique scar. When I learned that Trudy planned to have John cremated and buried in the national cemetery near Medford, Oregon, with full military honors, I moved quickly and squelched that effort. John was cremated. His ashes were released to Trudy, who put them on her mantel.

I sent Trudy a sympathy card with a handwritten note, extending my condolences for the pain she must now be feeling, pain that I knew firsthand. I offered to talk with her. As proof of John's impersonation and my good intentions, I enclosed the front-page newspaper article that was published when my law took effect. In it, the reporter used the trial transcript to point out that John was not who he said he was. Trudy never responded. Denial had its grip on her, and she didn't know how to escape its stranglehold. I understood that, too.

Three months later, the final autopsy reported that John died of an accidental drug overdose. I studied the detailed list of drugs found in him and was reminded of another time, another place, and a similar list. It was in Miami, in the summer of 1990, when John had had his supposed heart attack on our way to see the banker. I went to my file boxes and pulled out the list of the drugs I had found in John's briefcase while he was in the hospital. Most of them were the same. The old man just couldn't change. John wanted to trigger Trudy's sympathy, to bring her back under his control, by using his chemical cocktail to produce a fake heart attack and defuse the financial discussions. How many times had he done this in his life?

This time his trick didn't work. His timing was off, his body too old, or his dosage incorrect. Instead of continuing his charade, he died by his own hand. The prince who had charmed women his whole life ended up a pauper, with only the items he had manipulated from Trudy and me. In the end, he had died alone, a victim of one of his own schemes.

Unfortunately, my troubles didn't end with John's death. Five years later Trudy, working through John's divorce lawyer, continued John's vendetta to victimize me for company stock that John never collected from the final divorce agreement. Because Trudy had inherited his estate, she demanded her pound of flesh from the woman whom John had disparaged and almost murdered. She legally collected $8,000. I have no idea what was going through her mind—if greed spurred her on, or revenge for what she thought I did to John. What a sad commentary for a misguided woman in denial, and for the divorce laws of California.

The Victim and the Victor

Discovery of the truth returned my life. I fought hard to put the pieces together after living with and loving a man who was a socio-psychopath. It was exhilarating and exhausting, mind-boggling, and definitely enlightening to discover the connection between psy-chopathology and domestic abuse.

Once freed from my abuser, I put my life back on track slowly, one step at a time. I refused to remain the victim and embraced the journey. The results amaze me. I reencountered Rex, a former work-mate who deserved my trust, and we married in 1997. We travel at length to exotic places and enjoy the results of an award-winning home winemaking hobby.

Going beyond myself to help others is important to me, and I willingly share my story, which was featured on the Lifetime Televi-sion show *Final Justice*. As a member of the Speaker's Bureau for STAND! Against Domestic Violence, I deliver speeches to college classes, women's organizations, recovery groups, children's advo-cacy programs, and welfare programs. As a motivational speaker, I share my story as "One Person Can Make a Difference" and "From Victim to Victor" to Soroptimists, the International Women's Writing Guild, and the American Association of University Women, with audiences from ten to four hundred. Victory is sweet, and rewarding.

Domestic violence is abhorrent and costly to both victim and society. As awareness of this problem grows, so does help for abused women, children, and men who no longer have to go it alone. Abuse is toxic and damaging to body and soul. Extricating oneself mentally from a domestic abuser is challenging. Doing so physically can be dangerous and must be handled with great care. Both physical and mental help is now available from the National Domestic Violence Hotline (800-799-7233 or www.ndvh.org) and other such groups.

As concerned citizens, we can help eliminate domestic violence not only by refusing to condone it, but by acting on our knowledge. If we recognize a victim of domestic violence, we must be caring enough to appropriately approach the person, or, if we observe physical battering, to call the police.

My own journey has convinced me that it is possible to go from victim to victor. With passion, patience, and persistence, and planning and hard work, you, too, can make your dreams come true.

Survival Tips

Psychopaths exist and they continue to snare unsuspecting victims, as in the recent case of a woman from New York. She was middle-aged, with two grown children, and recently divorced. She turned to a Christian dating site on the Internet for solace. A man from Florida who purported to be a pastor with a ministry in music connected with her. He filled his e-mails with poetry, and he played on her love of music. Within a year he moved in with her. Six months later they married, and the following month she discovered he was a sex addict obsessed with Internet pornography. When confronted, the pastor killed her cat. He threatened to poison the rest of her animals. He behaved inappropriately with her daughter when she came to visit. He conned her and her friends out of money—she lost $20,000. In the summer of 2007 she found him in a grievous sexual lie and kicked him out, but not before he had abused her spiritually, financially, sexually, and physically. Stress crippled her. She is unable to work and remains in therapy. The pastor returned to Florida and now pursues other women over the Internet with his poems and lies.

We can take steps to protect ourselves from the wiles of the relationship psychopath and reduce our chances of being caught in his web by following these survival tips.

1. UNDERSTAND YOURSELF

Society sets up milestones but does not make sure we are mature enough to meet them. Most of us grow up without fully understanding ourselves. We ignore the events of the past. We are unaware of how they affect who we are or what we will become and are especially vulnerable when we are in a weakened emotional state—going through a divorce, breaking up, moving to another area, or mourning a death. The psychopath takes advantage of our weakened state. But by understanding ourselves, we create limits and boundaries based on our healthy beliefs and set up a defense zone against the psychopath's clandestine attacks. If we are unfortunate enough to become a victim of a psychopath, it is most important that we seek professional help and understand that it is not our fault.

2. UNDERSTAND PSYCHOPATHS

One of the strategies for success is to know your opponent, how he operates, and what he hopes to attain. But most of us are unprepared to encounter the cunning psychopath. We are trained by the media to think of psychopaths as serial killers, and we figure we will never be one of their victims. But we are wrong. Most psychopaths are not serial killers. They seem like ordinary citizens, but they operate out of greed and, most important, without conscience. We need to understand how psychopaths function in order to recognize their characteristic behaviors such as seeking pity, charming the birds out of the trees, and being the gregarious life of the party who always has an answer for every question, even if it isn't plausible. We need to understand how psychopaths draw us in by assuming positions of power. Without such understanding, the psychopath can finagle his way into our lives; then he will devastate our emotions and finances before moving on to the next victim.

3: BESTOW TRUST ONLY WHEN EARNED

When starting a new relationship, we can be caught up in the euphoria of learning about a new partner. We share stories back and forth. It's easy to believe everything we are told, and we automatically bestow trust when trust has not been earned. But it is our responsibility to protect ourselves. One way to do this is to validate stories. The Internet offers ways to check out facts for ourselves, or we can buy a background search for a reasonable amount. County offices offer accessible records for marriage, divorce, and property transactions. Remember, if the stories sound too good to be true, they probably are.

4. LISTEN TO YOUR INNER VOICE

If you feel unsettled or unsure about your relationship partner, if you have a feeling something isn't right, do not stuff the feelings into a denial sack. Investigate them. Listen to your inner voice and seek advice from a trusted friend, family member, clergyperson, or therapist. Share your feelings with more than one person. And be prepared to act on their advice. It may not be what you want to hear, but it will protect you from the devastation to come.

5. HEED THE WARNING SIGNALS

- You never meet or talk to his family.

- He's evasive about where he lives, and you are not allowed over to his house.

- He borrows your credit card and doesn't pay his debts.

- He makes you feel guilty about your feelings.

- He cons you into taking out a loan for him.

- He says he works for a government agency as a spy.

- He says he owns property, but he can't show proof.

- He moves into your home, and he doesn't come with much.

- He says he's divorced, widowed, or separated but is evasive about details.

- He uses threats to control you.

- He makes you feel like you're going crazy when you challenge him.

6. BECOME ONE PERSON WHO MADE A DIFFERENCE

Once we understand who we are, we must use our talents to go beyond ourselves to help others. To help others is to help ourselves. We build self-esteem and confidence, and society benefits. Find a cause you believe in, one that you are passionate about. Embrace it. Use patience and persistence to precipitate action. It's not the size of the project that matters, it's your involvement. Become one person who made a difference. If anyone you know is in a relationship like the one I found myself in, I urge you to share my story with her. Together we can protect those who would become victims and help them regain their lost strength.

EPILOGUE D

Resources

RECOMMENDED READING

The following references deal with issues touched on in this book. It is not an all-inclusive list, and it is important to seek a therapist who specializes in psychopath abuse to guide you.

Beattie, Melody. *Beyond Codependency and Getting Better All the Time.* Hazelden Foundation, 1989.

———. *Codependent No More: How to Stop Controlling Others and Start Caring for Yourself.* Hazelden Foundation, 1987, 1992.

———. *Codependents' Guide to the Twelve Steps.* Fireside, 1998.

Bradshaw, John. *Bradshaw on the Family: A Revolutionary Way of Self-Discovery.* Health Communications, 1988.

Brown, Sandra. *How to Spot a Dangerous Man before You Get Involved.* Hunter House, 2005.

Capacchione, Lucia. *Recovery of Your Inner Child: The Highly Acclaimed Method for Liberating Your Inner Self.* Simon and Schuster, 1991.

Carlson, Richard, and Kristine Carlson. *Don't Sweat the Small Stuff for Women: Simple and Practical Ways to Do What Matters Most and Find Time for You.* Hyperion, 2001.

Evans, Patricia. *Controlling People: How to Recognize, Understand, and Deal with People Who Try to Control You.* Adams Media, 2002.

———. *The Verbally Abusive Relationship: How to Recognize It and How to Respond.* Adams Media, 1992, 1996.

Hare, Robert D. *Without Conscience: The Disturbing World of the Psychopaths among Us.* Guilford Press, 1999.

———, and Paul Babiak. *Snakes in Suits: When Psychopaths Go to Work.* Regan Books, 2006.

Provost, Gary. *Make Your Words Work: Proven Techniques for Effective Writing—For Fiction and Nonfiction.* Writer's Digest Books, 1990, 1994.

———. *100 Ways to Improve Your Writing.* Penguin, 1985.

Stout, Martha. *The Sociopath Next Door.* Broadway Books/Random House, 2005.

RECOMMENDED WEBSITES

Beattie, Melody   www.melodybeattie.com
Bentley, Barbara   www.adancewiththedevil.com
Bradshaw, John   www.johnbradshaw.com
Brown, L. Sandra   www.saferelationships.com
Capacchione, Lucia   www.luciac.com
Evans, Patricia   www.verbalabuse.com
Hahn, Hannelore   www.iwwg.org
Hare, Dr. Robert   www.hare.org
Provost, Gail   www.writersretreatworkshop.com